LIVING ABROAD IN
ITALY

JOHN MORETTI

PRIME LIVING LOCATIONS IN ITALY

THE NORTHWEST

MILAN AND THE LAKES

THE NORTHEAST

THE CENTRAL REGIONS

ROME

SWITZERLAND

BERN ⊛

Lake Geneva

AUSTRIA

HUNGARY

SLOVENIA

LJUBLJANA ⊛

CROATIA

ZAGREB ⊛

BOSNIA AND HERZEGOVINA

SARAJEVO ⊛

A l p s

VALLE D'AOSTA

Aosta ●

PIEMONTE

Turin ●

FRANCE

MONACO

LIGURIA

Savona ●

Genoa ✈

Gulf of Genoa

CORSICA (FRANCE)

Ligurian Sea

LOMBARDIA

Varese ●
Lecco ●
Milan ✈

Lago Maggiore

Lago di Garda

TRENTINO-ALTO ADIGE

Bolzano ●

Trento ●

Verona ✈

VENETO

FRIULI-VENEZIA GIULIA

Trieste ✈

Gulf of Venice

Venice ●

Adige River

Po River

EMILIA-ROMAGNA

Parma ●

Bologna ●

Ravenna ○

Rimini ●

SAN MARINO

Adriatic Sea

Ancona ●

LE MARCHE

UMBRIA

Perugia ●

Lago Trasimeno

Lago di Bolsena

TOSCANA

Florence ●

Siena ○

Pisa ●

Livorno ●

Arno

Elba

Isola di Capraia

Isola del Giglio

Isola di Montecristo

Appennine Mountains

Tiber River

LAZIO

ROME ⊛

VATICAN CITY ⊛ ✈

Latina ●

ABRUZZO

L'Aquila ●

Pescara ●

MOLISE

Campobasso ●

Foggia ⊛

Manfredonia ●

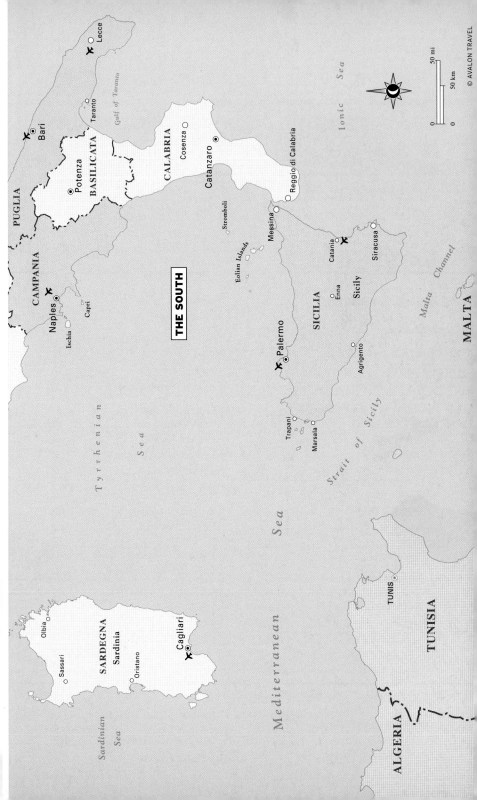

Contents

At Home in Italy

Sometimes when I'm mindlessly stirring cherry tomatoes in a saucepan, or ironing a favorite shirt that I bought at a wedding in Palermo, I think about what my life would be like had a string of coincidences not fallen into place a decade ago.

What if I hadn't been at a reporter's desk in Vermont at that time, contemplating a move, when my sister came around looking for a roommate in Italy? What if that job had never opened up in Milan just as I was considering the flight back home? What would life have been like then? It's like closing your eyes and pondering what would have happened if your parents had never met. Of course, I have no idea what I'd be doing now if I hadn't moved to Italy, but I know exactly what I would never have done. I would never have been able to drive to the Riviera on a whim. I would never have skied Mount Etna hours before it erupted. I doubt that I would have spared vacation time to walk through Venice on a silent, rainy weekday in February and seen *la Serenissima* the way it was meant to be seen. I can say with certainty that I would never have found myself pacing around Giorgio Armani's empty apartment, dodging cat litter boxes while I waited for him to show up for an interview. These are odd, once-in-a-lifetime experiences that the average traveler would see as a windfall, and the resident of Italy almost takes for granted.

You don't have to be an adventurer or a collector of bizarre experiences to appreciate Italy. There are as many reasons to move here as there are people who do: to ski in the Alps every weekend in the winter;

to cycle through the cypress-lined hills of Tuscany every weekend in spring; to spend your summers loafing on the rose-colored beaches of Sardinia; to eat porcini and drink Brunello di Montalcino in the Apennines; to spend years studying the frescoes of Giotto in the Scrovegni Chapel; to become an expert on a little-known quarter of Rome.

The pleasures and beauty of Italy are legendary, but the thing that really keeps you here is the people. The calm pace and perspective of the Italian people will rub off on even the most rigid and restless foreigner. Living in this beautiful country will also have some effect on your worldview. Whether you believe that Europe's mores represent the past and that the continentals look to the West for the future, or whether you are beginning to suspect that the opposite may be true, there is still no substitute for living in the cradle of Western civilization to grasp where we have been, how ideas and empires blossomed and died. Discussing current events, your convictions will be either strengthened or tested after sharing dinner tables with people who have survived a war in their backyards and who have lived under the specter of domestic terrorism throughout much of their lives. In the end, I think this is the part of living in Italy that I would have missed the most had I never landed here in the first place. I have made some very good friends.

▶ WHAT I LOVE ABOUT ITALY

- You don't leave home in the morning without your sunglasses.
- Espresso, cappuccino, and macchiato are perfect every time.
- When you order an orange juice, the bartender picks up an orange.
- Your 3 o'clock meeting is in a frescoed palace that is 700 years old.
- Everything is a work of art.
- Five weeks of vacation are the norm, and some of the nicest vacation spots in the world are only a few hours' drive away.
- Simple, traditional recipes + fresh, local ingredients = a great meal.
- You can still find a cobbler to repair a shoe, and it is done with care.
- A perfectly good bottle of wine at the supermarket costs €5.
- Friends and family greet you at the airport.
- Saturday: Ski a steep, powdery slope in the Alps. Sunday: Sunbathe on the Riviera.

WELCOME TO ITALY

INTRODUCTION

When you step off the plane in Italy, feel the balmy breeze, and hear the conversations of people who don't seem to have a care in the world, it's as if you've returned to a more innocent time. You can see the relief on Italians' faces when they hear their own language and share a wisecrack with a perfect stranger about a baggage belt that's taking hours to get rolling. This is our country, they think, warts and all, and we wouldn't have it any other way. They may have just returned from London or Munich or Brussels, all very orderly places where problems are quickly resolved and anyway don't seem to pop up quite as frequently, but where people seem to be more stressed nonetheless.

Sure, there are Italians who feel exasperated with a lot of things about their country, but they'll rarely complain about it. When faced with a long line at the post office, they don't fume over it and stamp their feet, but rather occupy themselves with more important thoughts, like where to go for dinner that night, or else strike up a conversation with the person next to them.

This human touch, a tolerance bordering on appreciation for the country's blissful imperfections, is what makes an everyday event such as grocery shopping more a recreational activity than a chore. In Italy, it's not a matter of driving to the supermarket and loading as many plastic bags into a minivan in as little time as possible. Instead,

you'll walk down cobblestone alleys to markets where vendors spend the time to tell you how to prepare a certain fish or which vegetable to choose as a side dish, even if it means that the person behind you has to wait a few more minutes.

The Lay of the Land

A patriotic poem written during the unification of Italy noted that the three colors of the Italian flag represent the variety of the country's geography: red, the glow of the South's volcanoes; white, the snow of the Alps; green, the Po River plain. The lines may come off as a little cloying, but once you set eyes on Italy, it is hard not to wax poetic. It is one of the most captivating landscapes in the world, containing every conceivable hue, altitude, temperature, and texture. In a rare instance of understatement, Italians call it simply *il bel paese* (the beautiful country).

All this is packed into a peninsula that, at 300,000 square kilometers (115,800 square miles), is about the size of Arizona and holds some 58 million inhabitants, or roughly one-quarter of the U.S. population.

Traveling its coastline and its mountainous surface, you'll see why Italian architects and road engineers had to be so talented. There is hardly a straight line or flat surface to be seen. The country has approximately 7,600 kilometers (4,722 miles) of jagged, mostly mountainous coastline (depending on how precisely you measure it). The only inland sections that aren't covered by mountains or foothills are the Po River plain and a few patches in the South. The country's mountainous spine runs from Liguria in the northwest to Reggio Calabria at the tip of the boot. Even the two island regions, Sicily and Sardinia, are nothing but hills and coast.

Unlike many Western European countries, Italy is not dominated by one capital city with the rest of the countryside bowing to it. Yes, all roads lead to Rome sooner or later, but all train tracks, you might say, lead to Bologna, the busiest station in the country, and much of the air traffic to Italy is now routed through Milan. Italy is sliced up into many spheres of influence that date back centuries, when the peninsula was a collection of fractious duchies, republics, and city-states.

Italians now mentally divide their unified country into North and South. You're either a northerner, a southerner, or from the boundary in between, namely Tuscany, Umbria, and Le Marche. (Le Marche even gets its name from the Germanic term for a borderland, *marka*.) This is how the prime living chapters of this book are organized: northwest, northeast, central regions, and south.

The North can be defined as those regions whose water flows into the Po, and, in fact, those who would like to see the industrial North separate from the rest of the country consider themselves part of a make-believe land called Padania, which takes its name from the Po River plain. There are no common ethnic or historical ties here, just a river that connects a string of prosperous peoples.

The Po starts high in the foothills of Piedmont, where the Italian Alps brush up against the French and Swiss borders. At the confluence of those three countries is Val d'Aosta, boasting the highest elevation in Europe (Mont Blanc, *detto* Monte Bianco, at 4,748 meters (15,580 ft) on the Italian side) and the lowest population of all Italian regions (about 120,000 inhabitants). From there, the melting snow makes its way downhill to Turin and weaves just south of the vineyards that produce some of Italy's most impressive wines. At the Lombardy border, it is joined by the Ticino, which brings frigid water down from the lakes region near the Swiss canton that gives the river its name. More powerful now, the Po rolls by small but historically significant cities: Pavia, the site of a very old university and one of the most important monasteries in Italy; Cremona, home of the Stradivarius violin; and Ferrara, which claims to have invented the modern theater. From there, the Po flows out into the Adriatic.

North of the river, a line of influential cities runs along the base of the Lombard Alps and the Dolomites of south Tyrol, historically part of Austria. These cities still carry the flavor of their Austrian and Venetian conquerors, as well as their Lombard settlers. Milan is Italy's financial capital and ground zero for fashion and design. Bergamo, a jewel of a walled city, produced artistic greats such as Caravaggio. Verona, fictional home of Romeo and Juliet, is set in the vineyards along the southern rim of Lake Garda, which reaches into the Teutonic-flavored region of Trentino-Alto Adige. Padua's university produced Galileo and others. Venice, the best known, perhaps needs no introduction at all.

North of Venice is a once-impoverished hinterland better known now for its family enterprises, operating in sectors ranging from furniture to liquor to shoes and clothing. A few of these small businesses have gone on to international acclaim. (The Benetton family, for example, from Treviso, started out with a small sweater-making business.) Farther north lies Friuli Venezia Giulia, the forests and vineyards that eventually give way to the Julian Alps in the north, and to the east is the limestone karst around Trieste. The landscape appears as foreign as the largely Slovenian-speaking population that inhabits it. The entire northern Adriatic coast, which swapped hands in a brutal manner through two world wars, seems to have more in common with parts of the Austro-Hungarian Empire than with Italy.

The Italian peninsula starts south of the Po, extending from Liguria, at the western end of the mountainous Italian Riviera, and sloping down into the plains of Emilia-Romagna, the breadbasket of Italy and home to some of the nation's wealthiest cities. Emilia's cities—Parma, Modena, Bologna, and Reggio Emilia—are known as places where you're guaranteed to eat and live well. Per-capita income here is pegged at about US$900 a month, which may not sound like a high number to a New Yorker, but it's more than twice the average found in the southern regions of Calabria and Basilicata and the island region of Sardinia. Romagna, along the coast, is best known for the teeming beach resort of Rimini and the ancient mosaics at Ravenna.

Tucked into the hills of Romagna, on the border with Le Marche, is the Republic of San Marino, a tax haven that doubles as an excuse for Italy to hold an extra Formula One Grand Prix every year. (It's not a novel idea. France does the same with Monaco.) In relation to the rest of Italy, San Marino is a small consideration, both culturally and geographically. If you swatted a fly on a map of Italy, it would cover more ground than this tiny republic.

South of Bologna, the Apennines spread out their hilly fingers from coast to coast. They define the northern border of central Italy, once the cradle of the Renaissance and now a hot spot for tourists and foreign homeowners. The attractions include not only the artistic treasures of Florence, but also the vineyards in the Tuscan countryside and the coast of Versilia in the summertime. Those crowded Mediterranean beaches stretch

© PURESTOCK

a vineyard in Tuscany

from the Gulf of Poets, in Liguria, to the port of Livorno. They pass by the inland cities of Pisa, with its famous tower, and Lucca, a classic medieval city that never fails to charm. On the other side of the peninsula, the regions of Umbria and Le Marche host fewer blockbuster attractions but have started to see new legions of house-shoppers drawn by the area's ideal climate and calming pastoral beauty.

Tuscany rolls downhill past the cape that juts toward the isle of Elba. The region passes through the scrub brush of the Maremma, the cowboy country of northern Lazio, until it meets the civilization of Rome. On the Adriatic side, the highlands of Le Marche heave up to the snowcapped peaks of Abruzzo, inhabited by bears, wolves, chamois, and bighorns. Maybe because of its untamed wilderness, Abruzzo is considered part of the South, though it lies on the exact latitude of Lazio, which is thought of as the center. More likely, Abruzzo is classified as southern because the rough-and-tumble people aren't as well-heeled as their neighbors.

Here begins the *Mezzogiorno,* or "Midday," so-named because the South is where the sun hovers at noon, at least from the point of view of Romans and their other geographic superiors. The expression has become a poetic euphemism for the poorest part of the peninsula. What the South lacks in lire, though, it more than makes up for in warm hospitality, ancient history, good food, and pristine beaches. The waters on either side of the boot's ankle compete for the title of Most Spectacular Coastline: the Gargano promontory's breathtaking and sparsely inhabited cliffs; and the stunning Amalfi coast, with its jubilant flower gardens and capricious summertime fun. The land becomes more mysterious as you move south into Calabria, Basilicata, and southern Puglia. The dome-shaped *trulli* (stone houses) and tarantella of Puglia still mystify guests with their Eastern flavor, while the mountain valleys of Basilicata and

Calabria retain the same sun-drenched silence they enjoyed in the days of the Greeks. Some ancient settlements still keep their secrets, buried for millennia under silt and only now beginning to see the light of day.

COUNTRY DIVISIONS

Each of Italy's 20 regions is divided into provinces, something like counties in the United States, in that they are based on population and share a *tribunale* (courthouse). A lot of national bureaucracy is administered at this level, such as car registration; every license plate carries the province's initials. The province is also a point of reference when talking about very small towns. For example, instead of naming the little village in Campania where a fire broke out, a newscaster will usually say *nel Casertano* (near Caserta). Any time you pick up a brochure for a hotel or restaurant in a small town, the name of the town will be accompanied by the province's initials, to give you some indication of where it is.

Each province is divided into *comuni* (towns), the lowest level of local government. The jurisdiction of the *comune* encompasses not only the village, but also outlying settlements known as *frazioni*. As a foreigner, you'll likely make several trips to the town's offices to register for a tax ID number; as a homeowner, you'll need to spend time at the offices to clear up permits for building, renovations, etc.

The most powerful local authority remains the region, which administers such state-run systems as education and health care. Each region has its own assembly and president, and handpicked by the president is an entourage of *assessori,* often translated into English as "inspectors." (Those who have seen Roberto Benigni's *Life Is Beautiful* might remember his charade as an *assessore* of education, visiting a grade school with the tricolor sash awkwardly tangled between his legs, but commanding the full attention of the schoolteachers nonetheless.) Regional authorities can wield considerable influence. For example, the long-standing president of Lombardy, Roberto Formigoni, is at the time of this writing still the head of a very wealthy region of more than eight million people, and therefore considers certain powers otherwise granted only to Rome, such as foreign relations, part of his own brief.

The regions may soon become even more powerful as they are granted more autonomy. Already the country has its autonomous and semiautonomous regions, designated as such because of their cultural distance from Rome: Trentino-Alto Adige, Val d'Aosta, Friuli Venezia Giulia, Sardinia, and Sicily. But the recent push for *federalismo,* a federal structure loosely based on the example of the United States, has less to do with culture than economics. The driving force behind federalism is the diverse character of regional balance sheets. Many northerners, especially from Piedmont, Lombardy, and the Veneto, believe that they contribute more than they benefit from national spending. Currently, regions have no tax-collecting authority, but rather rely on the distribution of national revenues, which is supposed to be proportionate. Federalists wish it were more so.

Southern politicians find themselves in a tough spot here because the South has little to gain from the movement. The former mayor of Catania, Enzo Bianco, who went on to become the Minister of the Interior in the late 1990s, tried to explain regionalization to a group of local students like this: People have different needs and customs in the North than they do in the South, and decision-making powers should reflect that.

Store hours are a good example. A shopkeeper in Milan may want to stay open during the traditional lunch break to attract more business, but it's too hot in the Sicilian city of Siracusa to be working at midday.

The real reason, of course, that northerners push so hard for a federal structure is that they prefer to spend money closer to where it is earned. They have found kindred spirits in the conservatives, which is only logical, considering the center-right coalition includes the formerly separatist Northern League (though, ironically, the fervently pro-unity National Alliance is also part of the coalition).

A Look at the Regions
ABRUZZO
- Population: 1,324,000; 122 people per square kilometer
- Provinces: Aquila (AQ), Chieti (CH), Pescara (PE), Teramo (TE)

BASILICATA
- Population: 591,000; 59 people per square kilometer
- Provinces: Matera (MT), Potenza (PZ)

CALABRIA
- Population: 2,007,000; 133 per square kilometer
- Provinces: Catanzaro (CZ), Cosenza (CS), Crotone (KR), Reggio Calabria (RC), Vibo Valentia (VV)

CAMPANIA
- Population: 5,811,000; 427 people per square kilometer
- Provinces: Avellino (AV), Benevento (BN), Caserta (CE), Naples (NA), Salerno (SA)

EMILIA-ROMAGNA
- Population: 4,276,000; 193 people per square kilometer
- Provinces: Bologna (BO), Ferrara (FE), Forli (FO), Modena (MO), Parma (PR), Piacenza (PC), Ravenna (RA), Reggio Emilia (RE), Rimini (RN)

FRIULI VENEZIA GIULIA
- Population: 1,222,000; 155 people per square kilometer
- Provinces: Gorizia (GO), Pordenone (PN), Trieste (TS), Udine (UD)

LAZIO
- Population: 5,561,000; 323 people per square kilometer
- Provinces: Frosinone (FR), Latina (LT), Rieti (RI), Rome (ROMA), Viterbo (VT)

LIGURIA
- Population: 1,640,000; 296 people per square kilometer
- Provinces: Genoa (GE), Imperia (IM), La Spezia (SP), Savona (SV)

LE MARCHE
- Population: 1,450,000; 150 people per square kilometer
- Provinces: Ancona (AN), Ascoli Piceno (AP), Macerata (MC), Pesaro-Urbino (PS)

LOMBARDY
- Population: 9,642,000; 404 people per square kilometer
- Provinces: Bergamo (BG), Brescia (BS), Como (CO), Cremona (CR), Lecco (LC), Lodi (LO), Mantua (MN), Milan (MI), Monza (MZ), Pavia (PV), Sondrio (SO), Varese (VA)

MOLISE
- Population: 320,000; 72 people per square kilometer
- Provinces: Campobasso (CB), Isernia (IS)

PIEDMONT
- Population: 4,400,000; 173 people per square kilometer
- Provinces: Alessandria (AL), Asti (AT), Biella (BI), Cuneo (CN), Novara (NO), Turin (TO), Verbana (VB), Vercelli (VC)

PUGLIA
- Population: 4,076,000; 210 people per square kilometer
- Provinces: Bari (BA), Brindisi (BR), Foggia (FG), Lecce (LE), Taranto (TA)

SARDINIA
- Population: 1,666,000; 69 people per square kilometer
- Provinces: Cagliari (CA), Nuoro (NU), Oristano (OR), Sassari (SS)

SICILY
- Population: 5,030,000; 195 people per square kilometer
- Provinces: Agrigento (AG), Caltanissetta (CL), Catania (CT), Enna (EN), Messina (ME), Palermo (PA), Ragusa (RG), Siracusa (SR), Trapani (TP)

TUSCANY
- Population: 3,677,000; 159 people per square kilometer

- Provinces: Arezzo (AR), Florence (FI), Grosetto (GR), Livorno (LI), Lucca (LU), Massa-Carrara (MS), Pisa (PI), Pistoia (PT), Prato (PO), Siena (SI)

TRENTINO-ALTO ADIGE
- Population: 924,000; 75 people per square kilometer
- Provinces: Bolzano (BZ), Trento (TN)

UMBRIA
- Population: 884,000; 104 people per square kilometer
- Provinces: Perugia (PG), Terni (TR)

VAL D'AOSTA
- Population: 126,000; 38 people per square kilometer
- Province: Aosta (AO)

VENETO
- Population: 4,832,000; 262 people per square kilometer
- Provinces: Belluno (BL), Padua (PD), Rovigo (RO), Treviso (TV), Venice (VE), Verona (VR), Vicenza (VI)

WEATHER
The Mediterranean climate is one of its greatest selling points. In the spring, it is warm and not too wet. In the fall, it is cool, sometimes a little damp, but not too windy. In

© LUCIE ERICKSEN

Escape to the beach in August.

the winter, well, the North and the mountains will get snow, but anyone who is used to brutally cold winters at home will find most of Italy very temperate. Summers are hot, except in the mountains and at the beach, where all Italians enjoy the month of August. Then come the rains, like clockwork on September 1, and tanned faces return to the city to do it all over again.

Italians can't complain, but sometimes they still do. Specifically, in the summertime. It cannot be stressed enough how infernally hot it can become in August. Coastal cities get a little bit of a reprieve, even in the South. Rome is not quite on the water, though, so summers there are not much more comfortable than in Bologna or Milan.

In Rome, the heat can come early. Even late May, walking down the street sometimes you have to seek shelter in the shade every five minutes. I mean it: If you are not a hot-weather person, carefully consider the summer temperatures of your new hometown unless you have a foolproof plan to get to the sea or mountains in July and August.

FLORA AND FAUNA

Because of this balmy Mediterranean weather and the vegetation it can support, Italy calls itself "the garden of Europe." All along the highways, in small towns, and everywhere in between, the country is teeming with azaleas, bougainvillea, roses, grapes, and palm trees. The hills are alive with olives, citrus, chestnuts, mushrooms, watermelons, cherries, pears, and apples. Corner vegetable stands overflow with locally grown bright yellow peppers, green onions, purple eggplant, many varieties of ripe tomatoes (in at least three different shapes), apricots, artichokes, green and white asparagus, and avocados. If you locked yourself in the kitchen with a full day's worth of groceries, you could prepare everything in your favorite cookbook and still have much of the bounty left over.

the shoreline of Lake Como

It may seem a little odd to begin a section on flora and fauna with a grocery list, but in a country where most available land is devoted to agriculture, flora and fauna mean food.

Fauna, especially. Coming to Italy from Vermont, where it seems a new species of animal crosses in front of your headlights every evening, I can't help but notice that almost the only mammals you see in Italy are livestock: sheep, goats, some cattle, and pigs. In fact, the only wild mammal I can remember seeing is the ubiquitous *cinghiale,* or wild boar, best-known for its starring role in stews and sausages.

If you want to spot a mammal in Italy that's not synonymous with a local specialty, Italy's network of national parks can offer at least a few. One of my favorites is the Gran Sasso park, in

Abruzzo. On your hike up the tallest peaks in the Apennines, you'll see plenty of chamois, and possibly a wolf or bear. Many of the Italian hikers you'll see in those mountains, running down the spine of the peninsula, are there to spot the fauna: again, mostly for food. Several varieties of edible mushrooms grow in the Apennines, making it a sort of national hobby on par with chestnut-gathering. The other precious flora is the truffle, whose hunters are there for the big payout that comes with every tiny tuber.

Italy has such a wide spectrum of altitudes and terrain in such a tight space that in a single day you can start off seeing tropical species in the morning, move through a stand of temperate, deciduous trees in the afternoon, and be in the midst of a boreal forest by dinner. The lakes region, especially the shores of Como and Maggiore, has a bizarre microclimate where palm trees and snow-covered firs fit in the same panorama. It's no wonder that camera-toting tourists flock to these shores.

Social Climate

AN AMERICAN IN ROME

Of all the patience Italians possess, they seem to reserve the most for their visitors from the United States. That says a lot about the Italian character. Relations have been tense under certain administrations, sometimes even chilly when it comes to foreign policy. But Italians are the eternal masters of mediation, and, on a personal level at least, they and Americans regularly come to the conclusion that they share more values than they harbor differences. Any minor deviation from Italian cultural norms is greeted with immense tolerance.

This is also good business sense. The millions of dollars that Americans spend in Italy—one of our favorite foreign destinations, perhaps because we are treated so well—represent a good portion of the nation's tourism income, which in turn is a significant source of total revenues. When Americans stop coming to Italy in large numbers, as happened in the months following September 11, 2001, and when the euro exchange crested 1.40 to the dollar, the service industry gets very jittery.

Italians have hosted Americans and U.S. businesses for a long time now and are used to their quirks. After World War II, U.S. soldiers patrolled the streets of Rome and Naples, followed by the expat café-dwellers of the roaring 1950s. The 1954 film *An American in Rome* is about an Italian so enamored with the United States that he pretends to be from Kansas City. The movie takes a few good-natured jabs at the baseball hat–wearing, spaghetti-slurping crowd, but the nasal American accent of actor Alberto Sordi is still endearing to the Italian ear. In the 1980s, McDonald's, basketball, and Coca-Cola were king, and to some extent they have endured the vicissitudes of style and the antiglobalization movement of the late 1990s. The symbols still conjure a Sordi-esque vision of a wide-eyed, youthfully energetic people.

ITALY AND FOREIGNERS

They may not always agree with Americans, and may point out domestic problems in the United States and other eyebrow-raising idiosyncrasies of American behavior, but on the whole, most Italians are willing to listen to American points of view with a certain deference. They reserve some respect for the people who helped them defeat

© TUPUNGATO/123RF

Rome's *centro storico*

Fascism and accommodated many of their own families during the mass migration at the turn of the 20th century. It's safe to say that, of all the nationalities that have relocated to Italy in the past decade, Americans enjoy a place of honor.

Others don't get the same warm welcome. Italy has only recently experienced the sort of immigration that has already changed the face of Germany, France, and the United Kingdom, and its response has been predictable. Italy considers itself a very tolerant country. At the same time, it is also one of the most Catholic nations in Western Europe, and the construction of mosques in the shadow of St. Peter's gets under the skin of a good portion of the electorate. The number of immigrants to Italy has risen dramatically over the last three decades, and some Italians immediately equate this with a perceived rise in the crime rate. Every time a Balkan immigrant lands in trouble—burglary, kidnapping, etc.—the papers have led with the story. This got the media into trouble when, after a mother and child were found dead in their bathroom in southeastern Piedmont, the headlines read: "Albanians on the Run." Turns out, it was actually the mother who killed the child and then herself. The mea culpa that followed was short-lived.

Such xenophobes have found an outlet in the Northern League. Once a separatist party fueled by small northern businesses irritated by national aid for the South, the group now has found an easier target in immigration. The Northern League makes a lot of headlines abroad and tends to paint Italy as a country of racists, but the party has lately garnered well under 10 percent of the national vote. Its power is mostly concentrated in small pockets of Veneto and Lombardy, two of the more prosperous regions where immigrants are lured to low-paying jobs.

HISTORY, GOVERNMENT, AND ECONOMY

Every day in Italy is a walk through history. Latin expressions are tossed around ad lib, medieval rivalries persist, ancient dialects are still spoken, post-Fascists and Communists remain in government, and streets bear the names of historical figures. The country's past is very much a part of its present, reexamined and reinterpreted in daily conversations.

Anyone who moves here should at least brush up on the basics. Only after you understand Italy's long and complicated history can you begin to understand why politicians say the things they do.

History

THE RISE AND FALL OF ROME

Passing over the peninsula's prehistoric inhabitants and the mysterious Etruscans of the Bronze Age, a good jumping-off point into Italy's history is the founding of the Roman Republic in 510 B.C. After the citizens of this small shepherding town overthrew their Etruscan overlords, they slowly grew an empire by forming alliances with other tribes in Latium, now known as Lazio. They built military roads and established colonies up and down the peninsula, offering Roman citizenship to the conquered inhabitants.

What the Romans lacked in culture, they more than made up for in government, engineering, and military prowess. In theory, political power in the republic lay with the people, who voted as centuries, or tribes. In practice, though, government was entrusted to the Senate, made up of aristocratic families. This arrangement caused tension between the patricians (the nobility) and the plebeians (the populace), and led to the Social Wars in 91 B.C. With the city in chaos, a military commander named Sulla staged a bloody coup and brought his armies within the city walls, long considered a religious taboo. His cohort, Pompey the Great, then took control of the city. The republic was passed down to Pompey's lieutenant and rival in the triumvirate, Julius Caesar.

Caesar was an intellectual who studied under Greek masters and could boast almost no military training, and yet he proved to be one of the republic's greatest generals, conquering Gaul and extending Rome's borders to the Rhine. But the height of expansion came under his grandnephew, Octavian, who renamed himself Caesar Augustus. The reign of Augustus (27 B.C. to A.D. 14) gave birth to a Pax Romana, when Rome's military dominance brought an end to major battles in Western Europe for close to two centuries. It also marked the decline of democratic institutions.

Augustus claimed to hold dear the values of the republic, all the while stripping the Senate of its power. He awarded himself titles and offices, and described his role as that of the "first citizen." (To this day in Italy, a mayor is often referred to as *il primo cittadino*.) The emperors that followed Augustus became nothing short of dictators. Some of them were enlightened leaders, others unscrupulous tyrants. The more colorful characters in the 1st century included Caligula, a murderous and chemically imbalanced emperor who managed to appoint his horse a lifetime member of the Senate,

a Greek temple in modern-day Calabria, hometown of Pythagoras

© JOHN MORETTI

© JOHN MORETTI

the "other" Roman coliseum, Verona

and Nero, whose contributions included (allegedly) burning down the city before he was driven from power. Nero committed suicide in A.D. 68, pronouncing, "What an artist I destroy."

The Flavian dynasty represented the better half of the century. The first of these emperors, Vespasian, built the Colosseum in A.D. 80. That dynasty was followed by Trajan, under whom the empire was at its height, geographically, and later by Hadrian, who oversaw the construction of Rome's most impressive engineering feat, the Pantheon. It is the largest dome ever built of concrete, a material the Romans invented.

Next came Marcus Aurelius, a Stoic philosopher and admired politician who built the walls that now demarcate the boundary of downtown Rome. Their construction coincided with a shift in Rome's military strategy from one of expansion to one of defensive isolation.

Things started falling apart for the empire in the 3rd century. The era was marked by one assassination after another, and also by the threat of attack—either from the Franks in the North or from the overtaxed populace itself. By the 4th century, the emperor, Diocletian, had to resort to severe legislation to maintain order. He fixed prices, passed a decree that every son must follow the profession of his father, and levied stiff taxes. To implement these, he created a bureaucracy that divided the empire into eastern and western halves. The western half was headquartered at Milan, and later at Ravenna, two important commercial centers at the time.

Constantine, instead, relied on religion to keep order. Christianity was never very popular in imperial Rome—Nero liked to use Christians as human torches to illuminate his garden at night—but now, spiritualism swept across the peninsula. In these troubled times for the empire, the Christians witnessed a reversal of fortune, as the pagans were now persecuted. Sensing this growing power base, Constantine issued an edict of toleration in 313 and established the eastern empire's capital in Byzantium.

Byzantium prospered as the western emperors' hold crumbled and the barbaric tribes north of the Alps showed more skill with the sword. The Goths, the Franks, and the Lombards had been overrunning the far reaches of the empire for a century, and were prepared to take the peninsula.

THE DARK AGES

Enter Alaric, a Visigoth. When he attacked Rome in 410, the citizens practically opened the gates for him—and then crept out themselves, fleeing to the hills. Their emperor, Honorius, had read the Vandals' writing on the wall already, and so was hiding out in Ravenna. Unlike some of the foreign occupiers to follow, Alaric wasn't too interested in ruling, mostly just in raiding, and the gold he looted from Rome is said to be buried still with his tomb under a river in Calabria.

Next came Attila the Hun, not much of a negotiator, but he was persuaded by Pope Leo not to sack the city. He was followed by Gaiseric the Vandal, and then a line of Goths leading to Theodoric. Theodoric set up shop in Ravenna, holding off the Lombards, who had taken control of the northern plains and had moved all the way south to Tuscany. Theodoric was one in a long line of Italianized foreigners: "An able Goth wants to be like a Roman," he said. "Only a poor Roman would want to be like a Goth."

The popes had their own ideas of how Italy should be run. They had taken the reins of an embattled Eternal City and stressed the notion that the church was not just a spiritual power, but also a temporal one. Pope Gregory II cut Rome's ties with Constantinople in 731 and started looking for military allies. He was most concerned with thwarting the advance of the Lombards, as well as Byzantium's legions of—imagine the irony—Roman troops. In 800, the pope named the king of the Franks, Charlemagne, as the new Roman emperor.

The 8th and 9th centuries embodied the depths of the Dark Ages for Italy. Rome was nearly abandoned, except for the popes, leaving the imperial buildings to decay while the clergy built hundreds of churches and cloisters. Most of the rest of the peninsula was overrun by barbarians, offering scant political or cultural contributions.

One place that did prosper was Venice. Over the next few hundred years, it rose to power with the other maritime republics—Amalfi, Pisa, and Genoa—whose four symbols now grace the flag of the Italian Navy. (Pisa was once on the sea.)

The end of the Dark Ages in Italy is usually defined as the birth of the Holy Roman Empire, commenced in 962 by Charlemagne's successor, Otto the Great. It saw a reorganization of power into fiefdoms, and the peninsula divided itself into a jigsaw puzzle of duchies, city-states, and republics. The fractiousness that resulted lasted until at least the unification of Italy in 1861. Many would argue it still exists today.

MEDIEVAL ITALY

When the Turks conquered the Holy Land in 1065, the popes found themselves in an enviable position. As the de facto organizing force behind the Crusades, the papacy attracted a lot of money to Italy. Indeed, they allowed for the first banking system in Europe. The title of the world's oldest institutional lender is generally credited to

TIMELINE

- **600 B.C.:** Etruscans make Rome their capital.

- **510 B.C.:** The Roman Republic is founded.

- **49 B.C.:** Rome, under Julius Caesar, rules the Mediterranean.

- **44 B.C.:** Caesar is dead, long live Caesar Augustus.

- **A.D. 80:** Colosseum is completed.

- **117 to 138:** Hadrian builds his mausoleum, wall, and villa.

- **249 to 250:** First empire-wide persecution of Christians occurs.

- **395:** Constantine establishes second Rome at Byzantium; Goths pour into the North.

- **410:** Rome is sacked by Alaric, falls to other invaders in 475.

- **800:** Charlemagne is crowned Holy Roman Emperor.

- **1065:** Crusades begin.

- **1091:** Normans take control of Sicily from Arabs.

- **1150 to 1300:** Clashes take place between Guelfs and Ghibellines.

- **1182:** Holy Roman Emperor Frederick Barbarossa recognizes autonomy of the Lombard League.

- **1222:** University of Padua is founded.

- **1303:** Popes vacate for Avignon; Giotto starts work on the Scrovegni Chapel.

- **1499:** Leonardo da Vinci completes *The Last Supper.*

- **1508:** Michelangelo starts the ceiling of the Sistine Chapel.

- **1513:** Machiavelli publishes *The Prince.*

- **1641:** Galileo applies the pendulum to clocks, a year before he dies.

- **1796:** Napoleon invades.

- **1853:** Giuseppe Verdi's *La Traviata* is first performed.

- **1861:** The Kingdom of Italy is born.

- **1915:** Italy enters World War I on the side of Britain and France.

- **1934:** Italy wins its first soccer World Cup (won again in 1938, 1982, and 2006).

- **1940:** Mussolini drags Italy into World War II on Germany's side.

- **1943:** Italy signs an armistice with the Allies; Mussolini is killed by partisans.

- **1961:** Federico Fellini directs *La Dolce Vita.*

- **1969:** A bomb in Milan's Piazza Fontana kills 16 and kicks off a decade of terrorism.

- **1978:** Prime Minister Aldo Moro is kidnapped and then murdered.

- **1993:** Prime Minister Bettino Craxi resigns on corruption charges.

- **1994:** Silvio Berlusconi's Forza Italia party wins elections; coalition later collapses.

- **2001:** Berlusconi is back in Palazzo Chigi after a brief, historic rule by the center-left.

- **2006:** Romano Prodi's center-left government returns to power after the Supreme Court upholds his razor-thin victory.

- **2008:** Berlusconi regains control as economy slides into recession.

- **2009:** A massive earthquake decimates the region of Abruzzo.

- **2011:** Italy's staggering debt crisis forces Berlusconi to resign; he is replaced by former EU commissioner Mario Monti.

Monte dei Paschi di Siena, born in the part of Italy that prospered the most from the foreign inflow of Christian capital, Tuscany. Some of the coffers went toward the cathedral and baptistry of Pisa.

The picture of a fallen and abandoned Rome is bleak enough, but the cities it spawned across the peninsula survived. Their aqueducts may not have worked as well as they had centuries before, but the municipalities functioned much as they did under Roman rule. This was especially true in the North. In the South, Amalfi was an exception. It did a roaring trade with the same Arab pirates who were looting Amalfi's neighbors, such as Salerno. Unfortunately for Amalfi, it had no other source of income, and so the end of this southern dream came in 1135, when the Pisans leveled its cliff-hanging shores. Today, it is little more than a tourist attraction. (Then again, the same can be said about modern-day Pisa. Genoa definitively rid itself of Pisa's pesky fleet in 1284.)

Venice was another trade-heavy republic. It considers itself the longest-standing republic in history. The Serenissima enjoyed profitable ties with Byzantium, becoming Europe's window on the East and giving birth to such Asiatic explorers as Marco Polo. (Actually, he was born on an island in modern-day Croatia, then under the Venetian flag.) The spice trade was lucrative, and the Italians also seemed to make good use of the noodles that the Polo family is said to have brought back from Asia.

But Venice really made hay by handling the passage of earnest knights traveling from Northern Europe to the Holy Land. So did Genoa, another seafaring giant and the hometown of a well-known explorer some three centuries later: Christopher Columbus. (Columbus came back from the New World with some interesting items himself. Where would Italy be today without the tomato?) The two cities competed to attract the Crusaders and their gold, not unlike the jockeying today to host the Olympic Games.

This kind of toll-booth income gave rise not only to the maritime cities, but also to the inland states of Cremona, Florence, Milan, Mantua, Piacenza, and Padua. Milan, for example, controlled the alpine passes. In terms of military power, though, the northern city-states had a little outside help.

The popes encouraged the autonomy of such *communi* because they weakened the hold of the Holy Roman Empire, which by then had gotten a little too powerful for the Vatican's tastes. The feud exploded into a war that lasted some 150 years between the Guelfs (representing the papacy, the freedom of city-states, the middle-class merchants, and, of course, religious domination) and the Ghibellines (on the side of the emperor, the nobility, and the freedom of religion).

It's interesting to note that the emperor met the toughest resistance in the North, where commercial interests were, and still are, the strongest. At the start of the Guelf-Ghibelline wars, in 1161, city-states around Milan bound themselves together in the Lombard League, which stopped the emperor, Frederick Barbarossa, in Legnano.

Northern populists are still very proud of this feat. If you buy a Legnano-brand bicycle, for example, on the fork will be the Lombard League's symbol, a soldier holding a sword high in the air. It's the same symbol borrowed by the formerly separatist and anti-immigrant Northern League party.

The signs of that medieval era are everywhere, especially in central Italy, where the fighting was at its fiercest. Cruising around the Tuscan countryside today, you can see which castles were loyal to which side. The ones with square turrets were Guelf; with swallow-tailed turrets, Ghibelline.

THE RENAISSANCE AND THE FOREIGN INVASION

All the banking and commerce that drove the rise of the *communi* also fueled the wealth of their principal families. These families demonstrated their wealth by commissioning art. The Sforza and Visconti families in Milan, the della Scala family of Verona, the d'Este family in Ferrara, the Medici in Florence—all were gearing up for the titles of duke and duchess. They required paintings and sculptures to dress up their power, and perhaps impart a few convenient social lessons in the process. The richest families—the Barberini, the Borgia, and the Medici—were awarded an even better feudal title, the pontificate, and the popes worked just as hard in that age to outdo each other with decorative contributions.

From its Renaissance right up to its unification in 1861, "Italy" continued to be a collection of Papal States, foreign-ruled kingdoms, and the odd republic. One historian pointed out that there were more independent states in Italy in the 14th century than there were in the entire world in 1934. This helped breed the phenomenon of *campanilismo* (the idea that Italians are loyal only to their local *campanile,* or bell tower). There was very little trade between the small states, contributing to a weak economy and consequently a slim chance of overthrowing their wealthy conquerors. Instead, they preferred to go to war with each other.

While fractious, each of them was more or less dominated by either the popes or Venice, Milan, Florence, or the Kingdom of Naples, which in turn had been ruled by a merry-go-round of foreigners since the Dark Ages. Only the republics of Venice, Siena, and Florence managed to keep some degree of independence. For example, in just 400 years, Naples passed through the hands of the Normans, the Spanish (specifically, the Aragonese), the French, the Spanish again, and then was ceded to the Austrians after the War of Spanish Succession. The Austrians then transferred Naples to the Bourbon kings before it landed in the hands of Napoleon in 1796. But Naples was just one illustration of the way Italy was humiliated by foreign powers after the Renaissance, just as Machiavelli had predicted. Throughout the 17th and 18th centuries, the city-states' industries were beaten out by foreign competition and French and Austrian military might, while the port towns suffered with the rise of Dutch, Spanish, and English maritime prowess.

© LUCIE ERICKSEN

the *campanile* in Siena

At one point, Spain was in control of

the entire peninsula, except for Venice. In 1519, Charles V purchased the crown of the Holy Roman Emperor and set his sights on northern Italy. He already ruled the South and held just about everything north of the Alps, all the way to Holland. Milan and the other French-held territories on the Po River plain were an inconvenient gap in his communications network, a sector that Charles V knew well. He spoke all of the languages, he said: Spanish to God, Italian to women, French to men, and German to his horse.

After he defeated the French at Pavia and stormed Rome two years later in 1527, he had done the impossible: unified Italy, albeit without Venice and for only a short period of time. Peasant revolts in Naples and elsewhere loosened Charles's grip, and the War of Spanish Succession would spin off many of those holdings to Austria. Napoleon was on the rise, and so was another new player on the geopolitical stage—the king of Piedmont. Under his flag, Giuseppe Garibaldi and his men would unify Italy again, this time for good.

UNIFICATION

The Italians have such a long history of infighting and divergent cultures that you can easily understand why patriotism is such a hard sell. Even today, the president of the republic has to plead with his citizens to hoist the tricolor flag and sing the national anthem.

Even after the country was unified, the royals who brought the warring factions together were unpopular in most of the peninsula, with the possible exceptions of Lombardy and Piedmont itself. Just like the Roman emperors and foreign kings before them, the Savoys were seen as another tax-collecting entity, a force to be subverted. There was, and always has been, some concept of "Italy" as a unit going back to the Romans, but as the historian Christopher Duggan argues in *A Concise History of Italy*, it was mostly relegated to the realm of philosophers and poets.

Dante Alighieri, who witnessed his share of poverty and factionalism living in the trenches between the Guelfs and the Ghibellines during the 14th century, lamented the lack of a strong leader to conquer the warring sides: "O servile Italy, breeding ground of misery, ship without a pilot in a mighty tempest," he wrote.

These same thoughts were shared by northern liberals in the Enlightenment of the 18th century, who wanted to see Italy united—except not by an outside emperor, as Dante had hoped, but by an Italian—and rid of its foreign-influenced nobility. In the early 19th century, the most prominent of these liberal thinkers were from the wealthy and independent kingdom of Piedmont, particularly Count Camillio Benso di Cavour, Giuseppe Mazzini, and his student, Giuseppe Garibaldi.

Cavour, at the time prime minister of Piedmont, was the first to plot to overthrow the Austrians. He struck a deal with Napoleon that if the French would march east toward Venice, Piedmont would cede him Nice and Savoy. The deal fell apart when Napoleon found out that Cavour was conspiring to annex the Papal States, and so halted his troops after they took Lombardy. Cavour was shamed, and he resigned. The war with Austria did provoke more popular uprisings, however, and when the Sicilians began getting restless under Spanish taxation, the next man to the fore was Garibaldi.

Born in Nice, he had been exiled from Piedmont on several occasions—once doing a stint as a candle-maker on Staten Island—but was perhaps the greatest patriot among the northern liberals. He would take on his mission with fervor: to bring a ragtag army of 1,000 men armed with bayonets to Sicily and liberate it.

He did, and then triumphantly crossed the Straits of Messina to march on Naples in 1860.

The Kingdom of Italy was thus born, ruled by Victor Emmanuel II of the House of Savoy, King of Piedmont and Sardinia. The Papal States having been annexed, the kingdom stretched from the Alps to Sicily, with the important exceptions of Rome and the Veneto, both taken in 1870.

THE RISE AND FALL OF FASCISM

Italians always loved a good entertainer who could stir their emotions and divert them from themselves.... They were always delighted by a talented painter, musician, sculptor, architect, actor, dancer, as long as he did not engage their higher faculties. They respected and admired great scientists, especially if their discoveries were abstract and incomprehensible. They endured and feared a forceful leader, but they always thoroughly enjoyed his fall.... It is true that in other countries, great men have also occasionally been persecuted and put to death. Nowhere else, however, has this happened with the same discrimination, regularity, and determination.

Luigi Barzini, *The Italians* (1964)

Benito Mussolini was born to a blacksmith's family in a small town near Forli, Emilia-Romagna. The region is known for its left-leaning tendencies today, and Mussolini fit the bill; he was a revolutionary, going unwashed and unshaven for weeks, and at one point living under a bridge in a cardboard box. He read rabble-rousing revolutionary literature voraciously and, like any good charismatic leader, skipped off to Switzerland to avoid the draft. Then he returned to Italy to become the editor of a Socialist newspaper, *Avanti! (Let's Go!)*.

The era that set the stage for Fascism was the turn-of-the-20th-century industrial boom in the North. The carmaker Fiat, still Italy's largest private employer, was founded in Turin. The agricultural South was mostly unaffected, and millions of southerners took off in this period for the United States, Northern Europe, and later Australia. The rise of industrialization was accompanied by restlessness on the part of laborers. Mussolini appealed to that crowd in his Communist propaganda, a genre that also typically denounces warmongers. "Who drives us to war betrays us," read one of his headlines.

But in 1914, he realized that he could gather more readers if he supported intervention against the Austrians in what would become World War I. He did, and was thrown out of the party, but he had chosen the winning side. The popularity of such Futurist poets as Gabriele D'Annunzio and Filippo Tommaso Marinetti showed that Mussolini's young audience was eager to be rid of unscrupulous Socialist leaders, such as Giovanni Giolitti, and their cozy relationships with the enlightened industrialist families of the left: the Agnellis, Olivettis, and Pirellis. The kids wanted lightning-quick modernization, and they wanted danger.

This they got in full. In 1915, Italy entered the war on the side of Britain and France. The fiercest fighting was along the border of modern-day Slovenia, then part of the Austro-Hungarian Empire, where 600,000 Italian soldiers are now buried. It was a giant disaster in that respect, but a much bigger success for the war supporters in another.

Italy had technically won, and had grown its industrial base exponentially in those years, thanks to the demand for planes, guns, and strong state controls on production. The values of war, militancy, and ruling with an iron fist would carry Mussolini and his Fascist blackshirts into Rome in a risky, but ultimately successful, march. (Actually, Mussolini stayed well behind in Milan and arrived by train once the dust had settled.) He took command in October 1922, and after a stirring speech to Parliament in 1925, he ruled as a modern-day Augustus until things went awry in July 1943.

In the late '30s, Italy fought alongside Germany in the Spanish Civil War, and a Fascist friendship grew. (Though it should be pointed out that Italians had their share of resistance fighters, too, rallying around the cry "Today in Spain, tomorrow in Italy.") This alliance became increasingly important when Hitler annexed Austria in 1938. The next year, Mussolini annexed Albania, which was already Italian in practice. In such matters, he avoided risk wherever he could—his contribution to colonialism was moving into Ethiopia—and once Hitler had conquered most of Europe by 1940, Mussolini thought there would be little risk in attacking Greece and joining the war on Germany's side.

After he lost battles in Africa (saved only by the Germans time after time) and faced strikes and food riots at home, revolts by the domestic Slavs, and a generally disenchanted Italian public, Fascism crumbled in July 1943. The king had Mussolini arrested and appointed Marshal Badoglio as prime minister. Badoglio pretended that he would continue to fight with the Germans while he arranged for an armistice with the Allies. The Germans rescued Mussolini from his prison in Abruzzo, eventually setting him up in a puppet state on Lake Garda.

The U.S.-led Allies had started moving up into the peninsula, closing in on the German-held North. Fighting alongside the partisans, the Allies bombed Rome and eventually ousted the Nazis. Badoglio and the king deserted Rome for Bari and signed an armistice on September 8, 1943.

Meanwhile, Mussolini had tried to flee to Switzerland, carrying a forged Spanish passport, along the western shore of Lake Como. He was captured by the partisans near the town of Dongo, held as a prisoner, and ultimately shot there. His corpse was dangled upside down, along with that of his mistress, Claretta Petacci, and fellow Fascists, from the roof of a Milan gas station. Il Duce was gone, but the scars of World War II remained.

RECONSTRUCTION

After the war, Italy created a constitution describing itself as a republic "founded on labor," opposed to military action as a way to resolve international conflicts, and free of the Savoy kings who had backed the man who dragged the country into war in the first place. No male heir to the Savoy throne was allowed to set foot on Italian soil, a ban that lasted until 2003.

Geographically and politically, Italy now sat on the front lines of a new international conflict that would last for another 40 years: the Cold War. Unrest at northern factories led to the creation of the Italian Communist Party, or PCI. It was well funded by the Soviets and would become the largest Communist Party in Western Europe. Meanwhile, the Americans who had helped liberate the country from the Germans would play an even more influential role in shaping the country's domestic politics.

The United States threw its weight behind the Christian Democrats, or DC, who more or less kept a grip on power until the fall of the Berlin Wall and would remain Italy's role model for decades. This relationship was "supported" by U.S. diplomats and intelligence services hard at work keeping the Communists at bay. Though it is impossible to prove, it can only be assumed that the CIA knew about most of the covert actions of the Italian intelligence agencies in the 1960s and 1970s, especially those surrounding what became known as the "strategy of tension."

THE YEARS OF LEAD

Much like in the United States, the late 1960s in Italy were years of near-revolution. Unrest at factories grew, accompanied by a rise in anarchists and leftist groups, the most famous of which became Lotta Continua (Enduring Struggle). The "hot autumn" of 1969, as it was called, came to a roaring crescendo on December 12, when a bomb ripped through a bank in Milan's Piazza Fontana, killing 16 people. Prosecutors were quick to blame the leftists and round them up for questioning. One of them, Giuseppe Pinelli, fell from the fourth floor office of police headquarters during an interrogation. The report said that he had committed suicide. The police official singled out by Lotta Continua as the one behind Pinelli's death (though he wasn't present during the famous defenestration) was soon murdered.

It was later determined that the leftists were not at all responsible for the bomb, but rather a far-right group from the Veneto was to blame. Further investigative journalism revealed that a member of Italy's secret service and indeed the government at large were part of the plot. The series of explosions that the state had in mind was referred to as the "strategy of tension"—that is, framing leftists for state-driven terrorism and hoping that the electorate would call for a strong conservative government in response.

There was indeed a shift to the far right in the next elections, but the country was splitting to extremes. This tension between the Communists, the Socialists, and the Christian Democrats prompted the Communists' secretary, Enrico Berlinguer, to draft what he termed a "historic compromise" between the parties in 1972 in order to increase stability and further economic growth. Though ultimately unrealized, it did bring a moderated Communism back into mainstream politics, and historians argue that it held back the reemergence of unrestrained authority and safeguarded democracy.

Still, the workers' strikes continued, and revolutionary groups grew. The early 1970s saw the appearance of the Red Brigades, who would terrorize Italy throughout the later part of the decade, known as the Years of Lead. In their early existence, they beat up managers and set their cars on fire. Later, they moved to "the heart of the state," killing political figures, kidnapping judges and, in March 1978, the prime minister, Aldo Moro. The assailants ambushed his car on his way to Parliament, killed his entourage, and held him prisoner for 54 days. They killed him on May 9 and stuffed his body into the trunk of a car. A number of mysteries still surround the government's handling of the Moro crisis, just as there were doubts about the real motives behind Piazza Fontana.

The decade's final tragedy took place on August 2, 1980, when a bomb in Bologna's train station killed 85 people, including some Americans. It was blamed on right-wing terrorists, and there has always been suspicion about the state's involvement. In fact, just a year after the bombing, the Italian public found out about a secretive Masonic lodge, P2, made up of the nation's most significant politicians and business leaders, whose mission was to rid the government of Communists. On the 20th anniversary of that bombing, leaders admitted that the whole truth about Bologna had still not yet been revealed.

CLEAN HANDS AND SILVIO BERLUSCONI

The 1980s in Italy will forever be remembered for the excesses and underhanded dealings of the Socialist government, thanks to the immense backlash against bribery in the 1990s. This scandal, dubbed *Tangentopoli* (Bribesville), was nothing particularly new to Italian politics, nor would it be to most any country for that matter, but prosecutors in the 1990s decided to do something about it. Lead prosecutor Antonio Di Pietro took on an establishment previously regarded as untouchable.

The *Mani Puliti* (Clean Hands) investigation overturned an entire political class, with some Socialist leaders so shamed by the accusations of bribery that they committed suicide, while others landed in jail. The prime minister, Bettino Craxi, was run out of the country and spent the rest of his days in exile, at a vacation home in Tunisia.

The late 1980s and early 1990s in Italy more likely will be remembered for the crackdown against the Cosa Nostra in Sicily, and the murders of two magistrates in that unlikely crusade: Giovanni Falcone and Paolo Borsellino. Both Palermo-born prosecutors rose to prominence in the "Anti-Mafia Pool" by orchestrating dozens of high-level arrests. The two were killed by separate bombs within a two-month span in 1992. In his last interview with Italian television, Borsellino warned that the ties between the Sicilian Mafia and wealthy businesspeople from the peninsula were stronger than anyone might have thought.

One of the northern businesspeople who would later be accused of harboring such ties was future prime minister Silvio Berlusconi. His party's sweep of all 61 of Sicily's parliamentary seats in 2001 led to allegations that his top aides in Sicily were in contact with none other than Toto Riina's right-hand man, Bernardo Provenzano.

Berlusconi's tenure had been marked from the start. As a budding real estate baron and aspiring media mogul, he enjoyed particularly friendly relations with Craxi before the height of the Bribesville scandal. His critics use this as a starting point to help explain the man's meteoric rise in the normally static world of Italian business.

After a short stint as a cruise-ship crooner, Berlusconi made his first fortune developing a residential area known as Milano 2. With the proceeds, he took on the task of creating a rival broadcaster to the state-run RAI. The largest hurdle was that it was illegal to operate a private national television network. But he and Craxi worked things out, and Berlusconi the builder was on his way to becoming a media tycoon, Italy's richest man, and, in 1994, its prime minister.

His holding company, Fininvest, extended into such sectors as insurance, films, food distribution, and even a soccer team, A.C. Milan, which played no small part in launching Berlusconi onto the political stage. He formed a conservative party, called Forza Italia, and swept to victory in the 1994 elections, along with the formerly Fascist National Alliance of Gianfranco Fini, and the populist and separatist Northern League of Umberto Bossi. Lingering charges against Berlusconi in the Clean Hands investigation, including the creation of a slush fund to avoid taxes and bribe judges and politicians, helped bring about his quick demise. The coup de grâce, however, was the withdrawal of the Northern League from the coalition, bringing an end to Berlusconi's first reign in December the same year.

After a year of Lamberto Dini's caretaker government, the left won the elections for the first time in its postwar history, led by "The Professor," Romano Prodi. His government lasted 28 months, a long haul by Italian standards. But in 1998, his reign suffered the same fate as Berlusconi's when its partners, the Refounded Communists, refused to sign his budget, pulling out of the coalition and forcing Prodi's resignation. The Communists were pushing for greater social spending at a time when Prodi had just brought the deficit under control, qualifying Italy to take part in Europe's single currency.

The next leader to the fore was Massimo D'Alema, a former Communist who went to summer camp in the Soviet Union. His tenure would coincide with a steep rise in immigration, and consequently a palpable rise in anti-immigrant sentiments. D'Alema's government lasted until elections in the spring of 2001, when Berlusconi, aka "The Knight," came galloping back with a surge of popular support, winning around 60 percent of the vote. Bossi's Northern League, no longer separatist and now running on a mostly anti-immigrant platform, was still in the coalition, but his slimmed-down power base no longer presented a threat of blackmail to Berlusconi.

The real threats to Berlusconi's government, in the end, were the charges of tax fraud and bribery brought against him in connection with his dealings with Craxi in the '80s. Berlusconi had already been acquitted for three charges of bribery, but had to rely on a statute of limitations to nullify a fourth. He still claims that judges in those cases were politically biased against him. It would, at any rate, cost him his post.

Once again under the stewardship of Prodi, and once again with the Refounded Communists as reluctant coalition partners, the center-left slipped into power with a wafer-thin majority in 2006. The results were upheld by the nation's highest appeals court. But in 2008, Prodi's feeble coalition splintered apart, and Berlusconi's renamed "People of Freedom" party won the national elections by a wide margin.

The next three years of Berlusconi's rule were marked by recession, more scandals that this time included allegations of paying for sex with a minor, and finally a Mediterranean-wide credit crisis that sent Italy to the brink of default, and ultimately cost Berlusconi his job. After his resignation in 2011, former European Commissioner and economist Mario Monti was installed as prime minister.

Government

Precarious alliances have resulted in the collapse of several Italian governments. Italy has in fact gone through more than 60 postwar governments, at last count, causing much grumbling abroad about the country's political instability. There are dozens of major parties (and hundreds of minor ones that rarely win any parliamentary seats), so no party has a very good chance of establishing a majority on its own. Coalitions are therefore composed of a half dozen parties, some of which share close ideologies, some of which do not.

In the conservative camp these days are Silvio Berlusconi's Forza Italia, the National Alliance, the Northern League, and two descendants of the once-unflappable Christian

Democrats: the CCD and the CDU, united in a party named the UCD. The center-left includes the Democrats of the Left, the Greens, the Socialists, and the Italian Communist Party. A number of other small groups flesh out the coalitions, but the two kingmakers, the fringe parties that have made or broken governments in the past, are the Northern League and the Refounded Communists. No mainstream party truly wants these outspoken groups in their coalition, but they rarely have much of a choice.

A technical note about Italian elections: The parliamentary seats are filled according to proportional representation in each region; that is, the parties in general are assigned seats depending on how well they did in the elections overall.

The other big players on the political scene are the lobbies. The most significant of these are the labor unions—especially the left-wing CGIL and the more centrist CISL and UIL—weighing in on the side of the liberals; the industrialists' group Confindustria, on the side of the conservatives; and the Catholic Church, which applies whatever pressure it can on either side of the spectrum, depending on the issue. Clearly, the Vatican is more at ease with the conservatives' social agenda, but more recently, it has shared common ground with the liberals on matters of foreign affairs.

The church, and the pope in particular, commonly speak out to promote pacifism whenever Italy is indirectly involved in an international conflict. And Italy is almost always indirectly involved in any international conflict, sandwiched between the formerly Communist world and the West, and hosting a handful of crucial NATO bases. In the great tradition of Italian diplomacy, prime ministers have always walked a tightrope between offending their neighbors and commercial interests in the Middle East, and appeasing the powerful victors of the Cold War. But Italian leaders will never offer their country's soldiers or weapons in direct combat, only peacekeeping, because they are expressly forbidden to do so in their 1948 constitution.

THE JUDICIARY

The constitution also has a few quirks reserved for other branches of government. There is not one but two Supreme Courts: one for reviewing the constitutionality of laws, the Constitutional Court, and another that acts as the nation's highest appeals court, the *Cassazione*. Appeals are considered entirely new trials, and cases commonly go through two or three appeals. In fact, only after an appeal can you be considered guilty, which is fortunate considering all charges are granted a trial, without preliminary judicial review to see if the plaintiff even has a case. Another unique trait of the Italian judiciary: A law student will become an attorney, a notary public, or a judge. Then, judge candidates follow one of two possible career paths: those of state prosecutors or actual judges. (Foreigners can be forgiven for scratching their heads when a prosecutor is referred to in the newspaper as a "magistrate." Even Italian critics argue that any system that groups together prosecutors and judges in the same career path does not exactly reassure defendants that they are innocent until proven guilty.)

A final constitutional trait that mystifies some Americans, who are accustomed to a strong executive, is the Italian presidency. The *Presidente della Repubblica* (the head of state) is not elected by the people, but rather by an assembly of representatives, and it is little more than a figurehead role. Aside from calling elections and receiving foreign heads of state (though just to shake their hands), the steward of the presidency does little more than expound on the virtues of patriotism and lay wreaths on soldiers' tombs. The architects of Italy's constitution had experienced problems with powerful heads of state in the past.

Economy

The earthquake that was the 2007 real estate collapse and subsequent debt crisis in the United States caused an economic tsunami that crashed on Southern European shores. Italy's economy is in tough shape these days. As of this printing, the formerly free-spending country was teetering on the precipice of credit default and was fighting to remain in the euro zone. Deep austerity measures that have public employees, especially, facing a frightening new reality, have been implemented to save the nation from financial ruin.

It was well known for decades that the Italian government was spending itself into a big problem. It struggled for years, but managed to keep its debt within European Union limits. But even at the height of the crisis, when Greece looked poised to return to its former currency and some bets were on Spain to do the same, even the hardiest cynics deep down could not fathom the euro zone without its third-largest economy. For one thing, the country is now also the world's fourth-largest issuer of bonds, but also because, unlike some of its Mediterranean brethren, Italy does actually manufacture goods that the rest of the world wants.

Any discussion about Italian production starts in Turin, the industrial city that gave birth to Fiat. The Turin carmaker, founded in 1899, was for many years the motor of the national economy. It sold cars to the average Italian in staggering numbers in the postwar years, becoming Italy's largest private employer—a title it has not yet surrendered.

But in 2002, faced with overwhelming competition from foreign cars and saddled with debt from unprofitable acquisitions, Fiat hit the breaking point. It announced plans to lay off some 8,000 workers, mainly in the South, and added fuel to the debate over selling the historic carmaker to a foreign company.

This was the final straw in Fiat's gradual acceptance of the fact that it would have to start thinking small. The adjustment period was painful. But by 2007, it saw some limited success with its more diminutive models (the classic Cinquecento, for example, got a closer look and a new design). And throughout, the brighter stars in the carmaker's galaxy, Ferrari and Alfa Romeo, continued to shine. This, after all, is what Italy does best: high-end, chic, boutique.

The company swiftly turned around its fortunes in this rapidly consolidating market, and in 2011 it completed its takeover of U.S. carmaker Chrysler when it purchased 6 percent of those shares from the U.S. government.

As in almost all Western economies, mass manufacturing has largely moved abroad from Italy and has been supplanted by the service industry (notably tourism, in this case), but the country can still boast a wide array of high-quality manufactured products, thanks to their cutting-edge design. These small and medium-sized companies have long been the country's bread and butter and probably represent its immediate future: high-end shoes and clothing, specialized machinery.

The rise to fame and fortune of these once-little ateliers, and how they plan to grow while not relinquishing control, is the second economic story of the budding century. Prada, Gucci, Versace, and Armani have similar beginnings, nurtured by a family or individual, but their plans as grown-up companies are varied.

Prada is probably the best example of a luxury-brand holding company that, despite its 2011 IPO in Hong Kong, is still run by the family and yet has grown to mammoth proportions: between US$10 billion and US$15 billion. Giorgio Armani is also still controlled by its founder, even though it now does nearly US$3 billion in annual sales.

Gucci and Bulgari are the ones that got away. While the names remain Italian, French companies now own them. This arrangement is what Italian family-held companies fear. In a larger sense, it is what Italy fears as a nation.

How long will Italy continue to defend its own, in the same manner that a family "bares its claws to protect its pups" in the words of one fashion CEO? Economists suspect that protectionists have learned their lesson and expect fewer barriers to foreign investment in the future. At least it's easy to understand why Italians can be so prickly about foreign power brokers meddling in their affairs—easy, that is, for those who have read their history.

PEOPLE AND CULTURE

For all its sleek technology, Italy is still an old country, not just in terms of buildings and art, but in more ways than meet the eye. The sewers of Rome use the same channels the ancients used to flush out the city's waste. Silversmiths and violin-makers use techniques developed in the Middle Ages. Family companies go back several hundred years. Mostly, though, Italy is an old place in terms of people's manners.

Italians abide by a time-tested decorum that governs every social gathering, every business deal, and every romantic interlude—the sorts of rules that, if they ever existed in North America, were thoroughly wiped out over the last century.

Certainly, some of these unwritten rules have changed in Italy, too. Young people don't speak to their elders as formally as they once did, for example. People don't go to church as often as they used to. That shift away from piety and ceremony has opened the gates for a number of changes, such as the cohabitation of unmarried couples, one of many social norms that were unheard of in Italy 50 years ago. But beware: Not every stratum of Italian society abides by the same rules. Values in Italy change from family to family. How you act and the things you should say in front of certain people also depend on considerations such as political affiliation, geography—the South tends to be more traditional than the North—and, above all, a person's upbringing.

© PURESTOCK

Ethnicity and Class

Everyone sees what you appear to be, few touch what you are.

Machiavelli, *The Prince*

To an outsider, the line between Italian classes can be difficult to distinguish, because everyone seems so effortlessly well dressed and well mannered. Most city-dwellers at least feign an interest in the arts, and all the other erstwhile hallmarks of the aristocracy have since been usurped by even the man on the street. Italians, however, are acutely aware and perceptive about a person's background and, more importantly, what people think about their own.

Unlike in the United States or much of Western Europe, in Italy scrutinizing someone's background does not often involve trying to decipher an ethnicity, for example, for the very simple reason that 90-something percent of the population is "ethnically" Italian. If you're not, it's pretty obvious.

Now, trying to define an "ethnic Italian" would be rather difficult. Right through the last century this region had always been the melting pot of the world for Etruscans, Gauls, Greeks, Sikuls, Romans, Huns, Goths, Lombards, Slavs, Austrians, French, Spanish, you name it; the list of tribes and nationalities to conquer and settle the peninsula is probably longer than in any other state in the Old World.

In the past 100 years, though, or at least right up to the 1990s, any significant migration was in the opposite direction. What was left in this ethnic and linguistic crucible—now more easily defined because people speak, for the most part, the same language—is what we will refer to here as an Italian ethnicity.

Until the 1990s, immigration to Italy was negligible, and even today it doesn't reach the levels of immigration to Northern Europe. While the more progressive Italians go to great lengths to pave the way for a multiethnic society, the reality is that anyone who is not an ethnic Italian is quite patently an outsider. Even those attempts to appear integrated come off as awkward. Recently, a "progressive" newspaper asked to interview two of my friends about the odd nature of their marriage: He is Milanese, she is a Londoner of Pakistani descent. Apparently this was newsworthy. (Wisely, they declined the interview.) Needless to say, in a country where a "mixed marriage" elicits a media circus, the small communities of non-Italians—most notably Chinese, Albanian, and South Asian—tend to keep to themselves.

If there is any ethnic sniffing-out among Italians themselves, it is aimed toward southerners in the North, but for the most part, this is a thing of the past. Sicilians and other southerners who migrated to Milan and Turin in the 1960s have integrated into northern society, even reaching high posts in the companies where their fathers worked as manual laborers.

Their children now speak with the same nasal accent and adopted local mannerisms. It should not have been too hard for them. Italians are masters of appearances, and most of all in matters of class. They go to great lengths to make themselves appear as well bred as possible. Trying to distinguish the rich from the poor is not so easy on first blush.

Attitudes toward money are giveaways to class anywhere in the world, but the verdict is a little trickier with Italians. They represent one of those rare nationalities with a reputation for being generous. The poorer a family is, sometimes the wealthier it will appear. Gifts are lavish, beyond the giver's means, and when it comes to hosting a party or a dinner, Italians spare no expense. Maybe it is culturally assumed that this is the way that the aristocracy would behave under similar circumstances. Ironically, the only outwardly frugal people in Italy are, in fact, the aristocrats themselves. Like something from the pages of Chekhov's *The Cherry Orchard,* noble families who don't have to work are often the most worried about squandering their dwindling capital.

Then there are more subtle clues into someone's upbringing that don't go unnoticed in Italian society: the manicure of someone's fingernails, their political leanings, and the way they speak—all things that don't require money, but indicate how someone was raised. Manners, not material wealth, are enough to convince people of your up-bringing in an era when anyone with some luck in the stock market can buy a castle at a public auction or a noble title from the back pages of *The Economist.*

In the past, one of the more entertaining litmus tests for class was soccer-team affiliation. For example, in cities with two Serie A teams, e.g., Rome, Milan, Turin, and (sometimes) Genoa, fan bases traditionally were split between the middle class on one side and the working class and aristocracy on the other. Take the example of Milan. Inter, a team owned for generations by an oil-refining family, was long seen as the bastion of the bourgeoisie, while A.C. Milan was the team of the working class—their fans were nicknamed "the screwdrivers"—and their political leanings were as red as the stripes on A.C.'s shirts. In Rome, the rabble-rousing proletariat rejoiced, in the most vulgar of terms, at every shortcoming suffered by S.S. Lazio, a favorite of the neatly dressed middle class. These days, even those lines have blurred, as ownership of clubs has swapped hands and technology has brought the games to anyone with a TV.

Anyway, who cares about class in this day and age? On the face of it, Italians seem so egalitarian and unassuming that you wouldn't think it matters a lick. But it does matter, and nowhere is pedigree more important than in the workplace, where nepotism is the name of the game. Admittedly, the old-boy network is alive and well in the United States in certain industries, but in Italy, all good jobs are relatively scarce. There just isn't the same selection there is in the United States, where new companies are born and grow every day. In Italy, the few new businesses that do grow very large tend to be family-run. The CEOs often have the same name as the company itself. Rarely do you hear of a tycoon who started from scratch. With a few notable exceptions, those who land the choicest jobs in the business world are *raccomandati;* that is, protégés of a well-connected clan.

In the workplace, everyone knows their part and plays it well. The boss is addressed as *"direttore"* (literally, "director"). Such democratic inventions as "flat" companies and glass doors between the management and the staff are laughable concepts in Italy, where firms are run like fiefdoms—the power is almighty, but so is the protection, namely, job security. For reasons discussed later, you wouldn't think of job-hunting if you already have a job.

For those in positions of authority, a business suit is obligatory, and you'll never really feel out of place in Italy if you're dressed to impress. If you walk into a store and are well dressed, you'll be addressed as *signore* or *signora.* The same people who wear jeans and T-shirts into the store can expect to be referred to as *il ragazzo* or *la ragazza.*

A HEALTHY ATTITUDE

The common stereotype about the cheese-eating and cigarette-smoking continentals is that they live life to the fullest and damn the consequences. It is true that diet soft drinks have little place in Europe and gyms still aren't quite as widespread as on the other side of the pond, but Italians seem to live to a ripe old age nonetheless. The 100-year-old Italians, when asked for their secret, routinely attribute their success to one glass of red wine per day. Maybe the toast *salute!* (to your health!) has some meaning after all.

Italians may smoke more than they should (though not more than the average European, according to EU surveys) and give off the impression that the present is more important than the future, but the reality is that they are adamant about keeping in shape and do a pretty good job of it. Whether it's the way they choose their food, how they dress for the cold, or what they put on their skin, they subscribe to the doctrine of preemptive health: It's better to keep the doctor away than run to the hospital for every ache and pain.

Popular wisdom about maintaining good health, though, contains a few traditions that can be dubious, or even downright superstitious at times. The most common threat to one's health is apparently the *colpo d'aria* (draft). Air-conditioning is widely believed to bring on a cold. Few public buildings use anything other than a fan, even in the dead of summer. Similarly, no one leaves the house with wet hair, regardless of the temperature outside. Grandmothers still scold young women for sitting on cold benches, as it allegedly renders them infertile. Do not be surprised to see these same women wearing fur coats in April.

(It's a very rejuvenating feeling to be a 30-something and still be referred to as "that boy over there who wants a coffee.") In Italy, it is not success, but merely the appearance of success, that counts.

In general, Italians work hard to make a good impression. Making *una bella figura* (a good impression) requires some practice. It is an air of confidence, patience, intelligence, and respect for other people, all delivered with a dazzling smile. It can also include more material representations of success, such as showing up in the right sort of car and wearing the right clothes. It's hard to put your finger on what exactly constitutes *una bella figura* in any given situation, but it will be painfully obvious when you've made a bad one. A few examples of making *una brutta* (ugly) *figura* would be showing up to a dinner without a bottle of wine, or with a clearly cheap one when the occasion calls for something nice; tripping and falling; confusing someone's name, or forgetting it altogether; letting out a closely guarded secret; forgetting someone's birthday—basically the same sort of buffoonery that gets you into trouble anywhere else in the world.

Birthday parties, incidentally, have their own peculiar nuances. You, as the person celebrating your birthday, host the party, or maybe even buy the dinner at a restaurant. Gifts are almost always presented in public. As a foreigner, you might consider it a little gauche if someone opens each of the presents in front of the invitees, but in Italy, this is standard operating procedure.

Outside of those sorts of celebrations, don't feel obliged to pick up the check at dinner if it was your idea. It's always a nice gesture, but Italians—young people, especially—will often decide to pay *alla romana* (the Roman way), which is to say everyone pays for themselves. Who knew the Romans were such cheapskates? In English jargon, it's usually the Dutch who are treated to this stereotype. (Guys, don't take this as an invitation to go *alla romana* on a date. You're usually expected to pick up the tab.)

Gender Roles

The divide between the sexes is still very deep in Italy. Men and women are different, and neither seems very disappointed in their role. Men are expected to be aggressive in courting women, and women are expected to parry with coquettish nonchalance, inventing themselves as objects of impossible desire and undertaking all the burdens and privileges pertaining thereto.

Take the Miss Italia pageant, for example. Every September, it draws tens of millions of television viewers—the majority of them women, apparently, judging from the shampoo and skin-cream commercials. It attracts more viewers than almost any other televised event. A few years ago, a contestant rose up against the establishment. She said that women were not objects to be judged, and that the inane questions asked of them were well beneath their intelligence. Silence. No one knew quite what to make of this irreverence, though the next day, a few observers applauded her for her pageant-ending performance. The next day, the judging resumed as usual, not a word more was spoken about it, and Miss Italia continues to be a teenage dream.

Italian women all over the peninsula are pushed to look stunning on a daily basis. The subways are filled with ads for diet programs that promise pounds lost by the week, skin creams that allegedly eliminate decades of aging, etc. Still, you will find very few women who would trade in their makeup for a flannel shirt and a pair of baggy pants. Sex appeal is an integral part of Italian culture on both sides of the gender divide. You won't find too many men with flannel shirts and baggy trousers either.

If you're single, be prepared for old-school courtship. You'll find flower vendors at every corner. Men use them frequently. They always hold doors open for women, call them on the phone regularly—though not too regularly, as the tightrope between interest and desperation is just as carefully walked in Italy as anywhere else in the world—and, on the whole, consider themselves to be pretty romantic guys. Apparently, they invented the term.

Italian women are not so easily convinced. They've been dealing with Italian men for a long time now, and they know every trick in the book. They are as savvy as they come. In turn, men have become even craftier. Which means women have to be even quicker. Which came first, the wayward rooster or the pecking hen? Who knows? All that's certain is that the woman's hesitance and the man's devious strategies to overcome it create a vicious circle leading to a deep but intriguing distrust between the sexes. It goes a long way toward explaining why Italian men have such an affinity for foreigners.

The art of picking up, or *rimorchiare* (literally, "to tow," as in a car), an out-of-towner is as carefully studied as the deliberate strokes of Giotto's brush. The infamous stories about sweet-talking Romans on the Spanish Steps waiting for an innocent Northern European or North American blonde to walk by are not at all apocryphal. They ring just as true today as they did back in the '50s, an era that spawned the "*rimorchio* generation," as one Italian-Scottish friend likes to refer to his parents.

Sometimes, though, the role-playing is no fun at all and borders on plain sexism.

The grumbles about the half-naked TV hostesses of prime-time quiz shows—think a dozen or so teenaged Vanna Whites minus most of their clothing—were pushed over the edge by one particular show that actually kept the young woman in a glass cage under the contestants' table, with airholes cut out for her to breathe. The producers protested that the setup was meant to be ironic, poking fun at the sexism in other shows, but the damage was already done. The glass cage has since disappeared. The bikini-clad hostesses remain.

There was nothing ironic, however, in a court decision in the late 1990s that ruled a woman cannot claim to have been raped if she was wearing denim at the time, because jeans are so tight-fitting that getting them off requires the consent of the wearer. Women parliamentarians, led by Alessandra Mussolini (yes, *that* Mussolini; she's his granddaughter), protested en masse and brought international attention to the whole ugly affair. Yet, at the same time, it highlighted the fact that Italy does have quite a few influential women in politics—not representative of the number of Italian women, perhaps, but still a relatively high number, many of whom hold key ministerial posts. One post that is almost always held by a woman is head of the ministry for equal opportunity, a brief partly designed to increase women's role in public affairs. In the private sector, women are not nearly on equal footing with men, but the country does have its share of companies run by women, especially those who inherited large family firms.

GAY AND LESBIAN CULTURE

Thirty years ago, if you had said that there would be a group of women holding ministerial posts in this decade, your prediction might have been met with a wry smile and a condescending pat on the shoulder. If you then added that an openly gay man would be a regional president in the staunchly conservative South, you could have expected a hearty guffaw.

Sure enough, in April 2005, the people of Puglia elected as their president 46-year-old Nicola Vendola, a gay man and a Communist to boot. What a difference a generation makes. That Vendola's election did not elicit more than casual attention shows just how openly accepted gay men can feel in Italy, even, amazingly, the South.

The North and Milan especially have hosted a very visible gay culture for years. This city obsessed with fashion, with Giorgio Armani as its king, has made sure that homosexuality was nothing other than mainstream. Its gay clubs are extremely popular with a diverse crowd, public displays of affection between men on the street are regular, and there are times when a straight man in the publishing world feels squarely in the minority at parties.

Turin, Venice, Florence, and Rome aren't much different in that regard. Each of them has a vibrant gay community, and even small cities like Bergamo, Treviso, Perugia, etc., have their own gay associations under the umbrella group, Arcigay (www.arcigay.it). Travel magazines regularly rate Italy as the top destination for gay travelers.

In fact, it seems almost silly to stress the point, but it's probably necessary when we consider that this is, after all, the home of the Roman Catholic Church. Roughly 50 percent of voters in the last national election chose a coalition that includes a number of Christian-oriented parties that, at least theoretically, believe that homosexuality is a sin. When that center-right coalition was in power, there were indeed police raids on popular late-night cruising grounds, and they installed lights in the darkest of them.

Religion

The modern state of Italy has had, of course, a very complicated relationship with the church, starting with the framing of its constitution. As we noted, the document states that the republic is "founded on labor," but then goes on to say, "whose sovereignty belongs to the people." That wording was a compromise between the two parties who signed the constitution, representing the Communists on the one side and the Catholics on the other.

The very road that leads from the center of Rome to St. Peter's Square is the Via della Conciliazione, a nod to the famous "compromise" of power between Pope Pius XI and Mussolini. Make no mistake; until very recently, the Catholic Church was a formidable force to be reckoned with, for both the left and the right.

The Vatican is literally a 15-minute walk from Parliament. Seminarians roam the streets in white collars, pilgrims flood into Assisi and Rome. Thousands of precious cathedrals and monuments at every turn give testimony to the 1,500 years that the Catholic Church ruled nearly every aspect of life on the peninsula. One would think that all this would have a profound influence on the spiritual lives of everyday citizens.

In reality, young Italians today are just not very religious. A good portion of them still marry in the church, even if that's one of the only times they'll go there in their adult lives, except for perhaps baptisms and the occasional Christmas concert. Even the local adoration of Pope John Paul II appeared to be a case of saluting the man, not the rank.

All this is to say that church attendance is very low for the under-60 set. Walk into a church in Poland on a Sunday and you'll be lucky to find standing room. Go to mass in Italy and you can choose just about any seat you like.

© OLENA KRYZHANOVSKA/123RF

Chairs are set up for a mass outside of the Vatican in St. Peter's Square in Rome.

This can be seen as good news for practicing Catholics planning to move to Italy. You will certainly feel welcome in church, and, besides, what a church it is! Your local parish might have been built in the 15th century, with Renaissance frescoes in the chapels and ceilings. For those who have never witnessed Easter Mass in St. Peter's Square—simply put, it is Super Bowl Sunday for even the moderately devout. Obviously, Italy offers a unique spiritual experience for Catholics.

For non-Catholics, well, not so much, though there is a little religious diversity. Rome has a historic Protestant presence. There are synagogues here and there in the major cities: Rome and Venice are home to centuries-old Jewish neighborhoods. Muslim communities are rapidly growing in the northern cities, with Milan hosting a very busy mosque.

To be honest, I've never been to that mosque, but I can't help but get the impression that Muslims don't feel embraced by Italian society. That may be comically understated. It's difficult to forget the 2003 rendition and subsequent torture of Milan's Muslim leader, Abu Omar, by CIA agents, who accused him of inciting terrorism. Or the 2010 arrest by Italian police of Abu Imad, the leader of Milan's largest mosque, on terrorism charges. In fact, it's surprising that his mosque was still in operation in the first place as authorities had threatened to close it for years. Other mosques have been closed down already, and construction of new ones has been effectively blocked across the country.

We hear similar stories around the continent, along with complaints that this "social experiment" of multiculturalism has gone too far. So, it's not going to be easy to be a practicing Muslim anywhere in Western Europe in this day and age, and Italy is no different.

The Arts

Italians are crazy about cinema—movie theaters are just about the only place in the country where everyone shows up on time. The masters of the silver screen found an eager public that didn't seem to exist for fiction writers, at least not in the same numbers, in linguistically divided Italy. Though the country has its share of literati, there never seemed to be the same popular passion for theater and literature as is in, say, France or Russia.

That said, there are some very well-known Italian authors. Much of the world has at least heard of the Renaissance authors Dante, Petrarch, and Boccaccio, and possibly have read works by Alessandro Manzoni, Italo Calvino, Primo Levi, Gabriele D'Anunzio, or Leonardo Sciascia, to name a handful. Contemporary Italian writers like Umberto Eco and Oriana Fallaci regularly make the *New York Times* best-seller lists. But the cultural treasures of Italy known far and wide are not its books, but its music, art, and architecture. Italians have contributed more to these fields than perhaps any other people throughout history.

The first hint of Italy's influence on music is in the terminology: It's all in Italian. From the musicians' guilds of Rome to the composers of religious madrigals of the Middle Ages, and onward to the inventors of opera in the 17th century, Italians steered music's evolution for centuries and gave name to their innovations. Indeed, one of the perks of living in places like Venice, Padua, Milan, Parma, Bologna, and Rome is the

© LUCIE ERICKSEN

Brunelleschi's dome in Florence

opportunity to hear the works of composers like Verdi, Rossini, and Vivaldi in the very cities that inspired the music—and perhaps even played on Stradivarius violins, still proudly crafted in Cremona.

The Italians' flair for creativity manifests itself everywhere. In architecture, the Romans borrowed much from the Greeks but made some very far-reaching improvements. For instance, they introduced a circular dimension to classic Greek colonnades, giving the world the arch—and, by extension, the vault and the dome. These became essential elements in the buildings of Christianity. Dating from the early Middle Ages, examples of this Romanesque style can be found in abundance in Ferrara, Florence, Lucca, Milan, Modena, Pisa, Pavia, and Venice, and, of course, in Rome itself. Some of the deepest impressions on the history of architecture, however, were made during Italy's Renaissance. Brunelleschi's dome in Florence, the ducal palace in Urbino by Luciano Laurana and Francesco di Giorgio, the ducal piazza of Vigevano by Donato Bramante—every Italian city, great and small, boasts at least one example of period architecture that is now closely studied around the world. The Baroque architecture of later generations—St. Peter's Square is the most obvious example—is also unequaled anywhere else.

As an unpatriotic people, though, Italians have little need to propagandize these innovations as "inventions." They rightly point out that visionaries in every field, such as Galileo, Leonardo da Vinci, and Michelangelo, all drew on the work of predecessors in order to create their own works of genius. Even Giotto had something to start with, having closely studied the paintings of Cimabue and Pietro Cavallini. Still, most experts on the subject divide the history of painting into what came before Giotto and his frescoes in the Scrovegni Chapel in Padua, and what came afterward. Following in the 14th-century master's footsteps were legions of Italian painters who continued to define the Renaissance: Masaccio, Sandro Botticelli, Piero di Cosimo, Piero della Francesca, and the sculptors Donatello and Luca Della Robbia. That period of rediscovery yielded to the High Renaissance of the 15th century, which gave the world Leonardo's *Mona Lisa* and *Last Supper,* Michelangelo's *David* and *The Last Judgment,* Raphael's *The Alba Madonna* and *The School of Athens,* and the works of Titian and Tintoretto. They were followed by Caravaggio in the Baroque period of the early 17th century and Canaletto's Rococo style of the 18th century.

If, when bombarded by such terms in Italy, you ever find yourself confused by the styles or can't remember who came when, all you need to do is open an Italian newspaper or magazine or turn on TV at prime time, all of which carry nonstop art coverage. The fact that a famous art critic has his own show on television in Italy, and that people actually watch it—or that there exists such a thing as a famous art critic at all—should give you some indication of just how seriously Italians take their painting, sculpture, and architecture.

If everything in the United States sooner or later boils down to business, everything in Italy is an art. The shape of a coffeepot, the line of a car, the taste of a simple pasta, the finish of a wine, the way a waiter scoops up the bill, and the flair of a soccer player tapping a pass into the net are all flourishes appreciated and practiced by everyday Botticellis. In Italy, more than anywhere else, style and image are everything.

PLANNING YOUR FACT-FINDING TRIP

Unless you know Italy very well already, you'll need to visit the areas where you might be interested in living. More than one trip will be necessary. The country is only the size of Arizona, but it's as varied as the entire United States. There is an Italy that speaks German and eats speck and sauerkraut in the foothills of the Dolomites, and one that uses Arabic fishing methods in the southern Mediterranean. There are farming plains, vineyards, fishing communities on rocky coasts, villages clinging to volcanoes, and alpine fields and valleys. Italy even claims its own Wild West, with rodeos and lots of beef, in the Maremma area of Tuscany.

Centuries of foreign occupation have left a mosaic of cultures with different values and priorities. You feel like you've just traveled to another country when you leave your office in Turin or Milan for a weekend in Bari or Palermo. The differences between the North and South are profound, and you'll only know which lifestyle suits you better after you've spent some time in each.

Mostly, though, the decision on where to live in Italy will be narrowed down by what sort of work you do, if you work at all, and how much you can afford to spend. If you're a career person, chances are you'll need to make your home in or near one of

the major cities. If you plan to open a bed-and-breakfast, you'll likely look for more bucolic settings where tourism flourishes. Entrepreneurs often feel more comfortable with the North, where the work ethic is assumed to be higher. If you're a student, you'll be confined to cities with a university program—for foreigners, this often means Padua, Rome, Bologna, Arezzo, Siena, Perugia, and above all, Florence.

If you're retired, well, you've earned the right to live just about anywhere you please, though it is a smart idea for homeowners of all walks of life to live somewhere near basic services, such as schools, hospitals, train stations, and airports. The dream of a country retreat can turn into a nightmare if the house is more than an hour from the nearest commercial center.

An initial fact-finding trip is a good time to check out the price of homes or apartments, meet professional contacts and potential employers (or examine the market for your business idea), and, hopefully, brush up on your language skills.

Reading English-language media about Italian current events and culture is one way to take the pulse of the country you're about to call home. Before arriving, scour maps, cookbooks, and guidebooks and read as much as possible on the art and history of the place—you won't know what you're looking at in Italy unless you know the past.

Preparing to Leave

Traveling to Italy in this day and age couldn't be much easier. There are several direct flights per week from the United States to Rome and Milan, even Pisa, and lots of connecting services to other cities. Plus, there is a field of low-fare airlines that fly from European cities to smaller Italian airports.

For European Union countries that adhere to the Schengen agreement, such as Italy, there are essentially no visa requirements for Americans staying fewer than 90 days. The only health issue is making sure your insurance covers you overseas—Medicare will not. Customs regulations are no stricter than they are in the United States—in fact, they are more lenient in many respects. After about a dozen flights to Italy, I've never actually had my suitcase checked by customs. One might assume that this has changed in a post–September 11 world, but for better or worse, it hasn't changed much in Italy. Just remember not to bring in perishable food items or huge stacks of currency.

CURRENCY

Everyone has a theory on the best way to bring money abroad, ranging from traveler's checks to stacks of greenbacks, but if you're the type of person who likes to rely on credit cards and ATMs, rest assured there are loads of bank machines in Italy, even in the smallest towns.

A few warnings, however. Some ATMs still go off-line at midnight, and often the international line falls for a few hours. It's not a foolproof system. It's a good idea to get a fresh card before any long trip overseas, in case the old one is almost demagnetized.

Check with your bank to make sure that the card can be used abroad. New ones often have to be activated at your own bank first, and some personal identification numbers (PINs) won't work overseas. Use a four-digit PIN, not six digits, and don't rely on letters on the keyboard to remember your PIN; some European ATMs have only numbers on the keys.

Still, the ATM and credit card combination is arguably the best strategy, and use that credit card wherever you can, as U.S. banks especially have been piling on higher ATM fees for international cash withdrawals. (Make sure the places you shop accept credit cards, and if the vendor says the credit card machine is broken, argue with him or her. It is not.) Traveler's checks are not common outside the major tourist destinations—and you will likely be looking off the beaten path for some of the best that Italy has to offer—and moving around any country with piles of dollars is never a sound plan. Stealing tourists' valuables is still a fairly common practice in almost every big city, especially Rome and Naples, and even Milan. (I had everything stolen out of my car once in downtown Milan, including my passport.) The name of the game is avoiding commissions at currency exchange booths and their awful exchange rates. It is true that using ATMs means paying the standard fee every time you withdraw, and some banks charge an extortionate percentage fee on top of that, but even €5 for of a €200 withdrawal is still better than the exchangers' rates, as you'll be getting a much better deal with your card. For a more complete look at banking in Italy, see *Banking* in the *Finance* chapter.

WHAT TO TAKE

You will need plug adapters for all of your U.S. electronics. For any large appliance, such as a printer or a blender, you should have a 110- to 240-volt transformer. Your laptop and other commonly portable devices should already come with one.

Remember that videocassettes and DVDs are on different systems in Europe. VCRs in Europe run on PAL, or Phase Alternating Line, not the U.S.-style NTSC, or National Television System Committee. (Italian camera operators, who swear that PAL offers more consistent quality, joke that NTSC should stand for Never Twice the Same Color.) Media companies have also set up separate DVD codes in Europe to prevent sneak previews of movies not yet released overseas. If your computer has a DVD player, be warned that you will be able to switch back and forth between European and U.S. systems only a few times, and then the computer will experience problems.

By all means, buy any accessories for your computer or digital camera before you leave; not only are they more expensive in Italy, but many brands are not as common here, and stores may not have what you're looking for. Also, pick up any software before you leave, unless you want the Italian-language version.

Other items that you should bring along for any extended stay include: tax documents, if you're traveling in the filing season (though the U.S. Embassy and Consulates have all the necessary forms); a résumé and any letters of recommendation; a photocopy of your passport (tucked in a separate suitcase) in case the original is lost or stolen. It's hard to get a replacement without the copy.

Packing a load of aspirin is a good idea, since it can only be bought at pharmacies, as well as any prescription medication you may need. Also, if you are particularly prone to colds, pack a good supply of decongestants. I still cannot explain why pseudoephedrine tablets (unless mixed in minuscule doses with unnecessary agents for fighting the flu) are so difficult to acquire in the average pharmacy. Other than that, the toiletry aisle of an Italian supermarket looks almost identical to one in the United States.

WELCOME TO ITALY

© PURESTOCK

Make sure to bring an umbrella if you're visiting Italy in the fall.

Dressing for the Weather

Depending on the time of year, packing clothes for Italy can be simple or very tricky. The dozens of different climates have their own weather patterns in different seasons. The only constants are that the Alps are very cold in the winter, and everywhere else is torrid in the summer. Especially in the North, the humidity can be suffocating. Rains there come like clockwork in early September and mid-November, and you can count on a snowstorm or two just after Christmas.

In the central regions and the South, you can usually get away with just a jacket in the spring and fall, and make sure to bring very light clothes for the summer. Except maybe during the week in early August, when the heat is absolutely dizzying, Italian men never wear shorts in the city. If you think it's important to fit in, bring along some light linen pants and a few dress shirts that breathe.

WHEN TO GO

Any experienced Italophile will tell you that late spring is the best time to visit. For Naples, Rome, Florence, Venice, and Milan, this is probably true. All of those places can be rainy in the fall, and summer, in my opinion, is out of the question.

But the harsh reality is that most people can only take time off in July and August, and if it's their first time here, they want to see the major attractions. The trouble is that not only is every other North American, Japanese, Australian, and German tourist here in the summer, but many Italians are on vacation, too, and a lot of the shops and cafés are closed for a few weeks at a time. If you must come in the summer, it's best to avoid the cities and head straight to the sea or the mountains. And book your hotels months in advance.

You will get much more out of your first stay in Italy if you come during the off-season. Every region has its own identity that expresses itself best in a particular time of year.

Early fall: Piedmont and Tuscany. These are the major winemaking regions, and if you want to taste Nobile di Montepulciano and Barolo, it's always nice to visit the vineyards when the grapes are still on the vine.

Late fall: Emilia-Romagna. This is when the *piadine* (roll-up) sandwiches and salads yield to the hearty, trademark dishes of the Po River plain: prosciutto and *culatello* (a prosciutto delicacy), followed by tortellini and ravioli with red Lambrusco wine. Universities are in session, which means a lively atmosphere. Emilia, Bologna especially, is often said to have the highest standard of living in Italy, and also tops the charts for the percentage of people that leave in the summer, when it is a ghost town.

NATIONAL HOLIDAYS

- **January 1:** New Year's Day
- **January 6:** Epiphany
- **March/April:** Easter Monday
- **April 25:** Liberation Day
- **May 1:** Labor Day
- **June 2:** Anniversary of the Founding of the Republic

- **August 15:** Feast of the Assumption
- **November 1:** All Saints' Day
- **December 8:** Feast of the Immaculate Conception
- **December 25:** Christmas Day
- **December 26:** St. Steven's Day

Most importantly, business is in full swing in the fall. To understand the glamorous reputation of Milan, you should see it when people return tanned and relaxed from summer vacation, the fashion models start to arrive, and the beautiful people put on parties. You might want to check out the calendar on the trade fair's website, www.fieramilano.it, to see when the fashion and design shows are. (Usually, the Salone del Mobile design fair begins in April, while the women's fashion shows are in late September and late February.) Conversely, you should stay away during those dates if you haven't yet booked a hotel. The best restaurants also fill up quickly.

Winter: Turin, Veneto, and Alto Adige. The Dolomites need to be seen in the snow. If Easter should be done in Rome, Christmas should be done in Trento, in a frosty town with alpine scenery and heavy meals. Plus, the skiing at Madonna di Campiglio and Cortina d'Ampezzo is some of the best in Italy.

Spring: Everywhere else. Rome, Florence, and Naples are fine to visit in the fall but are at their peak in the spring. So are the Cinque Terre area of Liguria and the lakes region of Lombardy, both of which are in full bloom and enjoy perfect weather. The same is true for almost any pastoral area, especially Abruzzo and Umbria, which holds its cherry festival just after the winter.

Every region hosts hundreds of festivals and events throughout the year. (A nice database of them is at www.whatsonwhen.com.) Many are held in the summer—most notably, Spoleto's music festival in June and the Umbria Jazz Festival and the Palio of Siena, which run in July and August—either for historical reasons or to dovetail with the tourist influx. Others, such as the Venice Film Festival in late August or early September, are timed to let the tourists get out first.

If, on your first trip, you've chosen a region and are reasonably sure this is where you'd like to live, it's always best to come a second time in a different season. You may have fallen in love with Puglia or the Italian Riviera during your stay in July, but do you realize how lonely it can get there in the winter? Like all resorts, the Italian lakes and coastlines are buzzing with festivals and activities in the summer, but it's all downhill from there.

Northern cities like Milan may seem an ideal choice for urbanites, with their swank shops, cafés, and cosmopolitan population, but most of these disappear in July and August, when the humidity and mosquitoes descend. Similarly, Venice—aka "la

Serenissima"—is indeed the most serene and romantic city in the world in the off-season, but feels more like Disneyland when the tourists start arriving in May.

A city or region that was off-putting on your first trip might take on redeeming qualities if you come back in a different season. You should try short-term rentals in a few places in various months before starting an earnest search for a house.

Again, keep in mind that you won't be able to get much real estate business done in the summer. In other seasons, a three-day weekend in Italy can magically turn into a week, so don't plan to reach agents or even homeowners in the periods around Christmas, New Year's Day, and Easter.

Arriving in Italy

PUBLIC TRANSPORTATION

It would be nice if we could take Europe's network of public transportation and make it work in the United States, but the expanses between cities usually make it more convenient to fly. Distances in Italy are small by comparison. It sometimes makes more sense to board a train in Rome's city center and get off in the center of Milan four and a half hours later than it does to get to Rome's airport 45 minutes out of town, board a plane 30 minutes later, take an hour's flight to Milan's Malpensa airport, and end up in the city center maybe an hour after that.

If you plan to visit cities and medium-sized towns on your initial trip, you should take the train. The railways go nearly everywhere and are relatively cheap. There is also always a reliable, though not always timely, network of buses.

Getting to the countryside to visit farmhouses is another story. For that, you'll need a car. Renting one in Italy is just as easy as in the United States, but if you're coming during tourist season, reserve well in advance. Agencies can sell out quickly, especially on the Ferragosto weekend starting August 15. If you're traveling in the winter, be sure to reserve snow chains also. There seems to be a short supply of these at rental companies, but chains are essential on wintry mountain roads. Actually, they are required by law.

Sample Itineraries

To get some feel for which area of Italy you like most, you really should shoot for a two-week stay. If one week is all the vacation time you have, you'll need to focus on just one particular area. I have listed a few suggestions below for weeklong trips. If you're scouting out a place to live, there just isn't time in one week to wait in line at the Vatican Museums, wander through the Forum, see the Uffizi in Florence, take a gondola ride in Venice, and still familiarize yourself with the countryside in between. The 10-day itinerary of northern and central Italy and the monthlong tour of the entire country have respectively wider scopes.

Beware; you will be spending a lot of time in the car, but if you hope to see enough countryside to get a feel for what the homes are like, there is really not much of an alternative. The best solution would be to sacrifice some sightseeing to spend an extra day in the town or city that you think could be your new home. The goal of this fact-finding trip is to pinpoint a location where you can eventually plan a short-term rental.

A WEEKLONG SAMPLER

Once you have some idea of the part of Italy that suits you best, you should plan to spend a week there to see some of the smaller cities and towns and get a feel for local flavors and rhythms. Below are four geographic options with ideas on how you might spend a week in each.

A Week in the Northeast
BEST TIME TO VISIT: FEBRUARY

Time your fact-finding trip to Lombardy and the Veneto to coincide with winter fun in the Dolomites and Carnival in Venice. The university life in Padua will be in full swing, everyone will be open for business, and, most importantly, the hotels will offer rock-bottom rates.

With a week's time, plan to spend: three nights in Milan, with a full day in the city and a day trip to Lake Como, a night in Verona, and two nights in Venice before making your way back.

Fly into Milan's Malpensa airport and spend a day in the nation's fashion and finance capital, where you might decide to go window-shopping for contemporary furniture for your new home. Delve into Milan's aperitif culture in the Brera district just after you've taken a look at the paintings inside the Pinacoteca di Brera and the galleries along that neighborhood's cobblestone streets.

Several trains per day leave both the Stazione Centrale and Cadorna station bound

© JOHN MORETTI

arriving in Menaggio, Lake Como

for Como, and you can take a boat to villages on the lakeshore from there. Of course, the best way to see everything is with a rental car, especially if you'd like to explore the hills above the lake and the suburban triangle between Como, Lecco, and Monza, the area known as Brianza. Those who plan to work in the big city but prefer more rural rhythms (and prices) will find Brianza a practical compromise, very close to both the urban center and the lakes' natural beauty. This suburban area is not the best place to spend the night. Rather, stay in Milan or in the Como area, both of which are just a 30- to 40-minute drive away.

The ideal time to visit the lakes region is really in March or early April when the wisteria start to bud. Still, Lake Como is no less beautiful in the winter, with its palm trees framed by snowcapped peaks and spectacular vistas. My favorite wintertime activity in the area is finding a plate of *pizzoccheri,* Lombardy's buckwheat pasta served with garlic, Savoy cabbage, and melted Bitto cheese.

Make your way east toward Verona. The opera season held at the Arena runs through July, but the splendidly preserved Roman amphitheater and the cozy downtown are enough to hold your attention in the off-season. Be sure to stop in the Bottega del Vino for an eye-opening enological experience. This area, too, has great urban and rural options. Nearby Lake Garda, a favorite retreat for Austrian and German tourists especially, is home to magnificent villas as well as more affordable housing. (As an added bonus, the adjacent Dolomites are a playground for snowboarders, skiers, or simply those who want to take a snowmobile ride up to a cozy lodge in the mountains for a fireside dinner.)

Padua makes for a great home base for exploring both Venice and Verona, as accommodations there are cheaper and more readily available in the high season. It is only about 30 minutes from the lagoon by train, and less than an hour from Verona. On the other hand, you might have your heart set on living in Venice itself, in which case you should spend a few days on the lagoon to make sure that a car-less existence is right for you.

Winter is truly the best time of year, maybe the only time of year, to tour Venice properly. The crowds are minimal and every *rio* and *calle* can be seen as they were meant to be seen. The revelry of Carnival, meanwhile, is legendary.

A Week in the Northwest
BEST TIME TO VISIT: LATE AUGUST, EARLY SEPTEMBER

Turin is no longer a mystery to most tourists thanks to the exposure it received during the 2006 Olympic Winter Games. And thanks to the Slow Food Movement (founded in Bra, Piedmont) and the growing international success of such local wines as Barolo and Barbaresco, the northwest corner of Italy features prominently on tourists' maps. They've been coming to Liguria's Cinque Terre for some time now already.

I recommend late summer as the best time to visit because if you're touring vineyards, you want to do so when the fruit is on the vine. By late August, the harvest is just around the corner. The only trouble with visiting in September is that rain is fairly likely in the North.

Fly into Milan's Malpensa airport and rent a car. On the way down to Turin, spend some time in Lake Maggiore, an idyllic respite just a quick drive from the city.

As much as I love the restaurants in this city and the royal palaces downtown, it has to be said the Turin doesn't have the same blockbuster attractions that other cities in Italy do (with the notable exception of the Shroud of Turin, the renowned Christian relic that only occasionally is on display.) Unless you plan to have a job here, Turin would be an unusual choice for a foreigner in search of a new life in Italy.

On the other hand, just south of the city is a magical area referred to as Le Langhe. Not only is it home to many of Piedmont's best wines, but also to the famous white truffle, celebrated in a festival in Alba every September. In nearby Bra, the Slow Food Movement holds two huge gastronomical festivals in alternate years: the Salone del Gusto, a massive banquet of foods from around the world, in even years (October), and Cheese, a celebration of, you guessed it—every type imaginable, in odd years (September). For gastronomes, this is a little piece of heaven. Because of this and the surrounding vineyards and castles, and its location midway between the Riviera and the Alps, Le Langhe has been attracting foreign homeowner attention.

Farther south, Liguria and its Riviera have been hosting foreign tourists for more than a century. Have a look around the coast between Camogli and Rapallo and you'll understand why. It is tempting for these same visitors, after hiking in the Cinque Terre and loafing around in around Portofino, to skip Genoa and shoot right up to San Remo and the beaches by the French border. That would be a mistake. Genoa has truly cleaned up its act—even UNESCO has recently named Via Garibaldi's row of merchants' palaces as one of its World Heritage sites.

A Week in Tuscany and Umbria
BEST TIME TO VISIT: JUNE

The international airport in Pisa is certainly closer to Florence, which also has its own air terminals, but Rome is just as easy if you plan to visit southern Tuscany. I would highly recommend that route. Northern Lazio and the Maremma are a great starting point for any visit to Tuscany for those planning a move. The countryside around Capalbio (a well-known retreat for leaders from the center-left, especially) has a number of *agriturismi* (rural bed-and-breakfasts) that run horseback tours of the area. Between the countryside trattorie, the thermal spa town of Saturnia, and the beaches nearby, you might well decide to spend the whole week there.

Though that may be tempting, you should head north toward Siena and enjoy an afternoon of wine-tasting and home shopping in Montalcino or Montepulciano along the way. Although prices there are for the most part prohibitively high, you should spend some time surveying farms in Chianti, if only to get an idea of what might be.

June is a great time to cruise through the countryside, with its sunflowers in bloom and its grapes just beginning to take shape. While the crowds will already have swelled in Florence, it's also a great season to visit the city. Florence holds the Regatta del Palio boat race and the Gioco di Calcio Storico rugby-like soccer match the third week of June.

My favorite city in Tuscany is Lucca, and the villages and nature in the Garfagnana are rustic, but with just a week I would recommend heading southeast toward Arezzo and on to Umbria.

The southeast corner of Tuscany is some of the choicest countryside for foreign homeowners, counting the rock star Sting among them, and of course Cortona is the setting for Frances Mayes's book *Under the Tuscan Sun*. Farther east, into Umbria, there may still be some deals you can uncover even today if you wander around enough. Todi

piazza in Lucca

has already been discovered by the international set: Serious home shoppers should have a closer look at the area around Terni, which is right on the way back to Rome.

A Week in the South
BEST TIME TO VISIT: LATE MAY

From the tip of Puglia to the western shores of Sicily, South Italy covers quite a long stretch. Add to that the lack of a good east–west highway in the South (or most anywhere on the mountainous peninsula, for that matter) and the hassle of catching a ferry from Sicily to the mainland, and any trip across the Mezzogiorno takes a very long time indeed.

I think it's much more prudent to concentrate on either Puglia or the coast of Campania and on to Sicily in order to get the most out of your trip. I'll focus on the latter one here.

The trip from Rome to Naples is only about two hours on the highway as it's pretty fast-moving traffic; it's the bit south of Naples that is infinitely slower. It is also one of the most spectacular coastlines in the world. In fact, the whole coast down to the tip of Calabria includes some spectacular, well-known resorts: Maratea and Tropea, especially. The adventurous beach house seekers might turn up something very interesting down here.

From Reggio, take the boat over to Sicily and explore the eastern coast: Siracusa, Catania and its volcano, and Taormina are the major points of interest. Just northwest, the Aeolian Islands are the highlight of any trip to Sicily in my opinion, with Stromboli as the crown jewel. From there, the northern coast to Palermo, in particular Cefalu, is studded with pleasant medieval towns, while Palermo itself will be one of the most unexpectedly magical cities you'll visit in Italy.

TEN DAYS IN ITALY

It's shocking how quickly a week will fly by in Italy. If you have 10 days, you'll probably want to stretch out your visit to the corner of the country that is your focus, even if there is a huge temptation to see what else the place has to offer. Italy is not a massive country geographically, but there are hundreds of sites that demand a visit. For first-time visitors, a 10-day trip should encompass the route from Naples to Rome to Florence, and then either the western route through Genoa and Turin, or northeast to Milan and Venice. Take a couple of days in each and refer to the weeklong itineraries above.

Days 1–2: Rome

A visit to the Vatican takes up much of the day in itself, and yet that's only the tip. Naturally, you can't leave Italy without having seen the Pantheon, Piazza Navona, the Trevi Fountain, and the Spanish Steps. Fortunately they're all within walking distance, and with the exception of the interior of the Pantheon, you can, and should, see those spotlit sites in the evening, gelato in hand, after an aperitif in Campo de' Fiori and a pizza in the alleyways between there and Piazza Navona. I would save daylight hours for a morning walk or inline skating in the Villa Borghese and exploring the neighborhood near the Colosseum: the crypts beneath San Clemente, the recently discovered Roman Houses nearby, and the Domus Aurea, Nero's underground palace, if it's not under restoration.

Day 3: Montalcino, Montepulciano, Siena, and Chianti

This is going to be an eating and driving day. Obviously you could and should spend a week in this part of Tuscany, but the basics are to see some vineyards, pick up a collection of wine, and spend the evening in one of Chianti's lovely *agriturismi*.

Day 4: Chianti and Florence

Spend the morning exploring the countryside and the afternoon and evening ticking off boxes in Florence. There's good reason for this. For purists, wine-tasting is done in the morning before breakfast, which incidentally is the worst possible time to try to visit the Uffizi in Florence. Spend the early afternoon visiting other sites in the city, and the line will be shortest an hour or two before the Uffizi closes. There's no sense in spending your day in line.

Day 5: Bologna, Verona, Vicenza, and Padua

This may seem at first glance like a lot to manage in one day, but these four small cities are each a quick trip from each other along the autostrada or train line. Aim for an early lunch of tortellini in Bologna before moving on to Verona for more serious sightseeing: the Arena for sure, Juliet's house if you must. Vicenza is worth at least a cup of coffee and a stroll down its main drag to admire the architecture, but Padua is where you should spend most of the late afternoon. Pop into the Scrovegni Chapel before it closes, and then enjoy the university atmosphere in the evening.

Venetian canal

Days 6-7: Venice

As with Rome, you'll need a bare minimum of two days in Venice, not so much because of all there is to see, but because there's so much to experience. You'll eat up a lot of time getting lost in its labyrinthine streets—even the best map won't remedy that—yet the idea is to relax and enjoy that experience.

Day 8: Lake Garda and Lake Como

Unless you're a sailing or windsurfing fanatic, in which case you might want to spend the whole day on Garda, I would recommend getting to Lake Como as quickly as possible to make the most of its unparalleled views. An afternoon hike in Menaggio, a ferry across to Bellagio, and another to the eastern side of the lake at the Vecchia Varenna restaurant ought to do the trick. It's also the most practical way to see the lake, since the train line and the highway back to Milan are on the eastern shore.

Day 9: Milan

Address all of your fashion needs here before departing Italy; make reservations well ahead of time to see Da Vinci's *The Last Supper,* and possibly a night out at La Scala or a soccer game at San Siro; be sure to have a Campari-based cocktail at an outdoor café in Brera, and you might even decide to sample some late-night clubs.

Day 10: Milan-Rome

Of course, it's best if you can arrange to fly out of Malpensa, but if you need to return to Rome, keep in mind that the high-speed train will get you to the Termini train station in 4.5 hours, but budget in another 45 minutes to Fiumicino. If you can make it a full travel day, take time to stop off in one of the cities along the way. Intercity trains stop in such worthy spots as Parma, Modena, Arezzo, and Orvieto, which you would have seen already had you been allowed more time.

A MONTH IN ITALY

If you want to see the whole country, this is the amount of time you'll need. And even then, it's going to be an aggressive campaign. From top to bottom, here are the places you don't want to miss.

Days 1-3: Milan and Lombardy

Milan is a tourist's gateway to northern Italy and a place to make money and spend it. Shopping will top the list of things to do, though there are a few must-see attractions:

Da Vinci's *The Last Supper* (which requires a reservation, so book ahead of time); the Pinacoteca di Brera, the city's best-known art museum; the Castello Sforzesco, the 15th-century castle; and, of course, the 14th-century Duomo, the fourth-largest cathedral in the world. Nearby is La Scala, Italy's premier opera house. If you're here during design week, you should stop by the Triennale contemporary art museum; or if it's fashion week, blend into the glamour on Via della Spiga and Via Monte Napoleone.

Bergamo might be one of the most overlooked artistic treasures of northern Italy, because it is so overshadowed by Milan. The province gave birth to Caravaggio (like many of his era, the artist took his name from the town where he was born), and the walled city holds what architects and art historians have described as the perfect central square.

About a 30-minute drive from Bergamo, and now famously frequented by Madonna and George Clooney, Lake Como is a top destination for tourists from the United States. The deepest lake in Europe, and maybe the most scenic, it flaunts opulent villas around Cernobbio, Bellagio, Menaggio, and Tremezzo, and tempers its materialism with nature trails leading to the Swiss border.

Days 4-5: Turin and Piedmont

As an industrial powerhouse and home of the carmaker Fiat, Turin has a gritty reputation, but remember that it was once home to the royal family of Italy. The historic center is still just as regal as it was in the 19th century. Aside from the royal palace, Turin's most famous attraction is the Shroud of Turin, a relic that is said to bear the imprint of Christ's face. Thanks to the exposure the area received during the 2006 Olympic Winter Games, Turin and its satellite winemaking towns no longer sit in an overlooked corner of Italy.

Heard of Asti Spumanti? The Langhe is the part of Piedmont where some of Italy's most celebrated wines are made, especially in Asti, Barolo, and Barbaresco, in the hills just southeast of Turin. The Barbera, Dolcetto, and Nebbiolo grapes have their origins here. Take a break from sightseeing to wine and dine your palate.

Days 6-7: The Riviera di Levante and the Cinque Terre

The stretch of coastline between Genoa and the Tuscan border has some of Italy's most spectacular maritime surroundings. Portofino welcomes celebrities and their yachts. Nearby Camogli is more humble but every bit as vibrant. The Cinque Terre has become a mainstay on the classic tour of Italy, thanks to panoramic hikes connecting the five tranquil villages; Lord Byron preferred Portovenere, where he embarked on his fatal late-night swim across the Gulf of Poets to Lerici.

Days 8-9: Parma, Modena, and Bologna

These three cities make up the culinary heart of northern Italy, known worldwide for their prosciutto, parmesan, and balsamic vinegar, and for the local pasta-making giant, Barilla. Opera also has deep roots here. Giuseppe Verdi was born near Parma, and the late Luciano Pavarotti hailed from Modena.

If you missed dinner in Parma, you won't be disappointed in Bologna, with its tortellini, green ravioli, truffles, and more. This is known as the wealthiest city in Italy, and the most progressive—it boasted the longest-standing Communist mayor—due in no small part to its university, which is among the oldest in Europe.

© JOHN MORETTI

the Duomo in Modena

Day 10: Ferrara

Here's a city you probably never gave much thought to, but it happens to have a wealthier history than many of its better-known neighbors, and the quality of life in the hometown of Lamborghini sports cars is second to none. Bicycle paths intertwine through the city center, past a beautiful cathedral and moated castle, and onward to the banks of the Po.

Days 11-12: Venice

Aside from the usual stops at Rialto and St. Mark's Square, be sure to visit some of the smaller islands in the lagoon and some of Venice's quieter quarters, such as the Ghetto and Cannaregio. By all means, try to time your visit with one of the major festivals. In the winter, it's February's Carnival. In the summer, La Festa del Redentore, a huge floating party on boats. Other biggies include the Biennale and the Venice Film Festival.

Days 13-14: Padua and Verona

The road from Venice back to Milan is spotted with some of Italy's most livable cities and fine works of art: the Scrovegni Chapel of Padua and its frescoes by Giotto; Verona, fictional home to Romeo and Juliet and quite factually the home of Italy's second-largest coliseum.

Days 15-16: Florence

In addition to the usual sights—the Duomo, the Accademia, and the Uffizi—be sure to take a stroll through the less-crowded neighborhoods of Santa Croce and the Oltrarno, stopping in the latter for a stroll through the Boboli gardens. It can't be stressed enough that Florence is positively mobbed in the warmer months; the earlier you arrive in the springtime, the better.

Days 17-18: Montepulciano, Siena, and Chianti

This is the Italian wine country you've dreamed about, and as clichéd as Chianti tends to be these days, it never ceases to please. In an ideal world, you would be visiting the Tuscan countryside by bicycle, with its challenging hills and leisurely freewheeling through the grape leaves, but there are any number of reasons why that might not be possible; limited time is the greatest culprit. The key to visiting Chianti is to find a nice place to have a lingering lunch and sip the local products. Unless you have great expectations and an even larger bank account, real-estate shopping here can be done from the car window with a heavy dose of imagination. In Siena, bring your

© LUCIE ERICKSEN

Siena, with the Tuscan wine country in the background

camera—especially if you're here for one of the two runnings of the Palio in summer—and your appetite. There are some great trattorie here at which to sample the
fruits of the Tuscan countryside. Fortunate American students often find themselves
at programs here, and if they ever feel the urge to leave, it's only because the area can
be very quiet after dark.

Day 19: Arezzo and Cortona

Arezzo would like to forget that it was long the younger sibling that Florence loved to
smack around during the Guelf and Ghibelline wars, and if Arezzo had won, foreign
students might now be flocking there for its architecture instead. It is still an impressive city of art, with some of the finest works by Piero della Francesca. It is also the
nation's best antiques market, and has enjoyed more recent fame as the backdrop for
Roberto Benigni's film *Life Is Beautiful*. Between Arezzo and Cortona are hills full of
magical country homes. Lose yourself in relaxing olive groves and wonder why you
didn't move here earlier.

Day 20: Todi and Orvieto

Here at the crossroads of Lazio, Umbria, and Tuscany, and in the heart of the Etruscan
homeland, you can still find good values on a rustic farmhouse near the haughtier
homes of Chianti. Todi is already overpriced, but certainly worth a look around.
Orvieto, nearby, is home to a pleasant white wine and boasts one of the more remark-
able cathedrals in all of Italy. Terni is not as well endowed architecturally, but it has a
distinct identity as the birthplace of St. Valentine and is spotted with country homes
just a 40-minute train ride from Rome.

Day 21: Perugia

Two things immediately come to mind when this city is mentioned—the university for foreigners, and Perugina chocolates (e.g., the Baci). Even if you miss the city's chocolate festival, you can still enjoy its papal fortress and works by native sons Perugino and Pinturicchio.

Day 22: Assisi and Spoleto

Assisi's role as an integral stop on any Christian pilgrimage is indebted to St. Francis, the wandering minstrel and self-styled monk, founder of a monastic order, protector of animals, and champion of the poor for whom the Basilica of San Francesco was built. It is indeed not to be missed on any trip to Italy. Its ceiling was toppled by an earthquake in 1997, but has been pieced back together. On your way to Rome, stop off in Spoleto. If you're traveling between June and July, you are practically obliged to see the town's Festival dei Due Mondi, considered the nation's most important performing arts festival. Otherwise, it is still one of the peninsula's most spectacular medieval hill towns, topped by a six-towered castle.

Days 23-25: Rome

Stroll through Piazza Navona and the Pantheon, past the Trevi Fountain, the Roman Forum, the Campus Martius, and the Colosseum. Next door to that, make reservations for the following day to visit the Domus Aurea, Nero's underground palace. Have dinner at an outdoor restaurant in Trastevere, Testaccio, or near the Campo de' Fiori, all of which have a number of open-air cafés for a drink. You could stay a month and not see everything here in the cradle of Western civilization, but at least make time to visit the Vatican Museums before you head south.

© JOHN MORETTI

the Amalfi coast

Day 27-28: The Amalfi Coast

Make one more tourist stop in Pompeii before your long-awaited vacation amid all this traveling. Pull up a deck chair on a hotel terrace in Positano or Amalfi and drink in the southern sun and a coastline like none other in the world.

Day 29-30: Either Sicily or Puglia

For reasons discussed earlier, going east to west in the South is a crusade in itself. Pick Sicily or Puglia—you can't go wrong with either choice—and enjoy a magical experience. Not to be missed in Puglia are the dome-shaped *trulli* of Alberobello and the beaches on the

PLANNING YOUR FACT-FINDING TRIP   **63**

WELCOME TO ITALY

Adriatic side (the Ionian, not so much). The Castel del Monte, in the province of Bari, is also a unique experience, with enticing olive plantations for house-seekers in the area. In Sicily, don't miss Taormina, Mount Etna, or the Aeolian Islands before capping it all off in Palermo.

Accommodations

There are loads of interesting options for accommodation in Italy, ranging from short-term rentals to bed-and-breakfasts to *agriturismi* to five-star hotels, and there are almost as many publications that suggest the best ones. Guidebooks are a popular option, but remember that each listing usually only represents what the authors managed to scrape together in their short stay. The most complete guides, in my opinion, are ones from the Touring Club Italiano (www.touringclub.it), a nonprofit group that has been scouring the country for the finest hotels and restaurants for decades. The only hitch is that many of its publications and its website are in Italian only.

Make use of the area's tourist board offices and websites, which have information on just about every hotel, campground, and bed-and-breakfast in the vicinity. This is the most democratic method, but there are no filters for what may turn out to be a dive.

Once upon a time, traveling in Italy was a lot more adventurous, especially in the South, where there were no real hotels to speak of. When the state put the first highway through Campania and Calabria in the 1960s, it also sponsored the construction of Jolly Hotels, a brand found all over the peninsula today. Just about every other chain is present in Italy, as well as luxury hotel associations such as Romantik Hotels and Compagnia Grandi Alberghi, which guarantee an opulent stay in family-run resorts, not cookie-cutter chains, for a not insignificant price.

A step below the *albergo* is the *pensione,* usually similar in quality to a two-star hotel, and then there is the *affitacamera,* or room rental. These are most common in budding tourist spots with insufficient beds in the summer. Room rentals can be a risk, but usually make budget travelers very happy.

The two relatively new entries in the world of Italian accommodations are the *agriturismo,* a family-run farm that serves homegrown produce and has a few rooms for rent, and the bed-and-breakfast, which might be thought of as the urban and suburban equivalent, although without the homegrown produce, of course, and not nearly as reliable in terms of quality. The *agriturismo* option has a lot of fans, and for good reason. The food will be authentic (if rustic), the rooms cozy, and the price reasonable. For more information about *agriturismi,* check with the national organization Agriturist at www.agriturist.it.

The final options are monasteries and convents. Pilgrims are often welcome to stay in them for a nominal fee, and the experience sometimes involves prayer and meditation. If you feel more religious than usual when visiting Rome, however, you can forget about the free accommodations. Many church-run residences around the Vatican now cost about €100 per night.

Practicalities

Obviously, you're going to need a comprehensive guidebook to find the best hotels and dining in Italy. The selection is vast. Below are a few of my suggestions.

ROME
Accommodations

The **Inn at the Roman Forum** (Via degli Ibernesi 30, tel. 06/6919-0970, www.theinnattheromanforum.com, €175 d) has a view of the Forum, a cozy environment with affable hosts, and even a nice little garden with fruit trees: That's about everything you could ask for and more in this excellent location.

In a quiet little square near Campo de' Fiori is **Hotel Teatro di Pompeo** (Largo del Pallaro 8, tel. 06/6830-0170, www.hotelteatrodipompeo.it, €195 d). This antique hidden gem has Renaissance-era exposed beams and old-fashioned furniture. It's cozy and quiet and set in an ideal location.

The **Villa Laetitia** (Lungotevere delle Armi 22-23, tel. 06/322-6776, www.villalaetitia.com, €180 d) is located on the banks of the Tiber between the Vatican and Piazza del Popolo. This boutique hotel/residence set up by the Fendi family of fashion fame is, of course, on the cutting edge of style. It breathes modern luxury for a price within reach. The chic studios are almost like apartments, and have access to terraces and gardens.

Food

Roscioli (Via dei Giubbonari 21-22, tel. 06/687-5287, www.salumeriaroscioli.com, 12:30–3 P.M. and 7–11 P.M. Mon.–Sat., €12–33) is a salumeria and bakery in the lively Campo de' Fiori square that has grown up to be a full-on restaurant these days, and an extremely popular one at that. It has Italian delicacies and also international foodie fare, from foie gras and Pacific salmon to the top Roman pasta specialties, amatriciana and carbonara.

Situated just behind the Colosseum, **Hostaria Nerone** (Via Terme di Tito 96, tel. 06/4817952, noon–3 P.M. and 7–11 P.M. daily, €8–12) sits on a hill that acts as the ceiling for Nero's underground palace. It is a classic Roman trattoria with the real deal as far as Roman specialties go, and at reasonable prices. If it's not too hot outside, the café tables have views of Ancient Rome's iconic stadium and the Baths of Trajan.

My old friends Aldo and Alessio Liberatore have done incredibly well with their little restaurant, **Taverna dei Fori Imperiali** (Via della Madonna dei Monti 9, tel. 06/6798643, www.latavernadeiforiimperiali.com, noon–3 P.M. and 7:30–10 P.M. Mon.–Wed., €12–16). Thanks to recent write-ups in the *New York Times* and other food sections, this neighborhood favorite has slowly gained international acclaim as a typical Roman trattoria with advanced culinary flourishes from around the peninsula. These days you'll have to make a reservation well in advance to secure one of the four outdoor tables on this cobblestone street in a neighborhood by the Colosseum. The cavatelli with spicy Calabrian 'nduja sausage is inimitable.

MILAN AND THE LAKES
Accommodations

These days, the best budget option is probably the **Hotel Girasole** (Via Doberdo 19, tel. 347/146-9721, www.bbilgirasole.it, €105–145 d). Milan isn't cheap. Don't expect an elegant atmosphere for that price, but it's clean, friendly, and very well-placed.

Sure, for €500 and up you easily could live well at the Four Seasons or the Grand Hotel et De Milan, or rub elbows with famous supermodels in the Principe di Savoia's elevator, but good, moderately priced hotels are hard to find, most of all during a trade show or fashion week. If you reserve in time, the most charm for your money in the city center is to be had at the **Antica Locanda Solferino** (Via Castelfidardo 2, tel. 02/657-0129, www.anticalocandasolferino.it, €130–200 d). It sits squarely in the middle of Milan's trendy Brera neighborhood, and the rooms are furnished as if you were one of the area's art-loving residents.

If you're planning to spend the night on the lakes, your best bet is called the **Hotel Milano & Apartments** (Via XX Settembre 29, tel. 0341/830-298, www.varenna.net, €125–200d) in Varenna. It is perched just above the lake in this cozy town with an eagle's-eye view of Bellagio's peninsula. Below the hotel is a little shoreline footbridge and walkway, called the Italian equivalent of "Lover's Lane."

Food

The soberly named **Trattoria Milanese** (Via Santa Marta 11, tel. 02/8645-1991, 12:30–3 p.m. and 7–11:30 p.m. Wed.–Mon., €9–24) has been a mainstay here for ages, hiding in a narrow lane just west of the Duomo. Nothing superbly inventive here, just a crash-course in Milanese cooking: The risotto alla Milanese, costolette alla Milanese, and the osso buco are as delicious and authentic as you can get.

Slightly more creative fare is at **Al Pont de Ferr** (Ripa di Porta Ticinese 55, tel. 02/8940-6277, noon–3 p.m. and 7–11 p.m. daily, €16–28) which stands head and shoulders above the rest of the lineup of restaurants in the Navigli neighborhood in terms of quality. If the mosquitoes aren't biting, sit outside and look over the canal while enjoying a plate of stewed rabbit or some Sicilian couscous. Have a good look at the quality wine list and extensive cheese selection.

Finally, there is a restaurant in Milan that I think is one-in-a-million, but you have to be somewhat selective, for political reasons, about whom you decide to invite, if you decide to go at all. **Da Oscar** (Via Palazzi 4, tel. 02/295-18806, 7 p.m.–midnight Wed.–Mon., €12–18) is run by a man named Oscar, a man nostalgic for the days of Mussolini. If the Duce memorabilia scattered around the joint doesn't tip you off that something very unusual is going on here, Oscar himself certainly will, the moment he walks out of the kitchen wearing a soiled white undershirt and wielding a very large knife, calling someone's wife a "filthy slut." The crowd loves it. You may or may not get a kick out of it, but while you're welcome to take your chances arguing with Oscar, there's no argument with his arrabbiata all'Oscar sauce, a spicy tomato-cream sauce laced with vodka.

Lake Como is full of great fish restaurants, but my favorite is far and away the **Vecchia Varenna** (Contrada Scoscesa 10, tel. 0341/830-793, www.vecchiavarenna.it, 12:30–3 p.m. and 6:30–10 p.m. daily, €12–16). One of your most memorable experiences here on the lake could be a meal at this romantic restaurant, which combines refined local cuisine with the lakefront charm of Varenna's oldest section, all at reasonable prices. The perfect dish for these parts in late summer is the risotto with wild mushrooms and lavarello (a white fish from the lake).

THE NORTHEAST
Veneto
ACCOMMODATIONS

Driving on the autostrada, the trip between Milan and Venice is only a few hours, so you can very easily spend the night in Milan the first night and one in Venice the second night. If you want to revisit something directly in between, it's less than 80 miles away from either city.

Even more conveniently, unless you have your heart absolutely set on Venice as your new home, spending the night in Padua as you research the Northeast will save you money. It's extremely close to both Venice and Verona, and you get much more for your money on the mainland than on the lagoon.

For example, the **Hotel Majestic Toscanelli** (Via dell'Arco 2, tel. 049/663-244, www.toscanelli.com, €149 d) is a four-star hotel in Padua with doubles starting at a figure that would be tripled in Venice for something this nice. It is loaded with old-world charm, with bright, tastefully furnished rooms and the best buffet breakfast in the area.

If on the other hand, you'd prefer to spend romantic evenings on the lagoon, well, that's a treat that's well worth the price. The mazelike streets over the canals are mesmerizing (if making it difficult to find addresses, thanks to Venice's archaic street-numbering system). For something with a romantic atmosphere, first try **Hotel Violino d'Oro** (San Marco 2091, Via XXII Marzo, tel. 041/277-0841, www.violin-odoro.com; €280 d, plus €30 for canal view). This is a little boutique hotel on a small square with a fountain, tucked between San Marco and the Accademia. The rooms are 18th-century Venetian, with Murano chandeliers and gilded details everywhere.

An excellent value for those on a tight budget is the **Foresteria Valdese** (Castello 5170, tel. 041/528-6797, www.foresteriavenezia.it, €100 d). A reservation is hard to come by in the high season, but those who do will find an elegant, 16th-century *palazzo* with simple accommodations. This is not a hotel but a foresteria, which is lodging traditionally given to religious pilgrims in Italy, taking its name from an old-fashioned word for foreigners. Most of these dormitory-style rooms give onto a balcony overlooking a canal and go for about the best price in this neighborhood.

Another great deal that hasn't gone unnoticed by U.S. travelers is the **Pensione Guerrato** (Calle Drio La Scimia 240a, tel. 041/522-7131, www.pensioneguerrato.it, starting at €100 d), right in the central San Polo district, with unmatched views of the finest palaces on the Grand Canal. For that price, you wouldn't expect to find the Guerrato furnished with taste and history, but it is. It's an especially excellent deal when you consider the location.

Finally, you might try the **Hotel Santa Lucia** in the Cannaregio neighborhood (Calle Della Misericordia 358, tel. 041/715-180, www.hotelslucia.com, starting at €50 d). Loaded with flowers and bright colors, this is a quiet, comfy, and very reasonably priced place to spend a few days.

FOOD

In Padua, it's hard to do better than **La Vecchia Enoteca** (Via San Martino e Solferino 32, tel. 049/875-28-56, noon–3 P.M. and 7–10:30 P.M. Tues.–Sat., noon–3 P.M. Mon., €12–22). This is wine country, after all, and the region's enological might is on full display here in a cozy but elegant atmosphere. Specialties of the area include polenta and risotto, as in much of the Northeast, but particular attention is paid to seafood offerings, such as the excellent sea bass in a light potato crust.

Venice is overflowing with restaurants, both outstanding and overwhelmingly touristy. A great restaurant can turn into a tourist trap overnight. Here are a couple of can't-miss bastions of Venetian cuisine. First, there is **Do Forni** (San Marco 468, tel. 041/523-2148, www.doforni.it, noon–3 P.M. and 7–11:30 P.M. daily, €8–20). The menu is outstanding and unadulterated Venetian, with a gigantic selection of seafood, such as linguine with lobster sauce and squid ink risotto, and a whirlwind of hungry locals coming in and out of the rustic dining room.

Another authentic choice, at even better prices, is **Ai Tre Spiedi** (Cannaregio 5906, tel. 041/520-8035, noon–3 P.M. and 7–10 P.M. Tues.–Sat., 7–10 P.M. Sun., €19–39) in the Cannaregio neighborhood. If you're feeling adventurous and want to eat like a real Venetian, try the braised eel with polenta, washed down with a glass of the local white. Otherwise you can't go wrong with my favorite fish, a grilled orata (sometimes called gilthead sea bream, sometimes John Dory, in English), a virtual steak of firm, white fish. And as almost anywhere else in Venice, you can just take it easy with a fritto misto, a mixed dish of fried seafood.

My first stop in Venice is usually at **Da Remigo** (Salizada dei Greci, tel. 041/523-0089, noon–2:30 P.M. and 7–10:30 P.M. Wed.–Sun., noon–2:30 P.M. Mon., €8–16). It's like an old friend. The same waiters wearing their same white jackets at the same no-nonsense white-linen covered tables serve an honest Venetian meal at acceptable prices. Last time I was there I was talked into the gnocchi and not at all disappointed, and followed it up with a faithful fish fry.

Sometimes the newcomers can be surprisingly good, and I was particularly impressed last time I was in Venice with **Taverna del Campiello Remer** (Canareggio 5701, tel. 349/336-5168, noon–3:30 P.M. and 5:30 P.M.–1 A.M. Tues.–Sun., 5:30 P.M.–1 A.M. Sun., €20 for buffet) in a hidden courtyard not far from the Rialto bridge. Opened in 2007, the Taverna indeed has managed a tavern-like atmosphere with candle-lit tables but a contemporary feel. Locals sit and have a spritz at the bar, listening to a tandem on guitar and drums in the corner (it hosts an open mike on Saturday nights), and pretty good food. An excellent place for a night out.

THE NORTHWEST
Piedmont
ACCOMMODATIONS

Again, industrial Turin would be an unusual (though certainly not bad) choice for a foreigner looking to experience a life in Italy, especially when pastoral beauty and culinary jewels await just outside the city in areas like Alba and Asti.

In Asti, the **Hotel Raniero** (Via Cavour 85, tel. 0141/353-866, www.hotelrainero. com, €85 d) makes its home in a centuries-old building in the best part of town. The rooms are modern and comfortable, if not very long on charm, but most importantly it is in a quiet pedestrian zone.

In Alba, the **Hotel Savona** (Via Roma 1, tel. 0173/440-440; www.hotelsavona.com, €100 d) is clean and bright, with modern amenities like whirlpool tubs in some rooms, as well as some terraces on an inner courtyard.

FOOD

With just a few tables and an authentic Piemontese repertoire, **Il Convivio** (Via G. B. Giuliani 4–6, tel. 0141/594-188, noon–2:30 P.M. and 8–10 P.M. Mon.–Sat., €8–12) in Asti is one of the top spots to enjoy the local specialties that may become your bread and butter. If it is on the constantly changing menu, try the braised rabbit with olives and white wine, and gnocchi with a sweet pepper sauce, for prices that will seem head-scratchingly low to a North American. It goes without saying that wine lovers will be on cloud nine when they see the list and are invited to tour the cellar.

Alba, home of the white truffle and neighbor to some of Italy's most prestigious wines, is ground zero for gourmands, which raises the bar in the restaurant category to new levels. Still, I can confidently recommend **Lalibera** (Via E. Pertinace 24, tel. 0173/293-155, www.lalibera.com, noon–2 P.M. and 8–10 P.M. Mon.–Sat., €9–21) as one of Alba's best. It is both stylish and comfortable at the same time, and the traditional Piemontese dishes are mercifully lighter than usual and given a special twist. You might want to start with zucchini flowers stuffed with a trout mousse, and move on to oversized ravioli stuffed with spinach, ricotta, and an egg yolk, and covered with shaved truffle.

Liguria
ACCOMMODATIONS

As long as you're on the coast, and don't need to be in the city, your time is best spent in the relaxing coastal town of Camogli, not far outside Genoa. Pass a night at a cute little hotel called **La Camogliese** (Via Garibaldi 55, tel. 0185/771-402, www.lacamogliese.it, €70 d). It's a one-minute walk to the beach, and the rooms are bright and airy, some with a balcony where you can catch a glimpse of the sea around the corner. It's not the height of pampering or decor, but just a cozy inn by the water for a small outlay.

FOOD

You should at least visit Genoa on your stay in Liguria, to see the aristocratic palaces and world-class aquarium, which is one of the best spots in all of Italy to take kids. It's also a good excuse to sample the fantastic Genoese cooking, which is exemplified by **Da Genio** (Salita San Leonardo 61r, tel. 010/588-463, noon–2 P.M. and 8–10 P.M. Mon.–Sat., €7–14) arguably the city's favorite trattoria. Start off with an antipasto assortment of sardines and vegetable pie, before you taste the definition of Ligurian cooking: trenette pasta with pesto. There is no better pesto on the planet.

THE CENTRAL REGIONS
Florence and Chianti
ACCOMMODATIONS

Florence has a huge selection of hotels, many of them overpriced and not so charming. Friends who are traveling there invariably ask me, "Can you recommend a nice *pensione?*" I can. **The Pensione Maria Luisa de' Medici** (Via del Corso 1, tel. 055/280-048, €120 d) is a quiet residence in the center of town with invaluable oil paintings in the halls contrasting with some basic, modern furniture in the rooms. If a tiptoe atmosphere and midnight curfew are not your thing, you can stay at its sister residence, the **Hotel Ferdinando II de' Medici** (Via del Presto 2, tel. 055/210-947, www. ferdinandodemedici.com, €95 d) next door.

An upscale option but still not overly expensive for Florence is the **Guelfo Bianco** (Via Cavour 29, tel. 055/288-330, www.ilguelfobianco.it, €99–190 d) on busy Via Cavour. The Rennaissance building holds on to some of its old charms, such as frescoes and period doorways, but the bathrooms and other amenities are impeccably modern. A good value.

Chianti has all sorts of *agriturismi* options; really all you have to do is follow the brown signs to one in any town along the way. Other fun options are old-fashioned country inns nestled in classic Tuscan villas. If you're in Panzano, I'd recommend the **Villa Rosa Boscorotondo** (Via San Leonina 59 on the SS222, Panzano-in-Chianti 50020, tel. 055/852-577, fax 055/856-0385, www.tuscany.net/rosaboscorotondo, €80–140 d), run by the owners of Florence's Torre Guelfa hotel. The price is right for a stately old pink villa on the country road toward Radda-in-Chianti. Enjoy the views, have a dip in the pool, or walk a path that leads through the vineyards into town. For a truly special gastronomic experience, stay with my friends the Grant family at **La Petraia** (on the SS222 about 4 km out of Radda-in-Chianti, tel. 0577/738-582, www. lapetraia.com, €250 pp based on double occupancy, breakfast and dinner included). The chef, Susan Grant, has worked at Michelin-rated restaurants around Europe and receives accolades for her dishes from the folks in town. Rarely will you taste such wonders created by ingredients found almost exclusively in her garden, fields, and forests. The rooms' decor is modern country chic, very comfortable.

FOOD

This is obviously an essential part of your stay, so you want to choose wisely. Staying in Chianti, you'll likely eat at least one meal at your *agriturismo,* but for a particularly memorable night out in Panzano-in-Chianti, visit the modern restaurant opened by the town's famous poet-butcher, Dario Cecchini. It is a three-story, glass-floored mecca of meat called **Solociccia** (Via Chiantigiana 5, Panzano-in-Chianti, tel. 055/852-727, www.solociccia.it, seatings at 7 and 9 p.m. Thurs.–Sat., Sun. lunch only, €30). You may be lucky to see him stand on a table and hear him recite verses from Dante's *Inferno,* and you will most certainly experience his famous cuts of beef and pork. Be sure to read the rules at the door; one of them is that the place is BYOB, a good thing for wine shoppers, and it's only open for dinner Thursday, Friday, and Saturday, with two seatings per night. Call ahead for reservations.

Florence has dozens of famous restaurants, not least of which is **Il Latini** (Via del Palchetti 6r, tel. 055/210-916, noon–2:30 p.m. and 7:30–10:30 p.m. Tues.–Sat., €6–16). It is a Florence institution for tourists and locals alike, seated alongside each other at long wooden tables with prosciutto dangling from the rafters. The Tuscan fare is authentic and well-priced, though the place can get a little loud and the service brisk when it's busy. The owner is Narcisso Latini, still opening the doors in the morning at 94 years old as of the printing of this book.

My personal favorite in Florence is a nearby restaurant opened by one of Narcisso's sons, Giovanni. He named the place, simply enough, **Osteria di Giovanni** (Via del Moro 22, tel. 055/284-897, www.osteriadigiovanni.it, noon–2:30 P.M. and 7:30–10 P.M. Tues.–Sat., €9–25). Giovanni married an American woman, and their two daughters, Caterina and Chiara, act as the chef and sommelier, respectively. The dishes are refined and creative, though thoroughly Tuscan in character, and the price is right.

Umbria and Le Marche
ACCOMMODATIONS
One good option is outside the hilltop city of Perugia, which is great news, as parking in the city is a hassle. Indeed the **Villa di Monte Solare** (Via Montali 7, Colle San Paolo, tel. 075/832-376, www.villamontesolare.com, €240), 25 minutes outside Perugia, is so far outside civilization, it is amazing that such a piece of luxury even exists here. Once you climb up the gravel road, past the olive trees and 17th-century farmhouses, it becomes clear that this is the true definition of civilization: nightly classical music concerts in the villa's frescoed chapel, spa treatments in a converted limonaia, jacket-and-tie dinners, etc. Try your hand at cooking classes or take one of the cycling tours. This is a spectacular Umbrian experience.

At the heart of Le Marche is the gorgeous medieval hill town of Urbino, and one of the best ways to enjoy the surroundings in peace is at the **Hotel Mamiani Urbino** (Via Bernini 6, tel. 0722/322-309, www.hotelmamiani.it, €85 d) just outside of town. With a modern, open villa feel amidst the greenery and views of the surrounding hillsides, the Mamiani caters to those looking to enjoy some fresh air and healthy living with guided bike tours and a full wellness center.

FOOD
One of Perugia's finest restaurants is **Il Falchetto** (Via Bartolo 20, tel. 075/573-1775, www.ilfalchetto.it, noon–2:30 P.M. and 7:30–10:30 P.M. Tues.–Sun., €8–15), just next to the Duomo. The medieval atmosphere is captivating, either inside the 14th-century stone dining room or on the tables along Piazza IV Novembre. De rigueur is the entrée falchetti verdi, a baked spinach and ricotta gnocchi with tomato sauce and cheeses. Try to save room for the grilled lamb or veal.

For an unforgettable meal in Le Marche, don't miss the **Antica Osteria da la Stella** (Via Santa Margerita 1, tel. 0722/320-228, www.anticaosteriadalastella.com, noon–2:30 P.M. and 7:30–10 P.M. Tues.–Sun., €12–15). The rustic dining room, with fireplaces and exposed brick, doesn't give you a hint as to how elegant the cuisine is, from the tagliatelle with white truffle to herb-filled buckwheat cannelloni, even ravioli with chocolate, which is much more refined and delicious than it sounds.

THE SOUTH
Naples
ACCOMMODATIONS
I wouldn't recommend staying in downtown Naples, you'll have a much more relaxing experience going a bit farther south toward the Amalfi coast. In high season you'll need to book well ahead for hotels, and prices, in general, aren't cheap. One reasonable

option, and a nice place for a family in Amalfi, is the **Sharon House** (Via dei Curiali 4, tel. 089/873-576, www.amalfisharonhouse.it, €120 d). No sweeping sea views here in the middle of town, but clean, vibrantly decorated rooms that make for a great base for exploring.

For roughly the same price, a little more romantic option is the **Villa Lara** (Via delle Cartiere 1, tel. 089/873-6358, www.vilalara.it, €90–195) which is a solid walk uphill. From the reception, you take an elevator carved into the rock up to the sweeping views from the terrace, and bright, colorful rooms.

FOOD

It's hard to go wrong in Amalfi, if you're after fresh seafood and great pizza, virtually everyone has it, but one of my favorites is **Taverna di Masaniello** (Vicolo Masaniello 14, no phone, noon–3 P.M. and 7–10 P.M. Tues.–Sun., €5–12). Have the catch of the day, followed by one of the freshest caprese salads you will ever taste, or just settle on a pizza (€5), better than any you will taste in North America.

Puglia
ACCOMMODATIONS

If you're going to spend some time in Puglia, you should stay at one of the *trulli*. It is an experience like no other. Many hotels and rental agencies offer *trulli* accommodation, one of the best of which in Alberobello is called, quite simply, **Trulli Holiday** (Piazza A. Curi, tel. 080/432-5970, www.trulliholiday.com, €59 two-bedroom unit). Here you can rent *trulli* of all sizes by the night, or by the week (or even buy one outright). There is also a beautiful new communal pool, with the little domes acting as the backdrop.

FOOD

Here, selecting a specialty off the menu is going to be a lot easier. Puglia has a lot to offer the culinary world, from fresh sea urchins to involtini to lovely cheese dishes, but if you're in Alberobello it is obligatory to have the orecchiette al ragu, the little ear-shaped pasta that comes with a spicy tomato sauce and small shreds of greens. And the best place to get it is at **La Cantina** (Vico Lippolis 8, tel. 080/432-3473, www. ilristorantelacantina.it, 12:30–3:30 P.M. and 7:30–10 P.M. Wed.–Mon., €10–16), an Alberobello institution.

Sicily
ACCOMMODATIONS

If you have already decided on Sicily as your new home, the best thing to do would be to rent a villa for a week. The past decade has seen countless ancient properties renovated, and prices for this kind of luxury are relatively affordable. Near Taormina, two- to five-bedroom villas start at €1,000 to €2,000 per week. If you're only here for a couple of days, use Palermo as a home base to explore the northern half of the island. The **Ambasciatori Hotel** (Via Roma 111, tel. 091/616-6881, www.ambasciatorihotelpalermo.com, €100 d, €60 apartment) is an excellent choice. The hotel is right in the downtown, but its rooftop terrace is an oasis of calm, overlooking the skyline of domes, bell towers, and mountains in the background.

WELCOME TO ITALY

FOOD

Palermo is overflowing with wonderful trattorie, serving the gamut of Sicilian specialties from seafood to couscous, all with a touch of citrus. One of the better choices downtown is **Ai Cascinari** (Via d'Ossuna 43–45, tel. 091/651-9804, 12:30–3:30 P.M. and 7:30–10 P.M. Tues.–Sun., €6–10). It has a simple, country-style menu with a mouthwatering variety of seafood in season: from red snapper and swordfish to stuffed calamari and sardines. Just down the road is another favorite, **Trattoria Mamma Ciccina** (Via d'Ossuna 15, tel. 091/212-011, www.trattoria-palermo.it), also serving typical seafood dishes, such as the classic pasta with sardines and fennel, but also an array of meat dishes, such as veal involtini and an excellent spezzatino, a stew of mixed meats.

DAILY LIFE

MAKING THE MOVE

When planning a move to Italy, the first thing to pack is patience. Navigating local customs and figuring out how things work is going to take time. The good news from the bureaucratic front is that recent laws have streamlined at least part of the paperwork. The bad news is that those same laws have tightened restrictions on foreigners.

For example, Italy now requires fingerprints for all non–European Union (EU) citizens—Americans, Senegalese, Norwegians, etc.—when they sign up for a stay permit. Especially after the events of September 11, authorities are more serious about stamping out illegals.

Once upon a time, lots of U.S. expats lived in Italy for long periods of time without ever announcing their presence. It's illegal, but it happens, and in all candor, Italians are much less worried about North Americans overstaying their welcome than other nationals from outside the EU. Don't take this as an open-ended invitation. I have seen at least one expat forcibly sent packing after her illegally procured job as a tour leader in Rome marched her past a group of police, who were paying unusually close attention to immigration laws that day. The penalties for overstaying your visa have become harsher, and you'd only be doing yourself a disservice by ignoring them in the long run. Once you've hacked through the bureaucracy, including multiple trips to the

© JOHN MORETTI

consulate, you will have many more freedoms and benefits than those who preferred to risk it and lived their lives in near-paranoia.

If you think it would be much more convenient to just become an Italian citizen, it just might be possible under the Italian policy of *jus sanguinis,* or "right of blood." This can go back generations as long as no ancestor in the chain lost his or her Italian citizenship before giving birth to the next generation. There seem to be different interpretations of this floating around, so here are criteria taken verbatim from a checklist provided by the Italian Consulate:

- Your father was an Italian citizen at the time for your birth and you never renounced the right to Italian citizenship.

- Your mother was an Italian citizen at the time of your birth, you were born after January 1st, 1948 and you never renounced the right to Italian citizenship.

- Your father was born in the United States, your paternal grandfather was an Italian citizen at the time of your father's birth, neither you nor your father ever renounced the right to Italian citizenship.

- Your mother was born in the United States, your maternal grandfather was an Italian citizen at the time of her birth, you were born after January 1, 1948 and neither you nor your mother ever renounced the right to Italian citizenship.

- Your paternal or maternal grandfather was born in the United States, your paternal great grandfather was an Italian citizen at the time of his birth, neither you nor your father nor your grandfather ever renounced the right to Italian citizenship (please note: a grandmother born before January 1, 1948 can claim the Italian citizenship only from her father and can transfer it to descendants born after January 1, 1948).

Note: "Italian citizen at the time of birth" means that he/she did not acquire any other citizenship through naturalization before the descendant's birth.

This last bit is very important. If the relative who came over from Italy was naturalized in the United States or any other country other than Italy, he or she effectively renounced Italian citizenship.

In the end, remember that mastering Italian bureaucracy is a lifelong pursuit. (Many have even turned it into a career.) You will constantly have questions about the fine print of laws on permits, visas, and residency, and will need to keep abreast of changes. A number of resources can help you. The best one I have found to date is *The Informer,* www.informer.it, founded by a Scottish expat a quarter-century ago.

Visas and Permits

All 15 signatory countries of the Schengen agreement, including Italy, allow U.S. residents to circulate freely within their borders for a maximum of 90 days at a time. If your vacation fits into that category, you need only a passport and a plane ticket. But Italy still has its own immigration laws, and even those travelers planning to stay for as little as two weeks are required, in theory, to apply for a stay visa within eight days of their arrival. Few people bother with the formalities. There are literally millions of North Americans who come every year for two-week vacations in Italy with no paperwork other than a passport.

If you plan to stay longer than 90 days, you are in effect planning a "long stay" and therefore need to apply for a long-stay permit in Italy, the infamous *permesso di soggiorno.* Before you can apply for your *permesso,* you have to obtain the appropriate visa from the Italian Embassy or local consulate in the United States. There are weeks, perhaps months, of footwork on that front to be done at home before you leave. Some cases drag on for years.

There are 21 types of visas in all, ranging from airport transit to sports-related, some easier to obtain than others. U.S. citizens looking to live, study, or work in Italy are most likely to apply for one of three types: a residency visa, a student visa, or a work visa. Different documentation is required for each, so check with your local consulate or the Italian Embassy's website (www.ambwashingtondc.esteri.it) before you make an appointment. All visas require a passport valid for at least three months past your application date.

STUDENT VISAS

Student visas are relatively easily obtained, provided you have been accepted into an Italian or Italy-based university and can provide proof of financial independence during that stay. Many U.S.-sponsored programs will handle your visa requirements for you.

There are hundreds of programs in Italy, and other Italian universities meant for foreigners. The best known among the latter are the Università per Stranieri in Perugia and the programs in Siena and Urbino.

If your program is more self-styled, you'll need to do the paperwork yourself. Be sure to bring to the embassy or consulate a letter of acceptance to an Italian university,

© PETER SPIRER/123RF

Student visas are relatively easy to obtain if you are attending an Italian university and can provide proof of financial independence.

proof of health insurance, and bank account information (it can be your parents' account) that shows you have enough money to live on once you're there.

RESIDENCY VISAS

"Elective residency" visas also require proof of independent income. It is, in fact, the operating principle behind this kind of visa, which does not allow you to work in Italy. You must prove that you have enough money to support yourself through the length of your stay, independent of any salaries you may be receiving at the moment. You also need to show either ownership of a home in Italy or a rental agreement. Plus, you will be asked to provide your criminal record, or proof of lack thereof. If you don't have an arrest record, the FBI has made this once-difficult operation much easier online at www.fbi.gov/hq/cjisd/fprequest.htm.

FAMILY VISAS

The family visa is for immediate family (spouse and/or children) of someone already working legally in Italy. If that person is an EU resident, the paperwork is quick: All you need is a letter from your spouse and the marriage certificate. You also need a *nulla osta* ("no obstacle") document from the local police headquarters if your spouse is not an EU resident but legally working there, plus any children's birth certificates if they are coming, too.

If, on the other hand, your spouse is still in the process of obtaining a work permit, you will need additional paperwork, such as proof of suitable family housing. In general, it is always easier applying for such residency once your family member has the job.

WORK VISAS

The work visa is the most difficult to obtain. It is divided into "dependent" and "independent" work, for employed and self-employed workers, respectively.

There are a limited number of such independent work visas afforded to U.S. citizens every year, and experience has shown that they disappear within a few hours after the quota is announced. The major challenge in landing a "dependent" visa is that you must have letters from the company saying it intends to hire you or bring you on as a consultant. This would be an unusual windfall for someone not already living in Italy.

In order to solve this paradox, many Americans arrange job contacts while on shorter vacations in Italy, and then fly back to the United States to straighten out their visas. Keep in mind that you should not overstay your three-month visit to be successful with this approach. For even more time, some people choose to sign up for a bona fide course in Italy, and then apply for a student visa. Many people manage to parlay the student permit into a work permit once the course is over.

Again, finding an employer who is willing to file the paperwork for an American has become more difficult recently, as there are new quotas set for foreigners allowed to fill Italian jobs. If you manage to qualify, you need to have your employer send the Labor Ministry a letter that says the company intends to hire you. When that has been approved, the ministry will issue a *nulla osta* document to police headquarters. The company will also send you a work contract to present to the embassy or consulate, along with proof of ministry approval, for your visa.

EXPAT PROFILE: THE IMPORTANCE OF BEING HEMINGWAY

Like many U.S. expatriates in Italy, he lives a life of anonymity, dividing his time between teaching English and doing translations. But what makes John Patrick Hemingway stand out from the crowd is his weighty surname. He is the grandson of Ernest, one of the 20th century's greatest writers.

Living in a modest apartment on Viale Monza in Milan, John does his best to stay out of the public eye. He shrugs off the coincidence that he lives in the same city where his grandfather convalesced from an injury sustained while serving as an ambulance worker in World War I.

Milan is the setting of a number of Ernest's writings, such as *In Another Country* and *A Farewell to Arms*, the latter of which describes a romance between a wounded soldier and a nurse. John scoffs at the coincidence that he is now married to a nurse. The two lives intertwine with uncanny similarities, but the last name John shares with his grandfather is no simple twist of fate. It is a constant reminder of the expectations he is asked to live up to.

Born in Miami, John is the son of Gregory Hemingway, the third son of Ernest's failed marriage to Pauline Pfeiffer. John came to Milan in 1984 after graduating from the University of California at Los Angeles. Two years later, he married his Canadian-born wife, Ornella, in Milan. In 1997, they had a son, and in 2003, a daughter.

On the side, almost clandestinely, he has penned short stories that have never seen the light of day. "It's a lottery of sorts," he says. "Certainly the name helps. With the stack of manuscripts on publisher's desks, it helps you get looked at as an author."

But for John, the surname is a bit like the marlin in *The Old Man and the Sea*. While it could land him professional fortune if he made the right moves, sometimes he thinks it would be easier to just cut this weighty inheritance free. "People are going to compare you to your grandfather, and obviously you're not going to come out looking very good in the comparison," he says. "You could be a very good writer, but it's unlikely you're going to become one of the greatest writers of the century."

Italy has provided something of a refuge from the fame and the infamy, he says. Although Italians place enormous emphasis on family ties and revere "Papa" Hemingway's works, they are more polite when approaching John about it than are people in the United States. Still, the subject comes up over and over again. "I try to explain this to people: I am I and he is he. You've got to concentrate on being your own person," he says. "Everyone's destiny is unique."

PERMITS

Again, only after you have the visa and are in Italy do you apply for the corresponding *permesso di soggiorno*. For student visas, you apply for the *permesso di soggiorno per studio;* the *permesso di soggiorno per dimora* is for those with a residency visa; and the *permesso di soggiorno per lavoro* is for those with a work visa.

All of the permits are obtained at the local *questura* (police headquarters). There, you will be asked to fill out an application, which includes three passport photographs plus a *marca da bollo* (a sort of administrative tax stamp available at the post office). You will also need some proof of health insurance.

If you are applying for a residency permit or student permit, the bureaucracy ends there. In the case of the work permit, upon being presented with your visa, police headquarters will provide you with an interim work permit that is good for 90 days. In the meantime, you acquire a *codice fiscale* (tax ID number), which you can do at the *ufficio delle imposte dirette* (local tax authority), to be found in the town's municipal buildings. It is an important card, as you will also need it for all kinds of purchases, such as a cell phone, a car, or a moped, and when opening a bank account. The documents you will need to show for the *codice fiscale* are limited to a passport and sometimes a stay permit, although many Americans are not asked for the latter, especially in small towns. The card will then be sent to you by mail.

The final step is to present your signed work contract to the local employment office, the Ispettorato Provinciale di Lavoro, for final approval of your application. (Ironically, that office represents the Labor Ministry, which issued the "no obstacle" document in the first place.) Once you have all those documents—the temporary permit, the *codice fiscale,* and the approval of the labor office—the *questura* will then award your efforts with the *permesso di lavoro,* available in two-year or five-year permits, or else the time period specified on your work contract, if any.

If you lose your job before the permit expires, you will need to find another one quickly. Recently passed legislation now gives employees just six months to land another job, or else the permit becomes void, whereas previously they could ride out its duration.

There is a legal alternative to the job hunt if you care for more time, though it's not entirely convenient. Once your work permit is up, you can apply as an independent worker for the *permesso di soggiorno per lavoro indipendente,* provided you have all the necessary skills.

Moving with Children

The thought of moving to another country with children can be daunting, but thousands of foreign couples raise their families in Italy and usually have positive things to say about the experience. Public education is very good, recreational opportunities abound, and most of all, family—and children in particular—is the number-one priority for Italians. Kids will never want for attention.

The most trying period for parents in Italy will usually coincide with their children's toddler years. There are almost always waiting lists to enroll your child into a public nursery school, and so candidates are assigned priority by a points system. It takes into consideration your financial status, your occupation, and whether there is a grandmother at home to watch over the kids, among other things.

For this reason, private nursery schools are also in high demand, and many middle-class or upper-middle-class families will find that a private nursery school tuition will cost the same as public one; count on about €400 per month. Naturally, the price increases the longer your child stays through the afternoon, though some mothers and fathers find that the money spent for the post-nap activities is a preferable alternative to babysitters.

DOMESTIC HELP

Many working couples and single parents rely on foreign au pairs, as a lot of them are native English-speakers themselves. Luckily for those young women, there are international standards for how much they are paid and what they are expected to do at the home. Those that live with the families can expect a monthly stipend of about €450, their working hours are limited to a half day, and they should not be asked to do any cleaning unless there is a specific agreement about such chores.

A housekeeper, on the other hand, could charge somewhere around €750 per month, but this of course depends on how often and how much the person is asked to clean. Some housekeepers in Rome, for example, are willing to charge just €30 per weekly, three-hour cleanup. Because most of the housekeepers are also foreign women, often from the Philippines or Eastern Europe, the authorities keep a close eye on the sector for illegal immigration. Those found hiring illegal help can face fines of up to €5,000. There are an estimated 100,000 immigrant women working as housekeepers in Italy, and polls show that about 3 percent of children are raised by an immigrant nanny.

Moving with Pets

There are no visa restrictions on pets, but they will be expected to have a clean bill of health from the vet and have had a rabies shot between 1 month and 12 months before departure.

Cat owners will find kindred sprits in Rome, a city where felines roam free and have a fan club of so-called *gattare* looking after their needs. In fact, you might even consider adopting one of the many stray cats, making a furry friend and helping to solve a growing problem at the same time. There are also many stray dogs in Italy, but those lucky enough to have owners enjoy a pampering unlike anywhere else in the world. In the cities, they are paraded around in small jackets and occasionally hats, carted here and there on subways and to those restaurants that accept them, of which

© JOHN MORETTI

Dogs will feel right at home in Italy.

there are many. Pet owners in Rome have even founded what they call "Bow Wow Beach," where canines frolic with their ilk and splash out the dog days of summer in the Mediterranean waves.

It is paradise for those puppies lucky enough to live in the countryside, but bringing a dog to Italy may not be a wise idea for those planning to live in a city. For one thing, police have started handing out long-overdue fines to dog owners who don't clean up after Pippo on the street. More importantly, many apartment buildings have laws against keeping pets, which could restrict your options drastically in what has been a seller's market in Rome and Milan.

What to Take

So, what should you take to Italy? The best answer: as little as possible. Shipping large and heavy things like furniture will be very expensive. Pound for pound, it can cost about as much as an airline ticket for a human being. For example, shipping a standard UPS Worldwide Express 25-kg (55-lb.) box from Boston to Rome can cost about US$500.

Many apartments for rent are fully furnished or at least equipped with the basics, like a bed, dresser, refrigerator, and often a washing machine. Unless you're planning to buy a house and absolutely must have your zebra-striped sofa, there really is no need to bring it. Between Arezzo's famous antiques and the contemporary furniture of Milan, there is a heavy temptation here to buy something local. Similarly, bringing clothes to Italy is like taking cheesesteaks to Philadelphia. Even if you don't describe yourself as a fashionista, chances are you will have bought a partial wardrobe after only a few months in Italy. The quality is good, and the prices are relatively low.

One thing that is less expensive in North America, however, is any sort of sporting goods. That includes just about everything, from fishing poles to running shoes to, believe it or not, bicycles. Bear in mind, though, that renting skis and snowboards costs much less in the Alps (as low as €20 per day for the whole kit) than in the Rockies, and renting them in situ is a lot more convenient than hauling them around in a car or train.

By all means, take along any expensive electronics, such as a laptop computer, as they are also pricey in Italy. You should pack them with your carry-on luggage: If you have them sent separately, you could incur a 20-percent import duty, which is a large figure when you're talking about computers.

These days, there are scant few things that you cannot find in Italy or order via the Internet. One of them is a decent bagel. (There's one business idea.) So, the best packing advice I can offer is: When in doubt, leave it out.

SHIPPING OPTIONS

These days, UPS (www.ups.com), FedEx (www.fedex.com), and DHL (www.dhl.com) are really the only games in town when it comes to private international shipping. The U.S. Postal Service (www.usps.com) could save you as much as 50 percent on your shipment, although I have never had great faith in the Italian postal service to take it the last leg, even if its service has improved significantly over the past two decades.

HOUSING CONSIDERATIONS

Renting or buying a house is the essence of living abroad; it's what separates you from the tourist. The experience of owning a home in the Italian countryside has become almost legendary, as have the headaches that go along with it. While renting an apartment is less of a responsibility, it also presents its pitfalls.

The same can be said about owning or renting property anywhere, but Italian real estate poses unique benefits and challenges. Italy has a historical claim to some of the most admired architecture in the world. This may be the reason you decided to live here. You wanted to carry your groceries from the open-air market past Baroque palaces and medieval frescoes, and step into your Liberty-style apartment building with a wrought-iron elevator shaft and bicycles parked in the courtyard. Or you wanted to hide away in a tile-roofed villa with terra-cotta floors surrounded by vineyards, where you can lean out your window to smell basil in the garden and hear the chatter of grandmothers.

These simple pleasures of domestic living in Italy make all the complications worthwhile. By complications, I don't mean the handheld shower heads and the three-kilowatt electrical outlets. These are local idiosyncrasies that most people would say lend a

characteristic touch to European living. If you were addicted to the consumer comforts of North America, such as crushed-ice dispensers and garbage disposals, you probably wouldn't have chosen to live in Italy in the first place.

Complications, rather, are the difficulties and bureaucratic underpinnings of buying and keeping up real estate here, the archaic methods of paying the bills, and the often frustrating attitude of repair people. The good news is that these drawbacks are slowly improving.

RENTING VS. BUYING

Whether you should rent or buy in Italy depends, naturally, on your future plans, and especially on the housing market. Trends in Italian real estate prices have more or less mirrored those in the United States: skyrocketing in Italy in the 1990s, but crashing closer to Earth in recent years with the global crisis. It is a good time to buy.

As a rule, Italians will always buy before they rent, no matter what. The nation has one of the highest homeownership rates in Europe. Italians are relatively new to investing in securities, anyway, and the near collapse of financial markets provided them with a frightful reminder of the inherent risks there.

Add in a national obsession with conservative investing and scraping savings, and you will understand why young Italians live with their families until they are well into their 30s, even 40s. At that point they are either married or simply tired of mom and dad's nagging and have enough money to buy some privacy. It may sound funny to an North American who moved out at age 18, but skipping the rental stage is a wise financial move for those with enough patience and humility to live at home as a grown adult.

Obviously, buying is almost always the smarter choice for foreigners as well, but there are a number of risks in Italy that can really burn you: buying in the wrong area, ignoring serious structural damage or shortcomings, or, worst of all, overlooking a legal morass. The advice that most property experts give is to rent first in an area where you think you might like to buy. If you feel the pressure to buy right off the bat, you should first get to know the neighborhood and the houses themselves by talking to the locals.

Renting

Families often own several floors of an apartment building—if not the entire *palazzo*—and rent out the parts that they don't live in. Foreigners are ideal tenants, since housing laws are so restrictive that it is very difficult to evict an Italian tenant. If Italian residents can prove that there's no other place to live in the vicinity, they can stay in that house until it is proven otherwise. Nonresidents are not protected by these laws, besides which they are sometimes willing to pay more than market price to settle disputes quickly.

Most short-term rental possibilities are well-furnished apartments in the city and private villas in tourist destinations, costing anywhere from 25 to 100 percent more than similar long-term rentals. Often located in nicer neighborhoods or resorts, short-term rentals are a comfortable solution for people fresh off the plane. It shouldn't take more than a month to find a cheaper apartment, and a month in a hotel would cost appreciably more.

These sorts of limited contracts are an obvious choice for vacationers in, say, Tuscany

COMMON HOUSING TERMS

- **affittare:** to rent
- **agriturismo:** rural bed-and-breakfast
- **arredato:** furnished
- **bollette:** utility bills (gas, electric, telephone, etc.)
- **bombola:** a tank (usually methane or propane for the home)
- **box:** garage
- **camera:** room
- **condominio:** homeowner's association, which collectively pays for such things as elevators, garbage removal, etc.
- **geometra:** surveyor/deputy architect
- **inquilino:** tenant
- **mansarda:** slanted ceilings

- **monolocale:** one-bedroom apartment (a two-bedroom is a *bilocale*, a three-bedroom is a *trilocale*, etc.)
- **palazzo:** a building
- **portinaio:** doorman/building superintendent
- **ristrutturato:** renovated
- **soffitta:** top-floor apartment; not a spacious penthouse, but a small converted attic
- **sottodichiarazione:** underdeclaring the value of a house during a sale for tax purposes (commonplace, but illegal)
- **spese:** in the case of housing, refers to utility costs
- **trulli:** stone houses

or Venice. For urban professionals, yet another such alternative is a residence. These are much like hotels, with a reception desk and laundry service, except that people stay in them longer—maybe a year or two. They are charmless and short on floor space, but they are inexpensive.

Many new arrivals with low expectations and less money choose to rent a room. If you look through the classifieds or university bulletin boards, you'll run into announcements from students looking for a fourth or fifth roommate, or else a family that has a spare bedroom with some privacy, possibly even an independent entrance. In Rome and Milan, these rooms can be found for as little as €500 per month in some of the outer neighborhoods, about 60 percent of the standard rent for a one-bedroom apartment.

But in the end, there's no substitute for your own place, if you can afford it. If you're dreaming of hardwood floors, a large terrace with grape leaves overhead and a view of the city, a huge shower with stone floors, and large closets in the bedroom to fit all the clothes you plan to purchase in Italy, you're half in luck. The large closets should be easy enough to find, and you may be able to land the terrace, for a price. Almost every apartment in Italy has some sort of balcony, except a few of the oldest ones in the historic center. The hardwood floors are more difficult to find—linoleum is par for the course, tiles if you're lucky—and you can forget about the big shower. Bathrooms in Italy are much more compact than the North American standard. If you have old-school taste, you may be pleasantly surprised by the gas stoves in the kitchen, and the latest kitchenware and stylish coffeemakers are just a quick shopping trip away.

The classified ads—discussed individually in the *Prime Living Locations* chapters—will tell you if it's a *monolocale* (one-bedroom) or *bilocale* (two-bedroom) apartment, the square meters of floor space, and whether it is *arredato* (furnished). There may

© LUCIE ERICKSEN

Fortunately, air-conditioning is becoming more common in Italy.

be some mention of parking if you live outside the city.

Another consideration is the heating, which may or may not be mentioned. Central heating—which is most often regulated by month of the year, not the temperature outside—is the most common. But you may have the luck to land an independent thermostat, in which case when the heat goes on and off is not at the discretion of the *Farmer's Almanac.*

Air-conditioning? If you're lucky. The exorbitant cost of electricity in Italy makes air-conditioning a luxury. It is therefore used mostly in workplaces when the outside temperature becomes truly unbearable. Even then, it breaks down periodically. On rare occasions, steamy weather can produce such a stress on utilities that they declare blackouts, when electricity is shut off in certain neighborhoods for hours at a time. Keep an ear out for such developments in the depths of summer. You don't want to be caught in an elevator when the power goes out.

Some conveniences, such as washing machines, are optional. Dryers are almost unheard of. Refrigerators will likely be smaller than you are used to, and in general, electric appliances are deemed unnecessary when a good old mechanical one will do the trick.

FINDING THE RIGHT PLACE

Any city-dweller knows the two secret ingredients to a comfortable apartment: lots of light and little noise. The former is relatively easy to find in Italy; the latter is nearly impossible.

It is no exaggeration of stereotypes to say that Italians are a boisterous people. There is some social value to understatement and subtlety, but for the most part, screaming over someone else's arguments is preferred. This makes for lively conversation, entertaining talk shows, and above all, noisy residential living. Try to get a feel from the outgoing tenant about the people living above and on either side of you and how much of a ruckus they make. Apartment buildings are almost always structured around a central courtyard, and the late-night conversations from adjacent balconies are projected directly onto your own. If there are a lot of children in the building, prepare yourself for evenings of soccer or volleyball games.

That said, most apartment complexes have condominium-style rules that forbid such things as taking your trash to the courtyard bins after a certain hour. But that won't protect you from the roaring motorcycles outside, nor the infamous local church bell. No matter how devout you may be, you should put as much real estate as possible

© PURESTOCK

rooms with a view

between you and the nearest place of worship, because the bell rings out to wake the slumbering sinners every 15 minutes, starting at 7 A.M.

Conversely, if you make too much noise at night, you will soon find yourself on the wrong end of a broomstick whacking on the ceiling below. Noise seems to travel downward, especially in flimsily built apartments, and if you have the misfortune to have light sleepers living beneath you, even the clicking of your shoes on the floor will be grounds for a cease-and-desist letter from their lawyer.

Italians of course pay close attention to which floor an apartment is on, and it may be mentioned straight away in the classified ads. Like anywhere else, a ground-level apartment on a busy street is going to be a nightmare, as is a sixth-story place in a building without an elevator.

RENTAL AGENTS AND CONTRACTS

Within the classifieds, many of the phone numbers will look suspiciously identical. Real estate agents hold the lion's share of what's available on the market, and that is mostly bad news for you. Agents will ask for a fee equal to one month's rent. So, if you lease the apartment for just six months, that's a 17 percent commission. It's important to remember that everything is negotiable in the universe of Italian real estate, especially the rent itself, and agents' commissions are no exception.

Even the outgoing tenants may ask for a cut—it's referred to as "key money," a fee to hand over the keys. This is illegal and has become less common in the past few years. Still, it can show up in different forms: If you take over an apartment contract from a friend, for example, you have essentially inherited that person's debts, such as lingering energy bills or any damage caused to the apartment, unless you specify your liabilities carefully—and in writing—with your landlord.

The most common contracts these days are four-year agreements, which make it easier for landlords to free themselves of a delinquent tenant, but don't necessarily mean that you need to be in there for four years. You are legally required to find another tenant to take your place if you want to leave sooner, but this is rarely a problem in the big cities, where a good apartment will be snatched up quickly.

You will be asked for at least one month's deposit from the owner, and sometimes as much as three months. Most contracts will stipulate that any repairs made to the apartment, including repainting or cleaning fees, will be deducted from your deposit when you move out.

If it is a furnished apartment, the owner keeps a detailed list of every item in there, right down to the last napkin holder, and will run through the list on move-out day. It's almost impossible to avoid losing some of your deposit; the owners' grievances can be outright comical; e.g., the sheets weren't ironed neatly enough, so you should negotiate for just one month's deposit if at all possible.

It may be included in your rent payment, and therefore goes unnoticed, but every apartment owner needs to pay a contribution to the *condominio* (association of apartment owners in the building). The associations pay for the *portinaio,* a sort of hybrid between a doorman, a building administrator, and a concierge; plus cleaning services, garbage removal, lights, elevators, etc. Some associations make you pay more for the elevator if you live on the upper floors.

Finally, prepare yourself for significant utility bills (see *Household Expenses*). They can reflect anywhere between 10 and 25 percent of your monthly rent.

Buying

There can be no better reward for a life well lived than a stone-walled farmhouse in the Italian countryside. Something with vines crawling up the sides, a wicker-covered jug of wine by the doorstep, and a garden full of cherry tomatoes and white asparagus. To complete the scene, you will need a wise old neighbor to remind you to keep your garden's mint from taking over the vegetables, and to show you how to prune your century-old olive tree correctly. With some money, some wisdom, and a lot of legal help, it can happen.

When buying their first place abroad, North Americans sometimes worry about a nation's political stability. They fear that their real estate may somehow be taken away from them in the future. This is not a concern in Italy, nor anywhere else in Western Europe, for that matter. But there is another fear that is well grounded—namely, that unfamiliarity with local laws might spell disaster.

The first thing to remember when settling on a home is that buyers and sellers will very often declare a price much lower than the one actually paid, to the tune of 50 percent or more. Sellers like this arrangement because it means declaring less income. Buyers, on the other hand, may be able to negotiate a lower price if they agree to do business this way (although housing prices in Italy, just as in the United States, are always negotiable). It is no different than getting a little discount in Italian restaurants for

DAILY LIFE

© PURESTOCK

Most property experts advise foreigners to get to know the neighborhood where they think they might want to purchase a home by renting first.

paying in cash, but on a much grander scale. This practice of recording a false sale price, known as *sottodichiarazione,* is illegal, and can present real problems for the buyer.

For example, if you buy property from a company that has recently gone belly up, creditors can reclaim the property when the company is liquidated. You will be reimbursed for the property, but at the lower declared value. *Sottodichiarazione* also creates a dilemma if you sell the property later and pay capital gains taxes. You will be taxed on an inflated figure, assuming you file the same declared value to the IRS.

The most common pitfall for Italian homeowners, and one that may be unavoidable, is the risk that the construction company goes bust after you have paid them a deposit, but before the home is finished (or even started!). You will be in court for a long time, and may never recuperate your down payment. In some cases, the deposit equals about half of the selling price.

Beware of wills. If you buy a home that is contested in a will, you could face angry co-beneficiaries who have five years to try to get the property back. Finally, for reasons described under *Renting,* never buy an occupied apartment or home in the hope that the tenants will move out. They won't, and will overcome even the most devious maneuvers, such as your shutting off the water or electricity. I have seen more than one apartment with a garden hose running through the bathroom window, and it wasn't there to water the geraniums.

SELECTING A HOUSE AND SIGNING THE CONTRACT

Window-shopping for Italian homes has become much easier with the Internet. No longer do you need to rely on a real estate agent's description of a place to find out whether it is simply a pile of rocks. Several sites have downloadable photos of all of their properties, sometimes accompanied by an asking price, which means you can start the first stage of your research from the comfort of your living room.

Once you have an idea of what sort of property costs how much, you can turn to a real estate agent to show you the houses firsthand. You have your choice between an Italian agent and a foreign agency. The advantage to dealing with the Italians is their in-depth knowledge of the area and ability to answer any question you may have. And there is an endless list of questions, for example: Do the owners owe any money in taxes or loan payments on the property? What other liabilities, such as condominium fees, does it have? Is the building structurally sound, and if not, how much will you need to spend to get it into livable condition? Is the water from a private well, and if so, are the pressure and quality acceptable? Is the property owned by a company or an individual? Do local zoning laws allow you to turn the residence into a business, such as a bed-and-breakfast or a workshop? Will you be allowed to do all the renovations and improvements you have planned, such as adding a swimming pool? If these renovations have already been done, have they been done legally, or will you have a liability on your hands? The trouble for foreign buyers is that many of the local agents don't speak fluent English, which is why many prospective homeowners turn to another foreigner.

There are two other professionals who will be able to answer these questions for you more thoroughly, and both play essential roles in every real estate transaction: the *geometra,* a sort of deputy architect and surveyor; and the *notaio,* a cross between a lawyer and a notary public. It is difficult to translate their titles into plain English because the professions simply don't exist in the English-speaking world. The *geometra* will survey the property, handle any subdivision issues, and, although not a professional architect, can give you a good idea of whether there are any structural faults, and how much the house will cost to renovate. In rural areas especially, the *geometra* often works in tandem with the local real estate agent, which of course raises red flags about the person's objectivity. There is always the option of finding someone from outside, though this will add to the cost, and an outsider will not know the local market and considerations as well as the agent-appointed person does.

Depending on the job, the survey will cost in the vicinity of €1,000. The report will be in Italian, so unless you have a very good command of the language, you should budget in some translation costs.

The major function of the *notaio* is to register the sale of the property with the state. The state land register is the basis for all tax calculations, and the *notaio,* as a public servant, is charged with assuring that you will be taxed on the property's full value. Because the fees of the *notaio* can be expensive (see *Purchase Fees*), because they double as a sort of tax collector, and because their services are essential for any legal maneuver, theirs is not the best-loved profession in Italy. It ranks down there with politicians. Still, they provide all the necessary documents about the property, and any contract must be signed in their presence.

The first thing to remember about real estate contracts in Italy is that they are divided into two stages—the *compromesso* (intent-to-buy document), which is not always binding, and the *rogito* (deed of sale), which is. The intent-to-buy is something used by real estate agents and developers to initiate the sale, and they're not always bulletproof. For example, if you're buying a preexisting building, the *compromesso* may come in the form of an offer to buy, which can be reworded to make it a nonbinding contract. Otherwise, it may be a full-fledged *compromesso,* which will outline all of the terms of the agreement, such as whether the property contains elements that are part of a cooperative (i.e., *condominio*), the price, the eventual date of sale, etc.

If, on the other hand, you are buying a property that is not yet completed, the agreements will either stipulate that you buy the property as is, or else after a specified time or a certain amount of work has been done to it. The latter, based on work completed, is always preferable to an agreement that is based on time, since Italian contractors and repair persons are not known for their punctuality.

There are obviously myriad questions to be asked before signing a contract, and only a good, English-speaking attorney will be able to make sure that all of your demands are met.

A few basics are often overlooked. For example, you should be aware of exactly what comes with the house. It is amazing what some homeowners think is valuable when they move out, and you may find your newly purchased home void of such assumed assets as light fixtures and toilets.

PURCHASE FEES

Once you have signed the deed of sale, it's time to settle up and pay all the assorted taxes. If you purchased the property from a company, there is a value-added tax to be paid, which is set at a higher rate if the property can be described as a "luxury." Otherwise, you will pay a duty, a real estate tax, and a local tax, all of which add up to somewhere around 10 percent.

Last, but not least: the notary's fees, which can vary according to the value of the property. For real estate worth under €500,000, the fee might amount to about 1 percent and would decrease as the property's value increased from there. Until recently these rates were set by law and were nonnegotiable, but now you can shop around.

Financially speaking, buying a property abroad is always more complicated than buying one at home, because it presents unique considerations. The first of these (unless you plan to pay for the home in cash) is where to get the money. One choice is whether to mortgage an existing property back home or take out a loan for the home you are about to buy in Italy. There are advantages and disadvantages to each.

There are currency risks involved. If you take out a mortgage for your Italian home, the monthly payments will be in euros. And, chances are, you're paying it off with dollars—unless you have an income source in euros, such as renting out part of the home, which can be risky in itself. The dollar–euro fluctuation can be damaging. When the dollar plummets about 25 percent against the euro, which certainly has happened in the past, a couple previously paying a euro-denominated mortgage of US$2,000 per month will suddenly find themselves forking over US$2,500.

The payments will likely come out of your Italian bank account. For those not working in Italy and depending on savings at home, this means picking the right time to transfer funds. Clearly, when the dollar is strong, you'll want to transfer as many dollars as possible into euros in your Italian account for future payments.

Keep in mind that there are always hefty fees on wire transfers, and there's really no way to avoid them, short of traveling with 3,500 one hundred-dollar bills in a carry-on bag, which is a pretty risky affair and won't go over well at the customs office. An alternative is to ask your bank for a certified check—an international draft—but this process can take a long time, the exchange rates are unfavorable at the Italian bank, and they will also exact a fee. In the end, a wire transfer is probably the best way to get the job done.

The other huge factor, of course, to consider when choosing whether to set up a mortgage in Italy or at home is whose interest rates are lower. As of press time, they were at rock bottom in both Italy and the United States.

BUILDING AND RESTORING

The processes of buying and building on land in the United States and buying and building on land in Italy are different. In rural U.S. towns with lax zoning laws, you can usually find a cheap piece of land and build whatever you want. Owning land in Italy is a different story, as lots of moneyed Italians and foreigners dream of nothing more than a nice plot in the countryside, and demand is considerably higher. Remember that there are nearly 60 million Italians (a quarter of the U.S. population) living on a peninsula about the size of Arizona, and there's not a vast amount of land left for construction.

That said, buying a cheap, run-down farmhouse is not much different than simply buying a plot of land. (That is, if you can find one of the remaining ruins. The secret, as always, is location.) In this case, you're going to have to start from scratch.

The first step is making sure, ahead of signing the contract, that you will be able to get the necessary building permits. "You really have no idea how much you can build on a property until you see the records and look at the local master plan," Rome-based architect Domenico Minchilli pointed out, "but a good real estate agent will be able to show you."

Permits are going to take a long time to nail down: no less than six months in even the most efficient parts of Italy. You should enlist the help of your architect or *geometra* for this. Keep in mind that if you buy property that is listed in the register of historic homes, it will be very difficult to make modifications to the exterior, and only minor ones to the interior, and sometimes difficult to put in a swimming pool. There are some parts of Italy where new pools are just not allowed.

Even after the initial permitting, there are a few more regulatory hoops to jump through.

For new construction in seismic areas (and as the recent earthquakes in Emilia-Romagna and Abruzzo illustrated, most of Italy does fall into seismic areas), two separate structural engineers will need to be hired by law

© LUCIE ERICKSEN

Tuscan farmhouse

DAILY LIFE

(besides the architect), one to do the initial structural seismic plan and another to review and test the completed work. The engineer requires that a geologist do soil-testing and write a report.

Then, for environmental reasons, there has to be a report on insulation and thermal losses prepared by a separate specialist.

The last step is the *riaccatastamento,* that is, a review of the finished product for the land registry. A surveyor will draw a new map of the house after works are completed, a new pool, etc., and the property will be reassessed accordingly for the annual tax.

Household Expenses

You'll find a few surprises when you open your first household bills: The phone bill isn't itemized, for example, and even many renters pay for their own water. Most shocking, though, will be the amount due, since energy in Europe costs a bundle. Utilities will be a significant line item in your budget, and if you're building or renovating a house, you should study your needs well before deciding what kinds of services will be most efficient.

More and more companies are setting up online bill payments, which is a long-awaited development, since paying the bills has traditionally been a pretty complicated affair. You never pay by mail, and checks are rarely accepted. If there is no online service, you have three ways to pay: You can go to the company headquarters itself, with the bill and a fistful of cash. You can arrange for a direct transfer from your bank account, which makes disputing a bill more difficult, since they already have your money. Or you can pay at the post office. The last option wouldn't be so bad if post offices were open for more than a few hours a day. But for now, expect massive lines come payment time.

© LUCIE ERICKSEN

un terrazzo (or balcone)

You can expect electricity bills to be the greatest expense, and there's not much you can do about it, short of buying a generator or running off solar power. The only way to save money is to remember to turn off lights and appliances when you're not using them.

ENEL (Ente Nazionale per l'Energia Elettrica) is the partly privatized former monopoly that still provides most of Italy with its power. The other major provider is Edison. They outfit the average household with three kilowatts, which is about enough to run three or four appliances (and pretty wimpy ones at that) at a time. This also helps explain why there are very few clothes dryers in Italy, and why air-conditioning is such an expense. Even without heavy appliances, you will often overload the circuit, so when moving into a new house or apartment, find out right away where the circuit breakers are.

Like most bills, the electricity *bollete* arrives every two months and is based on expected consumption. At the end of the year, the company calculates how much you actually used, and you will be either credited or debited accordingly. Mostly, you'll be debited. Indeed, electricity costs are so high that, whenever possible, Italians rely on natural gas. Heating is generally gas-powered, as are water heaters and stoves. This also makes it easier to save money by simply shutting off the boiler, or switching off the gas line altogether, when you leave the house for a long time. (Note: In many apartments, heating is central, which of course makes the question moot.)

As long as you live in the city or the center of town, your house should be on the gas network. If not, you can buy your methane in large tanks (called *bombole*) and run a line into the house. In general, it is a very cost-efficient and fairly clean energy source, but it can be dangerous. It seems that every year, there is a tragedy somewhere in Italy when a rickety old apartment building explodes because of a faulty gas line.

Next envelope, please: the water bill. Prices are laid out by local entities, and therefore vary according to where you live. Often, it is a pretty negligible expense, but could be as much as €50 a month if local prices are high and you do a lot of washing. Or worse, if your neighbors do a lot of washing, and the water bill happens to be shared by the *condominio* (owners' association).

Not everyone will get a water bill. It may be included in your electricity bill. Or, if you're a renter, your landlord might include it in the monthly rate. Homeowners in the country will likely have a private well and just pay for the electricity to pump it.

Aside from the phone bill and the television tax (see the *Communications* chapter), your final utility expenditure is the garbage tax. This calculation is based on the amount of floor space in your home, which has long been a bone of contention for those who would just prefer to see it based on the amount of trash produced. Renters are not likely to see an individual trash bill, since this is almost always paid by the owners' association and then passed along to tenants within the rent. As in the United States, garbage collection is seen—in the south of Italy especially—as the fiefdom of underworld dons. Naples therefore has a perennial problem with its garbage collection. This is passed off as a labor strike but quite transparently is an appalling Mafia power play. The trash always seems to pile up in the hottest months. In Rome, trash bins were once removed from public places, since they were considered an eyesore. This only made things worse when individual bags started appearing in the streets.

On the surface, at least, Italian cities have comprehensive recycling programs, with household bins for plastic, paper, and compost, and communal bins for tin and glass. But exposés in the past have shown that once the collectors haul it off, the stuff usually ends up in the trash, anyway. Hopefully, this is no longer the case.

LANGUAGE AND EDUCATION

If you were packing up to move to Northern Europe and didn't speak any of the local languages, you shouldn't be too worried. There aren't too many foreigners who can speak Swedish, Norwegian, Danish, or Dutch quite as well as those people speak English. The Germans are also known to be good English-speakers, and even the French understand you better than they might have you know.

The Italians, on the other hand, are often taken to task by their European peers for their lack of language skills, especially when, at European Union meetings, the steady chain of fluent English breaks down when the Italian delegate steps up to the podium.

It's not that English is rarely heard in Italy—between the millions of tourists that come each year and the English jargon that has sneaked into the workplace, Italians are regularly bombarded with foreign words. Businesspeople are swimming in them. On an average day, *un top manager* will be expected to *controllare l'email, scrollare, unzippare* and perhaps even *scannerizzare* just to send something to *il suo staff* to get *il loro input*. Then it's up to another department to *processare i raw data* before anyone can actually get to *la fase dell'implementation*. It's all so confusing to a nonnative speaker that financial dailies have started distributing pocket-sized glossaries with the latest terms.

Anyone who works in this kind of environment, or in tourism, or else has traveled a lot (loads of young Italians have spent extended periods of time in London, and many in the United States) has a good command of English. But others know just enough to get by. Why would they spend time perfecting it, they'd argue, if they're hardly going to use it? This brings up the more pertinent question: Why don't North Americans just learn to speak Italian?

Lots of North Americans who come to Italy on a one-way ticket do, and get on with their Italian lives right away. Others tend to embed themselves in a circle of fellow foreigners instead. It's only natural for immigrants to any country to band together to make the adjustment easier, but if you stay trapped in this cocoon for a while, you should ask yourself why you decided to move to Italy.

There's so much to gain by speaking the language well, and so much to lose if you don't. Every newscast you don't understand, every joke that goes over your head, and every other disappointment in life that results from poor communication will be patent reminders of how much you're missing.

After you've lived in Italy for a few years, you'll start to forget that you're speaking a different language altogether. Walking into a fruit-and-vegetable store, you won't pause at the door to remember how to say the word "basil." Your vocabulary will expand by the day. You'll start dreaming in Italian and maybe counting in Italian numbers by instinct (even though an Italian friend of mine living in London insists that this is never the case). You and your expat friends in Italy may even stop speaking to one another in English, and at some point, you'll feel as if you've lost your English altogether when the word *basilico* becomes firmly attached to that bundle of aromatic greens sitting next to the *peperoncino*. You know, next to the what's-it-called, the red stuff you add to a sauce to make it spicy.

Everyone plumps their own theory on the quickest and most efficient way to learn a foreign language. The throw-the-little-boy-into-the-pool-and-he'll-learn-to-swim approach may not be the best for every student, nor for every language, but it seems to work pretty well in Italy. For one thing, Italian is a relatively easy language to conquer, especially for those who speak a little French, Spanish, or any other Romance language. The grammar and lexicon are the same, and phonetically, Italian is about the easiest language there is. Every word is pronounced exactly as it is spelled. (English can be a nightmare in that regard. Just look at the word "nightmare.") On top of that, Italians are very patient with foreigners struggling with their native tongue. They're quite used to outsiders butchering Dante's language on a regular basis. For that matter, they're quite used to miscommunicating with other Italians.

If you don't speak any Italian and learning a new language is daunting for you, here's a hint: Watch as many Italian films as you can. It will help. Films clearly won't teach beginners the fundamentals, but they will give you a feel for the language. For those who studied Italian years ago but haven't spoken it in a while, watching movies is an excellent way to get back into practice. Fortunately, most of the Italian films available in the United States have English subtitles. In Italy, foreign films are almost always dubbed. In fact, the profession of dubbing movies here is something of a revered art in itself.

Regional Dialects

Italy has always been covered with a motley quilt of different languages, and thousands of dialects survive to this day. It's commonly pointed out that in the mountain valleys of the South, dialects could vary to such a degree that populations separated by as little as five kilometers couldn't understand each other.

Until the 1930s, literature was the only common linguistic thread. That is, the citizens of the newly formed nation could only communicate with each other through a Florentine dialect used by a Renaissance author, Dante Alighieri. Literary scholars estimate that 90 percent of the words in modern Italian can be found in Dante's works and those of his contemporaries. Later writers, such as Alessandro Manzoni, author of *The Betrothed,* may have thought up and written drafts in their native dialect—in Manzoni's case, the one from the lakes region—and then chosen Florentine for the finished product.

But literature was read only by a very slim minority in what was, until the mid-20th century, a mostly poor, agricultural country. Furthermore, books can only exert so much influence on how a language is actually spoken, and Italian in the 19th century was almost the Latin of its day: spoken by the educated class, used in the courts and for all other official business—but by and large ignored by the masses, who conversed in the vernacular.

That all changed when the radio came to town. The Fascists, in their push to create a national identity in the 1930s, were very fortunate in rising to power at a time when radio audiences were swelling and the first televisions were about to arrive in Italy.

© PERSEOMEDUSA/123RF

statue of Dante in front of Santa Croce church in Florence

Radio brought Italian to previously impenetrable towns, and video threatened to kill off dialects altogether. Before the 1950s, some 80 percent of the peninsula's population could not speak Italian. Now, official figures say, only about 5 percent of the population does not speak Italian on a regular basis.

That's not to say that only 5 percent of the population speaks in dialect. Millions of Italians still do, and consider themselves bilingual. Census data counts about 1.3 million people who speak Sardinian; 500,000 who speak Friulian; 300,000 who speak German in the region of Alto-Adige, and, in that same area, some 55,000 who speak an ancient language called Ladino; about 300,000 who use one of several French dialects in Piedmont and Val d'Aosta; 70,000 Slovenian-speakers in the northeast; 18,000 Catalan-speakers in Sardinia; 2,600 Croatian-speakers in Molise; and 20,000 Ancient Greek-speakers in Calabria and Puglia, where another 100,000 have retained Albaresh, the language of their Albanian ancestors who arrived in Italy in the 14th century. These languages were officially recognized by the state as "protected" in a 1999 law, following a European Union directive that aimed to preserve some of the continent's disappearing tongues, of which Italy probably has more than any other country in the EU.

Chances are, though, you won't run into a native Albaresh- or Ladino-speaker unless you go specifically to those enclaves. More often, you'll hear some of the more diffuse dialects, like Venetian, Milanese, Bergamasco, Genoese, Roman, Neapolitan, and Sicilian (to name some of the more recognizable ones), especially if you talk with older people. Remember that almost everyone in Italy over the age of 65 spoke something other than Italian at home when they were children.

Television may have brought a common language to successive generations, but many younger people still speak with their elders in dialect. The so-called protected

road sign in Italian and Albaresh

languages are even taught at school. In Alto-Adige, for example, students have their choice between a German-speaking school and an Italian-speaking one, and more often than not, they choose the former, because job opportunities are seen as greater in the Teutonic world than in points south.

Other idioms aren't so welcome in class. In one highly publicized case not so long ago, a high school principal near Vicenza in the Veneto fined his pupils a few cents for every word spoken in dialect. It's only natural in a country where people pride themselves on their hometowns that a little good-natured provinciality shines through. Even celebrities on television, the great linguistic equalizer, give some hint of their roots when they open their mouths, if not an overpowering accent that lends itself openly to caricature. Silvio Berlusconi's nasal Brianzolo and soccer star Francesco Totti's Roman drawl are just two of the easier targets. They don't try to hide it, as a matter of principle. The only exception might be southerners who moved to Turin or Milan for jobs, and who want to conceal their backgrounds for fear of being labeled a *terrone* (peasant), a form of intra-Italian racism that grew in the 1960s and still pervades the North. On the other side of the coin, finding a fellow Sicilian in a position of power might just be an islander's ticket to the top.

In general, you'll make more friends in Italy if you speak with an honest accent and use simple words, rather than try to churn out polished verse. High school principals and other scholarly types may speak the language of Dante, but average Italians will snicker under their breath when they hear the perfect tense too many times, or suffer through a pedantic insistence on the subjunctive clause. Both of these are so correct that they come off as awkward.

Unfortunately, this kind of populist attitude won't get you very far with an Italian professor, and for all the bravado and braggadocio about learning Italian on the fly, there really is no substitute for a language class.

Learning the Language

Italian courses are easy to find in the United States. Just about every local college offers a class at night or on the weekends, and any independent language institute will certainly feature it on its brochure. Learning the basics before you come is a smart idea. Mastering the grammar should only take a few months, and then you'll be free to improve your pronunciation and build your vocabulary by the time you arrive in Italy, rather than poring through lists of irregular verbs—something that could just as easily be done at home.

If you're a college student and are considering a move to Italy after graduation, obviously the wisest option is to take a semester abroad in Italy. You may end up speaking a lot of English with your cohorts, but at least you'll be surrounded by Italian-speakers for a few consecutive months.

Italy remains the second most popular destinations for U.S. students abroad, after the United Kingdom (13 percent of all students abroad go to Italy, versus 15 percent in Britain.) It's amazing how many of them fall in love with Florence or Rome on their junior year abroad and then decide to move back for good. That field is destined to grow as more students keep flowing in. In 1985, U.S. undergraduates studying in Italy

TU AND LEI

For English-speakers, the trickiest parts of mastering any Romance language are remembering a noun's gender and deciding whether to use the formal or informal version of the pronoun "you." The first distinction is pretty straightforward in Italian: Ninety-nine percent of the time, if the word ends in an "a," it's feminine; if it ends in an "o," it's masculine.

The second dilemma is more difficult, because there are no hard-and-fast rules. It's a social judgment, not a linguistic one, which means that the guidelines used in one generation may not be good for the next. For instance, in the past, it was always proper to use the formal *lei* to address your elders. That's not necessarily the case today. Many of today's "elders," especially those who grew up in the 1960s, shudder at the formality and will insist that you address them as *tu*. Some of your friends' parents, however, will have been brought up with a certain decorum at home, and will expect everyone but close friends to

address them as *lei*. The safest bet is to err on the side of formality, then switch over to the informal if you get the green light.

Then there are nuances that have little to do with age or respect. The *lei* form is a convenient way to put distance between yourself and a person with whom you don't want to be too familiar, especially in a business setting. Suppose you have a problem with something you bought, and you call customer support for assistance. An operator that genuinely wants to help you may switch to the informal right off the bat to establish a close rapport. If, on the other hand, you run into an operator who just wants to get you off the phone at all costs, expect a generous helping of polite distance. Another example: You walk into a restaurant when the kitchen is about to close. If you hear the *tu* form, there may be some room for negotiation, and the right smile and joke may get you a table. But if you hear a stern *lei* immediately, just say thank you and head for the door.

numbered around 4,000. By 2010, there were about 32,000 of them at some 400 U.S. programs or in a curriculum of their own design.

Two popular self-styled options are the universities for foreigners in Siena (www.unistrasi.it) and Perugia (www.unistrapg.it). Both offer three-month beginner courses in Italian, as well as more advanced programs. Both cost in the vicinity of €1,500. There are dozens of other institutes spread throughout Italy. Two examples are the Dante Alighieri Society (www.dantealighieri.com) in Siena, and Lingua Due (linguadue.com) in Milan. Both offer two-, three-, and four-week courses for about €150–200 per week.

A number of private U.S. companies also offer language courses in Italy. One of the more reputable is Education First (www.ef.com), based in Boston. It conducts both a year-abroad program and shorter-term classes at its school in Rome.

Education

PRIMARY AND SECONDARY EDUCATION

The progression through schools in Italy is not so different from in North America, in that there is an elementary school, a middle school, and a high school. The ages roughly correspond: elementary school is for five years, ages 6–10; middle school is three years, ages 11–13; and high school is five years, ages 14–18. That's more or less where the similarities end.

For one thing, students choose to go to a high school for either science or humanities, or else for vocational training. Not so long ago, that choice definitively determined your course of study in university as well. Now, a student from a scientific high school, for example, can theoretically choose to study journalism at university, but conventional wisdom still states that a scientific high school will prepare you less well for a humanities degree, and vice versa.

Just how well you perform on the *maturità,* the exam at the end of high school, will determine which fields of study you are allowed to pursue at university.

There has been continual debate in parliament for the last few years over proposed reforms to the system, especially the transition from middle school to high school. Whether the test that students are subjected to at the end of middle school can keep them from entering a certain type of high school, and instead determine that they are to go to vocational school, is still undecided as of the writing of this book. This uncertainty is likely to continue: Reforms under one government are regularly overturned in the next, and that cycle in Italy is relatively frequent.

Public Schools vs. Private Schools

Public schools are often at their best at the first two levels: the *scuola materna,* for three- to five-year-olds, and elementary school, which in Italy runs from first to fifth grade. According to some parents I interviewed, their elementary school students were even studying Greek and Latin (!), while recent reforms have made English and computer classes compulsory. In general, parents feel that students start to receive less attention as they progress into *scuola media* (middle school), *liceo* (high school), and beyond, culminating in a university system where—depending, of course, on the sort of program you attend—professors are often hard to track down for questions, much being less available for counseling.

Private schools are not necessarily the best place to send a gifted student. Run for the most part by religious orders, they tend to cater to those with short attention spans or disciplinary problems. That said, there are a number of private schools with highly regarded curricula, where a top-flight education costs top euro.

The third possibility is a private English-language school, which seems the most logical option for expatriates but is also a popular option for Italian families willing to pay top euro for their children's command of English. There are British, U.S., and international schools in the major cities, some with better reputations than others. (A comprehensive listing of those schools is available in the English Yellow Pages at www. intoitaly.it.) One occasional lament from parents, however, is that there are so many

Italian students in these academies that classes can sometimes move slowly to accommodate nonnative speakers.

HIGHER EDUCATION

Math classes, on the other hand, progress at what we might consider a breakneck speed. Anyone who has been to the Old World on a high school exchange program will be the first to admit that European teens are well ahead of their North American peers in mathematics. This is hardly surprising when you consider just how prepared scientific students need to be to enter their first university course. Degrees in Italy are highly specialized. Students in medicine, for example, graduate directly with an MD. European university degrees are essentially considered master's degrees.

First, though, we need to take a step back and define what constitutes an Italian diploma. Incidentally, the word *diploma* in Italian refers to the thing you receive when you complete high school. After graduating from university, you receive a *laurea,* and there are now two different kinds: a three-year degree, known familiarly as the *laurea breve,* or the full-fledged, specialized degree, or *laurea specialistica* which requires five or more years. Some students drag out the process well into their thirties.

Those who complete either can at last call themselves *dottore* or *dottoressa,* but recipients of the *laurea breve*—now a decade after the reforms that introduced this two-tier system—are realizing that they really need to have the specialized degree in order to find a job.

DAILY LIFE

HEALTH

Health insurance is one of the first concerns of people who move to Italy. Your policy in the United States may not cover you abroad, and if you rely on Medicare, it certainly won't.

Travel insurance is typically good for about a six-month sojourn, and is the best way to get started. After all, you want to make sure that you and your family are covered from the moment you step foot on Italian soil. In the meantime, you can start preparing to enter into the Italian health care system, which has both public and private options.

If you have a job in Italy and therefore make regular payments to the health care system, you will automatically be provided with the same public coverage extended to those Italians who were employed at some point in their lives, plus their dependents. If you're not regularly employed, there is always the option of independently buying a plan that covers you through that same public system.

Alternatively, you can take out a private health insurance policy, which is going to be more expensive but offers more benefits. Many Italians buy private policies in addition to the state-provided coverage. The costs and comparative advantages of each sector are described in *Types of Insurance*.

Types of Insurance

PUBLIC VS. PRIVATE CARE

Health care is free to all Italian citizens, regardless of how much they contribute in income taxes. Part of every worker's salary goes to the national health service, the Servizio Sanitario Nazionale (SSN), though insurance is administered at the local level. This means that (1) the quality of care can vary according to the region—in general, northern hospitals are said to be in better shape than southern ones—and (2) all of your questions are answered by your local health authority, or the Azienda Sanità Locale (ASL).

If you are regularly employed, you will receive public health insurance automatically. The only expense you are expected to pay is a nominal copay fee. To register for this insurance, you need to go to the local ASL office and pick a primary care physician from a list. The doctor will be your reference point from then on—writing your prescriptions, referring you to specialists, and ordering your hospitalization if necessary.

The largest complaints about the public system are that the hospitals are not always the cleanest-looking places and the lines can be long. Waiting several hours in pain is not uncommon, as long as the injury or illness is not life-threatening.

Italians have similar gripes about public universities. Though public education, which is free, has a certain level of prestige in Italy, professors—like doctors working in public hospitals—are given little incentive to make themselves available. When it comes to health, those who can afford it don't take chances. They sign up for additional coverage at private clinics, where the wait is usually less tedious and the hospital rooms can even be luxurious.

While Italian health care, even private, is rarely compared favorably with the U.S. system in terms of technology and research, certain Italian clinics are way ahead of the game. On a recent trip to a private clinic in Milan, a dermatologist who had trained in top programs in the United States was surprised to see a computerized scope that she had never laid eyes on back home. Don't assume, however, that doctors in private clinics will have better credentials than those in public hospitals. For one thing, many doctors work in both sectors. Also, some regions have worked out deals with the local clinics to send public-care patients there for certain procedures. Finally, the public domain is the stronghold of academia, and so the brightest lights in their fields—if they haven't already been lured away by big money in the United States or Germany—prefer the prestige of working in a state-run university hospital over higher salaries in a clinic.

SELF-SERVE INSURANCE

If you don't have a job, you have a number of other health insurance options in Italy. These include paying for public care, paying for private care, or taking out traveler's health insurance at home before you leave.

The last option is the best way to get started, as well as the obvious choice for those who plan to stay only a few months. Many U.S. health insurance companies offer plans with the following services: nonemergency and emergency medical expenses, medical evacuation, and prescription drugs. (They also include repatriation of remains, given the worst-case scenario.) But travel insurance policies are usually only good for up to six consecutive months or multiple shorter trips. The other disadvantage of this approach is that you will have to pay up front for any medical expenses incurred in Italy. You could be stuck holding the debt for seven or eight months before the company pays you back.

Many people who do not have a regular job, and therefore do not contribute to the SSN, can take out an insurance policy with the public health system. Present your stay permit at the local ASL office, and pay a set fee of about €300. The catch is that you need to have some sort of proof of health insurance to qualify for the stay permit in the first place. You will not be issued one without insurance. A temporary policy from the U.S. will do the trick.

Alternatively, you can enroll in a private plan. These start at about €1,000 annually, available at any major Italian insurance company. One advantage is that you have your choice of clinics, an important consideration for those who suffer from a chronic illness. But bear in mind that even the public system goes a long way. Many of my friends who have both health insurance in the United States and public coverage in Italy (through their jobs) prefer to have some operations done on the Old Continent. Laser surgery to correct your vision, for example, can be expensive in the United States, because many insurance policies will not cover such elective procedures. That is not necessarily the case in Italy. And although that kind of corrective surgery can be hit-or-miss, my friends, at least, had positive results—for free.

TAKING YOUR CHANCES

Of course, your last option is to take your chances and not hold any medical insurance at all. Note that Medicare will cover only a very small fraction of your hospital

BENESSERE: THE ART OF FEELING GOOD

Italians are on a perpetual crusade for both comfort and beauty. It is only fitting that a country with some of the most beautiful scenery in the world should have beautiful people as well, and that the pleasant climate should be matched by a general sense of *benessere* (well-being).

This ideal state of mind and body involves eating right, staying trim, keeping skin flake-free and well-tanned, and, above all, keeping stress at a minimum. The nation's fitness centers offer so-called relax rooms, with soothing colors and music for a post-workout calm.

Nothing in the world, however, can compare to Italy's spas, where stressed-out city slickers get massaged and soak up sulfuric waters. It is a tradition dating back to antiquity, when Roman soldiers would go to Tuscan springs for "the cure" after defeating a legion of Goths or the

like. The mountainous peninsula is loaded with thermal springs, concentrated mostly in central Italy and the Alps. A weekend retreat often includes mud baths, massages, and aromatherapy. Some hotels even propose bathing in wine or hay.

The search for good health begins at the supermarket, where herbal treatments line the aisles. Food magazines regularly include recipes using such greenery as birch leaves and witch hazel to deliver softer skin and improved circulation, or to cure kidney ailments and gout.

If this all seems too newfangled for Italy, a country previously associated with rotund, mustachioed pizza chefs feeding roly-poly mammas and their pudgy kids, you must remember that Italy revised its diet long ago, following the French lead of nouvelle cuisine and these days its eating habits are among the healthiest in Europe.

Shop for healthy food at your local fruit market.

costs abroad, if at all. Also remember that this hands-off approach will pose a problem when you apply for your long-stay permit.

There is technically one other alternative for those without insurance: free health care for illegal immigrants. It is a shaky option at best. Italy has a reputation for being a compassionate country. This might seem undeserved praise, if one considers that there is no welfare program for those who have never had a job and therefore have never contributed to Social Security. The assumption here is that their families support those who cannot or will not work. And to a large extent, this holds true for those who have relations in Italy. But for the hundreds of thousands who don't—including the growing number of single male immigrants—the state provides nothing. De facto welfare comes in the form of Catholic charities. Numerous church-run organizations sponsor free hospitals for immigrants and the homeless. It is indeed a warm gesture, but suffice it to say that you never want to rely on free care.

Rest assured that you will receive emergency medical attention if you happen to be run over by a car or hit by a stray bullet—regardless of your insurance or residency status. Even illegal immigrants with no insurance are covered for ambulance and emergency room bills, as is generally the case in the United States. But don't expect a free ride in a helicopter after a skiing accident, for example.

Pharmacies and Prescriptions

Public health care covers most of your prescription drug costs. Once your doctor writes you a prescription, you will be ushered into the world of Italian pharmacies, where medicine is dispensed with a serious air and quaint packaging. Prepare for an adventure.

Pharmacy schedules are confusing, but there will be at least one open at any time in any given city or town. Just look for an illuminated green cross. If the sign is turned off, it's closed. Especially late at night, you may have to check several locations, as pharmacies take turns filling the night shift.

This can be frustrating, since pharmacies are the only places in town that sell aspirin. They are also among the few places that sell mosquito spray and plug-in vapor repellents—indispensable urban survival gear in the summer, especially in the North. The moral is: Don't wait until you have a headache or mosquito problem to go looking for relief. Always keep a supply of medicine on hand.

Once you find an open pharmacy, you'll notice that it isn't the sort of place with greeting cards and cigarettes for sale with a drug counter tucked in the back. Italian pharmacists take their vocation very seriously, and their customers afford them due respect. Theirs is one of the most sought-after fields of scientific study, ranking just after medicine among high school students aspiring to university. Candidates need to score rather high on entrance exams to be admitted to a pharmacy program.

Your pharmacist, invariably dressed in a white lab coat, will act as a sort of physician for minor ailments such as the flu or diarrhea. If you have a cold, a stomachache, or mild headache, spare yourself the hassle of going to the hospital and head directly to the pharmacist for a quick diagnosis and over-the-counter pills. Be warned that what might be done with a tablet or capsule back home may take a more frightening form in Italy. Italians are not hesitant to administer an injection. Seek out someone's mother for help.

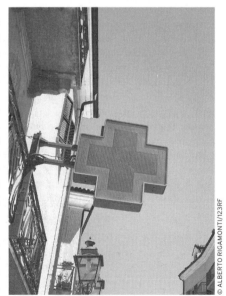

If you take a particular medicine back home, make sure to jot down the generic name, as brand names are rarely the same in Europe. Also, because Italian food and drug regulations are different, you will have access to medicines that might be awaiting FDA approval in the United States.

Aside from traditional cures, Italian pharmacies always stock a wide array of "alternative" treatments, such as herbs and homeopathy. Both are very popular in Italy. Your quack detector may start

the green *farmacia* cross

MEDICINE, SCHMEDICINE

Italians are turning to alternative medicine in increasing numbers. According to a survey in 2000 by the National Statistics Institute, ISTAT, up to three times as many people chose alternatives to traditional medicine in 1999 than in 1991; roughly nine million Italians in all, almost one-sixth of the population, preferred to go to someone other than a medical doctor to treat an ailment.

The study was based on a sample of 30,000 families. Women led the trend, especially those with a relatively high level of education who resided in the northeast. The most typically cited cures were homeopathy, massage therapy, acupuncture, and phytotherapy (a somewhat rarer approach based on the curative power of plants).

Homeopathy—treating a disease with small doses of the same disease—has seen the greatest increase in popularity over the last decade. In 1991, 2.5 percent of the Italian population used that method; by the end of the decade, 8.2 percent did.

While northerners were described as the most eager to try new methods, one out of six people in the central regions did the same, as compared to one out of 15 in the South. More than 60 percent of those who sought alternative treatment were women.

About 40 percent of respondents said they approved of alternative medicine, and 23 percent said they did not, while the rest passed no judgment. As for those who had actually tried it at some point, 91 percent said they were pleased with the results.

beeping if a pharmacist suggests a sort of potion or oil that you've never heard of, but anything new is worth a try if nothing else seems to help (and as long as your life is not on the line). You could be pleasantly surprised by the results.

When picking up a prescription at the counter, you normally have to pay a fee of about €2 along with your "ticket" for the subsidized medicine. If the prescription is for a serious illness, such as a heart condition, often there will be no fee at all. The government also subsidizes treatments for drug addicts.

Unfortunately, this system has been plagued by scandals. Courts have issued hundreds of indictments for fraud and bribery in the health industry, ranging from pharmacists who cashed in bogus "tickets" for state-subsidized prescriptions they claimed to have filled, to more subtle cases involving doctors accused of accepting what judges called "bribes" from drug companies, usually in the form of all-expenses paid vacations, in exchange for pushing their brands. The Health Ministry said it plans to clear up rules about promotional offers for doctors in the future.

Potential Hazards

The biggest health scare in Italy in the past decade has been Creutzfeldt-Jakob disease, caused by the so-called "mad cow" brain-wasting virus found in infected meat. The riskiest parts of the animal are bone marrow and especially cerebral and spinal fluids. For about a year in 2000–2001, the venerated Fiorentina T-bone steak was taken off menus in Florence as a result, and sheep brains, a delicacy in Rome, were temporarily banned. Though they have since reappeared, many similar specialties are still hard to find.

AIDS levels are about at the European average. The last available data are from 2001, which put the number of people in Italy living with HIV/AIDS at about 140,000, which was well below the figure for Spain and roughly on par with France.

The Health Ministry runs a very active safe-sex campaign, with posters canvassing the subways and public buildings. But this is one of the areas where proximity to the Vatican makes such initiatives politically delicate. Vatican officials repeat that the use of condoms in curbing AIDS is not "ethically admissible," and its influence on Catholic members of Parliament should not be underestimated. This is not to say that condoms or other forms of birth control are not readily available—they are—but there appears to be a lingering taboo under the surface.

It may come as a surprise, then, that the Vatican runs one of the largest and best-equipped pharmacies on the peninsula, where many experimental treatments and pharmaceuticals pass under the radar of Italian drug laws.

Environmental Factors

One recent skirmish between the church and the government highlighted the state of environmental affairs in Italy. The Vatican transmitter towers that broadcast the church's Radio Maria channel were thought to be linked with higher-than-average rates of leukemia in the region of Lazio. For months, Italians were jittery about so-called "electrosmog." In the end, the claims were neither proven nor disproven scientifically. Accusations were thrown around, and then the whole affair just disappeared, as do most impulsive urges to make Italy a greener place—sort of like New Year's resolutions, except on a parliamentary level.

One resolution that has finally stuck is Italy's resolve to quit smoking. The baby-boom generation has witnessed at least three attempts to ban smoking in public places, and this last time, it has worked. No restaurant allows smoking indoors. At outside tables, however, it is pervasive. This area of a restaurant is seen as the de facto smoking section.

Moreover, don't expect the same level of courtesy smokers may show in the United States toward nonsmokers. Cigarettes aren't seen as the demonic vice that they are in North America. Italians may casually light up in your home, even if it has been made clear that you are a nonsmoker, but don't take that to be an extremely rude gesture, just a simple misunderstanding of cultures.

Italy has also vowed to make a better effort at recycling, and it has an impressive program—in theory, at least. Every apartment building is equipped with separate bins for paper, plastic, glass, and aluminum, although there is some question as to where that recycling ultimately ends up.

Critics of U.S. environmental policy will make the claim that, although Italy may be slightly behind the rest of Europe in terms of conservation and protection, at least their hearts are in the right place. They will point to the Kyoto accords, which Italy happily signed along with its European neighbors to curb greenhouse gases, while the United States huffed and puffed. However, total carbon dioxide emissions in Italy are down about 2 percent between 1990 and 2012, well short of the 6.5 percent target set in Kyoto.

Most of Italy's greatest environmental villains are found in the industrial North. Biochemical plants just outside Venice are perennially plagued by dumping scandals or caught with illegal emissions. Residents of towns near the lagoon have been asked in the past to tape their windows shut, after one such refinery went up in flames. Milan and Turin have the worst air-pollution problems. The grandmother of a friend of mine recently went to the doctor with a worrying cough, and after looking at her chest X-ray, the doctor said she would do well to stop smoking two packs a day. The grandmother said she had never touched a cigarette—but had spent her entire life in Milan.

Not so long ago, on select Sundays, the city limited traffic to those cars with either odd- or even-numbered plates when pollution levels reached a critical level. Sometimes it banned traffic altogether. Lawmakers recognized that this is a short-term solution, and lately it seems the practice has disappeared. But they made their point. Italy is one of several European countries developing effective hydrogen-powered cars, and several hydrogen buses are already in circulation in northern cities. Smaller, battery-powered buses are common all over the country.

© VALERY VOENNYY/123RF

When pollution levels reach a critical level, Rome limits traffic to cars with either odd- or even-numbered plates.

DAILY LIFE

Like everything else in Italy, environmentalism is an area of sharp contrasts. Leaded gasoline has been definitively banned, catalytic converters are obligatory, more and more land is protected every year, and so on. Yet change has been slow. Until 2005, Milan was the only major European city without a sewage treatment plant, for example. Its waste ran directly into the Lambro River, cut across the width of northern Italy, and came to a swirling stop on the Adriatic coast among the eels and rice paddies of the Po River delta.

EMPLOYMENT

The best thing that can be said about being an employee in Italy is that they have long enjoyed a very comfortable lifestyle. They've had monthlong vacations, complete job security, above-par dining at the cafeteria, and countless benefits that range from full health care to the occasional company-provided mortgage and lifelong pensions for some.

Enjoy it while it lasts. The strength of the unions in Italy may never allow for a completely free labor market, but the desperate condition of Italy's balance sheets led to austerity measures that have succeeded where successive conservative governments have failed: In 2012, Mario Monti's caretaker government passed laws that made it easier to hire and fire workers. Public sector employees are already feeling the squeeze.

The traditional security and comfort afforded to Italian employees have come at another cost. The average monthly salary is well below what you'd find in the United States for a similar post, and there's little chance you'll ever make it to the inner circle of top earners.

Whether an unintended consequence of socialist labor laws, or a by-product of centuries of feudalism, or, in many cases, just plain laziness, social mobility is a rare phenomenon in this part of the world. Rags-to-riches stories are almost unheard of. Admission to Italy's elite is by invitation only, and all the seats in the so-called *salotto buono,* or "fine drawing room," are already comfortably occupied.

The highest echelons of business surround themselves in an impenetrable fortress

of power. The Agnelli family and their circle of friends, most notably the heads of creditor banks such as Mediobanca, still control the country's corporate giants. These include the consolidated mega-banks and insurance companies as well as the utilities and telecoms that were privatized in the 1990s. The *salotto* safeguards its interests through shareholder pacts to defend against takeovers by the wrong sort of people.

The great majority of all Italian companies are private, midsized, and still family-held, and thus there is little chance you'll see the inside of the boardroom unless your last name is the same as the founder's. These are deep-rooted traits in the Italian economy that may never change.

At the lowest levels, that of the *operai,* or manual laborers, well, they seem to harbor few aspirations, at least in the eyes of managers, who assume that workers are easily contented with the company-provided ski trips and intramural soccer games on Saturdays.

If this strikes you as an overly cynical assessment of a Western economy, note the success enjoyed by the best-selling 2007 book *The Caste,* by Sergio Rizzo and Gian Antonio Stella, and the political frenzy it engendered. This indictment of the de facto class system in Italy explains why politicians are "untouchable" and why the moneyed class is so deeply entrenched.

Seeing the writing on the wall, the business community starting making overtures toward a more equitable distribution of fortune. In a December 2007 speech, Luca Cordero di Montezemolo, the leader of the nation's industrialists' lobby, lamented that 6 in 10 children of manual laborers go on to do the same work as their parents, as do 7 in 10 children of professionals and managers. "We live in a caste system," he said.

So what does all this mean for a foreigner looking for a job in Italy? Well, you will be the consummate outsider in a system run by insiders. On the other hand, as U.S. expat, your outsider status may actually work to your advantage. Italian employers' respect for the American work ethic and English-language skills is discussed under *The Job Hunt.*

As a business owner, being an outsider simply means that you have a lot to learn about your new country.

Self-Employment

Despite the considerable challenges, many foreigners have chosen to *mettersi in proprio* (start their own businesses), ranging from web design to goat farming. Lots of them cater to a North American clientele in such fields as wine export, relocation services, and travel agencies. These are, for the most part, small businesses, employing only the owner and perhaps a spouse or children, a practice that can be chalked up to strict hiring laws and expensive benefits for employees. Businesses with fewer than 15 employees are immune from many restrictions.

LABOR LAWS

The sorts of contracts handed out to employees are described in more detail in *The Job Hunt* section, but suffice to say that, compared to the United States, they are designed to favor employees. Put another way, salaries are much lower in Italy than in the United States because many of the benefits that Italian workers enjoy, such as long vacations and free health care, are subsidized by businesses.

A worker's salary is only one of many obligations a potential employer should keep in mind. Others include:

- The "13th month," which is essentially a month's bonus tacked on at the end of the year. In some cases, there is a 14th and even a 15th month, depending on the kind of contract.

- Liquidation: Labor laws state that early termination of any contract requires a payment that amounts to roughly 10 percent of an employee's earnings over the duration spent at the business.

- Every month, there are pension payments to the social security system—called INPS—taken out of a worker's salary and matched by the employer.

- In those workplaces with a relatively high risk of injury, an employer needs to set aside what can amount to 50 percent of an employee's salary and hand it over to the state body for worker's compensation, called Inail.

The first step for anyone committed to opening a business is to get the appropriate permits and licenses from the town or city. In Italy, you don't just find a spot that you think would be ideal for an ice cream store and set up shop; the local government will make that decision for you. In theory, at least, this decision is based on the location of other ice cream stands nearby and whether the market can support another. Every type of business is therefore registered at the local chamber of commerce.

After you have the local court's approval for the existence of your business, there are four offices with whom you must register: the Registro delle Imprese (Registrar of Businesses), the Registro delle Ditte (Registrar of Companies), the Registro delle Imposte (Tax Registrar), and the Ufficio Registri (Tax Registrar's Office).

Next, you need to decide on a corporate structure. The simplest of these is declaring

Even neighborhood markets are registered at the local chamber of commerce.

yourself a self-employed freelancer; for example, a web designer, translator, or consultant. Why bother with the formalities? Because when you perform work for a company, it will ask you to file an invoice and will need a tax ID number in order to pay you. So, to become a legal freelancer, you must register for a *partita IVA* (value-added-tax number), and your clients will withhold 20 percent tax on every invoice you file.

Alternatively, you can incorporate your private business into a partnership; that is, a *società* in *nome collettivo* (SNC). The only real difference between this arrangement and the freelancing option is that, with an SNC, the IVA number is assigned to the company, not the individual—and therefore the company will pay taxes in May and November, rather than having them withheld as an individual.

Farther up the entrepreneurial food chain is the corporation. These come in two forms: *società a responsibilità limitata* (SRL), which is a limited liability corporation, and the *società per azioni* (SpA), a joint stock company. The first is a private company—therefore divided into quotas, not shares—that has initial working capital of at least €10,000. The second has a minimum working capital of €100,000, is divided into shares, and is the only type of company that can be taken public.

Again, the whole process of setting up a business is complicated, and there is no substitute for getting some professional help. Registering your company, for example, is best done through a *notaio* (notary public). Fees for registering a corporation will amount to a few thousand dollars. Accounting is also a very delicate operation in Italy and is best left to a *commercialista* (accountant). These may be the only people in Italy who fully understand how the tax system works.

Before you even get to that stage, however, you should do some research with the chamber of commerce. A preferred option among foreigners is the American Chamber of Commerce in Italy (www.amcham.it). (Their events are also a good networking resource.) Better, a consultant from one of the big U.S. firms can offer you some professional help, if you can afford it. The Big Four accounting and consulting firms are very active in Italy.

TYPES OF BUSINESSES

The types of businesses that foreigners own in Italy often fall into one of two categories: taking America to Italy or taking Italy to America. Just 10 years ago, you could walk around the streets of Rome and imagine a dozen kinds of shops that might have made money and now do: video rentals, one-hour photo kiosks, gyms, sushi restaurants, etc. These products of globalization are only slowly cropping up in smaller cities, representing what might be an emerging market for retail entrepreneurs.

For professionals, it seems that there is still a sizable market for North American things in Italy. All sorts of U.S. technology, know-how, and the English language itself are still very marketable here, even if the gap between the two continents has closed considerably in those respects in recent decades. Indeed, in many cases, the United States could stand to gain from importing certain methods and products developed in a country that isn't as old-fashioned as many North Americans think.

Italy's classic products, such as its wine, food, fashion, cars, and bicycles, were introduced to the United States long ago, but the more you look around the world of crafts here, the more secrets you will find and may decide to bring home. The same goes for

COACH G, WHIPPING ROME INTO SHAPE

Some people are born Romans, some become Romans, and some have Rome thrust upon them. Gerard Burley falls squarely into the third category. When his partner was assigned to the U.S. Embassy in Rome, Gerard was faced with two options: Stay home and risk an almost certain end to the relationship, or move to Italy.

He decided to pack up his stuff. He rented out his home in Washington, D.C., and in a matter of weeks, he had assumed a new life abroad, and a new identity as "Coach G."

Coach G's business plan was bulletproof. Everyone knows that pasta and wine are some of Italy's biggest draws, but also hazardous to your waistline. So Coach G parlayed his background in athletics into a career as a personal trainer to the well-fed.

While a life in Italy was never on his radar, personal training was his calling. His passion for fitness initially brought him to study sports medicine at UNC-Chapel Hill, and later he worked as a trainer at a Division II school, Bowie State University. With his summers free, Coach G found a part-time job at a local gym and learned what it took to get people in shape.

Coach G managed to establish a small clientele in the United States in short order, but duplicating this success in Italy was really raising the bar. He knew virtually nobody, and very little Italian. So he went to cocktail parties hosted by the English Yellow Pages, inserted himself in the network of English-speaking expats, and soon found a few takers. Then he looked up every U.S.-run business in the capital and showed up at their doors, armed only with a handful of business cards and a lot of charisma.

What he had to offer were the most modern training methods from the New World, an ebullient, almost preternaturally positive attitude, and rock-solid reliability. Coach G shows up on time, all the time. In Rome, these qualities are in short supply.

He comes to people's homes armed with a scale and tape measures to get the "Before" picture. The next time he shows up with kettle bells, weights and mats, and of course a no-nonsense, no-excuses attitude. And if you don't take his instruction seriously, you won't be his client for very long.

In a matter of weeks, the scales and tape measures, register smaller numbers.

These days, Coach G has to turn down business. He is starting to hire instead.

the tourist industry: There are still a few corners of Italy waiting to be discovered by travelers who would pay good money to do so.

Then again, you may decide to forgo the import/export sector altogether and compete with Italians at their own games. One expat in Venice, Thomas Price, is regularly interviewed on Italian television to talk about his gondola-making business.

Another option is what you might call A2A: American to American. Some examples would be an English-speaking real estate service, a wine-tour company for visitors, an English-language newsletter, etc. These ideas are not novel, by any means—there are hundreds of expats in Italy doing this kind of thing already—but maybe you can come up with a new slant?

The Job Hunt

EMPLOYERS

While the thought of being your own boss in Italy may sound exciting, the reality is that most of the foreigners you run into here are working for someone else. They are often found teaching English, translating, designing web pages, working in marketing or public relations, consulting for a multinational, teaching at a university, writing for a newspaper or magazine, or working with a governmental organization.

Fortunately for those Anglophones without an illustrious career behind them already, the very act of speaking perfect English lends one a certain credibility. Italians may be suspicious of U.S. foreign policy and not particularly fond of U.S. food and fashion, but they do regularly defer to U.S. business sense.

Also, employers admire the professional habits cultivated in the United States. When compared to European workers nursed on labor-friendly hiring laws, prospective North American employees have a leg up on the competition, as they come from a culture where efficiency is king and are accustomed to the kind of laissez-faire capitalism where hiring and firing are quick and easy processes.

Even the most venerated institutions of traditional Italian sectors often have a native English-speaker in their top brass. But unless you have outstanding contacts or credentials, or else were sent to Italy by your U.S. company, chances are that you will have to start the way most expats did: translating or teaching English while scouring the Help Wanted ads for something that fits your background more closely. (Then again, many people feel that they were cut out for teaching or translating and build it into a career.)

In Rome, a good place to start looking is an expat magazine called *Wanted in Rome* (www.wantedinrome.com). It has classified ads for short-term or long-term apartment rentals and a list of jobs for native English-speakers. Its counterpart in Milan is *Easy Milano* (www.easymilano.it).

The Monster board has an Italian site at www.monster.it, focused on an international crowd, while for Italians, the most popular venue is Corriere Lavoro (www.corriere.it/lavoro).

A second possibility for those starting off is to go to a temp agency. The two best known in Italy are Adecco (www.adecco.it) and Vedior (www.vedior.it), where candidates can upload their résumés and await a temporary assignment, which often turns into a full-time position. As lifetime contracts are on the

English-speaking businesses can be successful in Italy.

ALL IN THE FAMILY

The old adage in Italy is that the first generation founds a company, the second generation grows it, and the third one runs it into the ground. But for every family business that fails, another one crops up to take its place. As a result, when compared to the rest of Europe and North America, Italy remains a land of small- and medium-sized firms.

It is estimated that 90 percent of all companies in Italy are family-held. The tradition goes back centuries. The oldest is thought to be Barolvier & Toso, a glassmaker founded in 1295. Another ancient example is Beretta, an arms-producing dynasty that has invoices going back to 1526, and whose guns were used in the American Revolution.

Today, the phenomenon exists in virtually every sector. In fashion, the dynasties include Versace, Prada, and the Delvecchio family of Luxottica eyewear. In the food sector, there is the Barilla family. The Alessi and Merloni clans dominate design and household appliances. And the biggest names in Italian finance—Agnelli, Benetton, Pirelli, and De Benedetti—refer not only to an individual, but a family.

Alberto Falck, patriarch of the industrial group Falck SpA and chairman of the Italian Association of Family Businesses, says the reason such businesses do so well is that "in times of crisis, they bare their claws and protect their pups." That is to say, families protect their livelihoods more vehemently than a CEO might protect a corporation. An outside manager can walk away from a crisis and take his lumps. On the other hand, protective patriarchs tend to shy away from rapid growth. "Italian family companies are cautious," says Guido Corbetta, a professor of economics at Bocconi University who specializes in dynasties. "American companies can grow much faster, but they take on more risk."

One high-profile case is Versace, which, in 2002, turned down investors looking to give the fashion house €200 million to buy back control of its brand from franchisees. "We're not looking for investors," Donatella Versace said in October of that year. "For three years, investors have wanted to come into our company, and we always said no."

The Milanese stock market has tried to woo large- and medium-sized family companies to list their shares, but it, too, found more reservation than enthusiasm. Fiat remains the only Italian company among the world's largest multinationals, ranking 11th in total assets with €93.9 billion (US$122 billion). Italy has just 15 multinational corporations.

wane in Italy, these stopgap measures have become more useful for employers. The disadvantage for foreigners, however, is that the employers are quite unlikely to undertake the hassle of getting you the necessary paperwork for what is supposed to be a short-term position.

The best bet is to spend the first few months making personal contacts while earning some money on the side. Fresh off the plane, young travelers can usually expect to find immediate employment at a bar, guiding tours, or working as a nanny, while those with some experience might land a job doing public relations, marketing, or web design for an international company.

The fashion industry is particularly fond of hiring internationals to work in showrooms, especially if they are young, attractive women: Remember that most Europeans do not see anything wrong with what North Americans might deem overt sexism and ageism. In a classified ad for a receptionist, for example, it is common practice in Italy to require that the applicant be "a friendly girl between the ages of 23 and 27."

© PURESTOCK

walking home from work

LANDING THE JOB

A résumé in Italy includes the candidate's gender, date of birth, marital status, and almost always a photo. They are longer than the average U.S. CV (two pages at least) and will include the type of high school attended and the score received at college graduation.

As the taste for things American grows in Italian business, a résumé that focuses on what the candidate accomplished at various jobs and internships will be viewed more favorably. But don't expect a pure meritocracy: A personal contact will always beat an ace of a different suit.

When interviewing or sending a cover letter, be as respectful and professional as possible, as nothing turns off a prospective employer in Italy more than excessive in-formality. Needless to say, you should always use the *lei* form, and always address your interviewer as *dottore* or *dottoressa,* titles that assume they have graduated from college. Even for low-level and mid-level positions, the interview process will likely take a few weeks. Most of that time will be spent negotiating the salary and the type of contract that would be offered.

Because Italy is a land of small- and medium-sized family firms, pockets are not as deep as they are in big U.S. corporations. Coupled with the lower cost of living in Italy, somewhere near 80 percent of that in the United States, your salary will ap-pear exceedingly slim at first. Pay for many professions is based on a national sched-ule known as the *tabelle professionali.* Entry-level workers will receive the minimum wage of that category, and unionized professionals can expect a raise every two years. Your salary will be paid by the month and will be accompanied by a receipt that out-lines how much has been taken out for taxes, social security, health benefits, and any extra days off not granted in your contract. Once you have the job and want to see how your package stacks up against similar ones, a resource you can consult is www. quantomipagano.it.

Types of contracts are becoming more varied. Until the late 1990s, almost every full-time contract at firms with more than 15 employees entailed *posto fisso* (employment for life). Now, large employers are permitted to offer contracts for a fixed duration, sometimes as little as six months. However, an employee can only renew a time-limited contract once. After that, the company must offer *posto fisso*.

The relative relaxation of labor laws has also given rise to almost U.S.-style contracts, where the hours an employee puts in are less important than the work that is actually accomplished. One example is the *collaborazione a progetto* or "Co.Co.Pro" contracts, a "per-project" contract. It is a legal hybrid between freelance and full-time work, releasing the employer from certain payments and responsibilities. In general, though, the majority of contracts are full-time, complete with all the union-guaranteed benefits.

BENEFITS

For starters, you can expect 12 national holidays and at least four weeks of vacation, often five or six, depending on your contract. Many people end up taking off two weeks around Christmas and most of the month of August. Italian cities traditionally close down in August, although this is slowly changing. More companies have decided to spread out their employees' vacations to alleviate the frustration of international clients. (It also means less summer traffic on highways and fully booked resorts.) If you don't use up all four or five weeks in a year, you can theoretically carry over your vacation days into the next year, though many companies require you to periodically go on vacation to make bookkeeping easier.

There are 12 bank holidays nationwide, and each city also gets its patron saint's day off. Romans, for example, celebrate Saints Peter and Paul (June 29), while workers in Milan get Saint Ambrose's day off (December 7). If a saint's day or national holiday falls on a Friday or Monday, workers naturally get a three-day weekend. Even better, if it falls on a Tuesday or Thursday, it generally becomes a *ponte* (bridge)—a four-day weekend. For Romans, it means a fortuitous beach holiday, while Saint Ambrose marks the beginning of ski season for the Milanese.

Maternity entails five months of paid leave, spread out on either side of giving birth. Women on maternity leave receive 80 percent of their salary. Furthermore, they can request an additional six months off at 30 percent pay and be guaranteed their jobs when they want to return to work. It is not uncommon for a woman to file for extra sick days above and beyond those nine months. Like any other sick day in Italy, it needs to be backed up by a doctor's note. A company can send a state inspector to the person's home as well, to make sure that it is not just an excuse to go shopping.

In general, employees are allowed 180 days of paid sick leave. Above and beyond that, the matter is referred to the pensions office, as the person is considered disabled. Either way, Italians don't need to worry too much about staying healthy in order to keep their salaries.

Indeed, job security is so solid in Italy that companies must prove a "just cause" bordering on an egregious breach, such as breaking the law, in order to fire somebody. Countless lawsuits—or even the threat thereof—have resulted in a fired employee's reinstatement. One such high-profile case involved baggage handlers at an airport in

Milan. They were caught on videotape stealing valuables such as cash and jewels from passengers' luggage, found guilty in court, but never fired.

In fact, it is nearly impossible to terminate an employee's lifetime contract, as even the "justified motive" of downsizing has to be cleared with the unions first. Most companies prefer to just brush the worker aside by keeping up salary payments but not requiring his or her presence at work.

WORKING *IN NERO*

It is no wonder, then, that many Italian companies prefer to take the illegal route and pay their employees *in nero* (under the table). Figures from the Italian Institute of Economic and Social Research (IRES) in 2009 pinned the underground economy at about 15 percent of the GDP, while police stings nationwide regularly reveal that about half of the companies probed are paying employees under the table, 10 percent of whom are foreigners according to IRES. That makes Italy one of the worst offenders in Western Europe, and the real numbers are probably even higher. Large companies periodically hold "appreciation days" for local law enforcement communities, inviting them to sample the goods, ostensibly in return for lenient inspections.

The lack of an outcry against laws that engender such behavior means that things aren't likely to change soon. Prime Minister Silvio Berlusconi, who ran on an antiestablishment platform, was only codifying a time-honored tradition when he decriminalized false accounting. Cooking the books has always been seen in Italy as a necessary evil in the face of an oppressive state. It remains to be seen whether that law will be revisited now that Berlusconi has faded from public life.

While working under the table may be a tempting offer in order to avoid the hassle of never-ending Italian paperwork, the truth is that an employee has little to gain by taking such a risk. "Freelancers," as they are euphemistically known, do not have access to the extensive health care that full-time contracts provide, nor will they receive social security payments when they retire.

It's not altogether different from the situation in the United States, with one important exception: Italians depend almost exclusively on state pensions for their retirement. The concept of the private retirement fund is only slowly catching on, and frankly, it's hard to save for your golden years when your pretax income is only €1,250 a month.

FINANCE

Some very dark thunderclouds have been gathering around Italy's finances for many years now, but in 2012, as this edition went to print, it seemed like the storm would break any minute. Economic growth has remained at a standstill for longer than anyone cares to remember. Debt has mounted to preternatural levels, but while there are serious doubts on the street about an economic recovery any time soon, only the most pessimistic would forecast that the coming rains will wash Italy out of the euro zone.

Italy is one of the world's largest economies—"too big to fail," as they say—but it's also one of the world's biggest public spenders. Changes are all but inevitable. What seems certain from even the rosiest forecasts is that jobs and investment in Italy will not be on the upswing in the next few years, but then, nor is the euro going away. Italy has been comfortably earning and spending the common currency for a decade, and by all accounts this is likely to continue.

Cost of Living

The euro-to-U.S. dollar exchange has oscillated around 1.30 for the past few years, meaning that Italy is still expensive for anyone earning greenbacks. Whereas some shoppers might remember everything from a cappuccino to a leather jacket as a good buy in Italy, now travelers are counting their coins much more carefully.

This is not to say that everything in Europe is out of financial reach. Renting a home in the largest Italian cities is doable when compared to New York or San Francisco. In the most expensive cities, Rome and Milan, €1,000 per month should land you a single-bedroom apartment somewhere near downtown. (Keep in mind, though, that this figure represents about an entire monthly salary in Italy.)

The longer you stay, the more hidden costs you will find. More often than not, they take the form of taxes. Like most European governments, Italy likes to discourage the abuse of its most precious commodity, energy. Heating a modest apartment of 70 square meters, for example, will cost at least €100 per month in the winter (and Italy is not a very cold place), thanks to high fuel taxes. For that reason, electricity is just as costly. No Italian would ever leave the house without first turning off all the lights.

Cars can almost be considered a luxury. Gasoline prices are more than twice what they are in the United States, and insurance doesn't come cheap either. To insure a 10-year-old Volkswagen in the city, a young person will spend about €1,000 per year for the minimum coverage—again a monthly salary for the typical Italian under 30.

How much you should budget per month depends, of course, on how much you earn and where you want to live. As a rule of thumb, the farther south you go, the cheaper life becomes. To get some idea of the discrepancy, rent in Naples costs about half as much as it does in Milan. And even Naples can be out of reach for those who live in small towns in Calabria and Basilicata.

Not coincidentally, the cheapest place to live is also where there are the fewest jobs. In 2012, unemployment in Italy among people in their 20s stood at 30 percent. In Sicily, that number was 40 percent. That bears repeating. Close to half of Sicily's young people have no jobs.

The figures are lower than the national average in Milan and Turin, which is easily understood when you consider that, of the 30 companies that traditionally made up the benchmark index on Italy's stock exchange, 17 have their headquarters in one of those two cities. None have their headquarters in the South.

The smoggy North may appear to be an unpleasant place to spend your time when compared to the sunny lemon groves of Sicily, but then again, so is New Jersey when compared to the Florida Keys. Floridians can expect to be paid in "sunshine dollars." So can Sicilians.

Your compensation will depend on a lot of things: the kind of job, your skills and experience, whether the company is Italian or North American, etc. But in the broadest terms, a college graduate with five years' experience who makes US$50,000 per year in a major North American city might expect to be paid half of that in Italy. The majority of Italian blue-collar workers and many entry-level white-collar workers earn in the vicinity of €1,000 per month.

EXPENSES: DIVIDING YOUR DAILY BREAD

When you hear Italians complain about the cost of living, you might groan to yourself that life is tough all over. But when you consider that most annual salaries in Italy are well under €2,000 a month after taxes, you start to realize that in order for that kind of dough to feed a household here, it would take the miracle of five loaves and two fish.

For simplicity's sake, let's look at the numbers for a single person renting an average apartment of 60 square meters in the capital.

- Rent: the average rent in the center of Rome is about €20 per square meter, which would put this apartment at about €1,200 per month.

- Electricity: Definitely varies according to usage, but an average of €50 a month is a conservative bet.

- Television: The yearly tax to support the state broadcaster is €110 (for whomever bought the television) and, depending on the sort of package, satellite TV will be about €30 per month.

- Public transportation: A single bus ticket is €1.50, and a monthly pass is €40.

- Internet and Telephone: About €40 per month.

- Natural Gas: about €30 per month.

- Water: about €20 a month.

- Groceries: This is also hugely variable, but you won't be eating very well on less than €200 per month.

- Total: €1,610

Homeowner costs, of course, greatly depend on the type of mortgage and the buying price of the home, but those who plan to own an apartment in the city should also budget at least €1,000 per year on condominium fees and €300 per year on trash collection.

It's a good thing coffee's cheap: only €1.20 for an espresso at the local bar.

DAILY LIFE

Banking

The advent of the ATM, or Bancomat as it is known in Italy, has made banking from abroad a snap. Even foreigners who spend months at a time in Italy don't bother opening an Italian account. As long as you have an ATM or debit card, you can pull out cash on demand. Before you plan to rely on a card as your lifeline, though, check a few things:

- If the card is new, make sure you first activate the PIN in a local branch. You won't be able to activate it from abroad. Some banks also have a distinct PIN for international withdrawals.

- Don't memorize the code using letters to guide you: Letters often aren't included on Bancomat keyboards.

- Your card must work with either CIRRUS or NYCE, as most do, or else be a debit card from Visa or MasterCard.

It is also a good idea to keep an extra card on hand in case one is lost, crushed, or demagnetized. Sometimes, a confused Bancomat will eat your card for no good reason, and the Italian bank will send it back to the United States for verification—no matter how much you plead that there is no problem with your account and you are who you say you are.

The downsides to this home-banking strategy are (1) there is a fee, usually €2, every time you withdraw on a foreign account, and (2) keeping track of the paperwork

ATMs (or Bancomats) make banking from abroad easy.

from abroad can be a hassle. Many U.S. banks have not yet made online banking available for those living abroad, though some lenders offer a service—again, for a fee—that sends your statements to an Italian address.

For those who don't plan to settle down for the long term, opening an Italian bank account should not be a priority. If you work for an Italian company as a freelancer whose legal residence is in the United States, your payment will be sent to a U.S. bank via wire transfer.

But if you have a regular job contract, and therefore have a registered tax ID number on file with the government, your employer will pay you either by check or by a deposit in an Italian bank. Most Italian firms won't pay a full-time employee through a foreign account, as that would suggest that they and the employee are evading taxes. And a check made out in euros is worth zero in North America. In this case, opening an Italian account is a necessity. The process is easy. The only paperwork the bank will ask for is a passport and a tax ID number. Just as in the United States, you have your choice between savings and checking accounts, along with a number of investment options. If you want to bet on U.S. dollars over euros, for example, you can open a foreign currency account. This will allow you to deposit your dollars directly and convert them to euros only when you make a withdrawal.

Here again, there is a big hidden cost—namely, the fees to hold an account. One consumer group found that fees for a single account reached €400 per year. And you will be hard-pressed to find any type of savings account in Italy that actually pays you interest.

Checking accounts of course almost never provide interest payments either. But the value of writing checks should not be underestimated. It is one of the easiest ways to pay. More importantly, with a checking account you'll also have access to an Italian Bancomat card, which is accepted even more frequently at stores than Visa and MasterCard.

An example: I once found myself visiting an isolated monastery on the Ligurian coast, the kind of place you can only get to by boat. My friend and I ordered sandwiches, ate them in a hurry, and then realized neither of us had any cash. There was certainly no bank machine in this town of fewer than 50 inhabitants, and the nearest one was a ferry ride away. The snack bar was smack in the middle of the beach and didn't accept credit cards, but it did, miraculously, accept Bancomat cards. You will find this to be true even in urban areas.

Absurdly, many travel agencies do not accept credit cards. The culprit is the same: merchant fees. The travel agents complain that the amount they pay to the card

ITALY BY THE NUMBERS

- **Population:** 60.63 million
- **Population growth rate:** 0.42 percent
- **Birth rate:** 9.06 births per thousand people
- **Death rate:** 9.93 deaths per thousand people
- **Net migration rate:** 4.67 migrants per thousand people
- **GDP:** US$2.20 trillion (€1.76 trillion)
- **GDP per capita (PPP):** US$30,100 (€24,720)

GDP by sector:

- **Agriculture:** 2.0 percent
- **Industry:** 24.7 percent
- **Services:** 73.4 percent
- **Industries:** Tourism, machinery, chemicals, food processing, iron and steel, beverages, textiles, motor vehicles, clothing, footwear, ceramics
- **Unemployment:** 8.4 percent
- **Inflation:** 2.8 percent
- **Public debt:** 120 percent of GDP
- **Export partners:** Germany 13.0 percent, France 11.6 percent, United States 6.0 percent, Spain 5.9 percent, United Kingdom 5.2 percent
- **Import partners:** Germany 16.1 percent, France 8.8 percent, China 7.8 percent, Netherlands 5.4 percent, Spain 4.6 percent
- **Cell phones:** 82.0 million
- **Internet users:** 29.2 million

(Source: CIA Factbook)

company totally wipes out their commissions. But then, they should ask themselves, how many foreigners are prepared to pay for a transatlantic flight with cash? For that matter, how were Italians expected to pay for a ticket without a credit card in the days before the Bancomat?

The answer, again, is cash, and lots of it. Stacks of bills in large denominations still swap hands every day in the typical Italian store, as some customers still distrust plastic. For the store owners, cash also means no paper trail, and therefore no real incentive to report the income. But tax police have cracked down on under-the-table transactions in recent years, sending in plainclothes officers to check whether they are offered a receipt. These days, stores are legally required to give every customer a receipt, and it is the customer's responsibility to have that receipt in hand when walking out the door. The store owner will sometimes run after you if you forget to take it off the counter.

Credit cards won't be very helpful when it comes time to pay household expenses, such as heating, electricity, and phone bills. This is done at the post office, and the only accepted forms of payment there are cash or a Bancomat card. (You cannot send a check to the utility company itself, though you are certainly welcome to walk to its local headquarters and pay by cash if you wish.) Just bring your bill, and a lot of patience for long lines, to the nearest post office, and they will explain the procedure.

Post offices also act as a kind of alternative bank, offering accounts with post-office checks. Like banks, their hours are short: 8 A.M.–2 P.M. weekdays, though some are open on Saturday as well. There is no fixed schedule as to which branches are open on Saturday, but you can check the hours of individual offices at www.poste.it.

Banks are open 8:30 A.M.–1:30 P.M. and 2:45–3:45 P.M. on weekdays. Again, some are open on Saturday.

Taxes

ITALIAN TAXES

Italy has long held a reputation as a nation of tax evaders. Having the head of government under such accusations certainly didn't help, nor do the now regular amnesties that allow them to wipe the slate clean. Instead of sending them to already crowded prisons, the government now asks tax evaders to pay a small fine. The Swiss francs soon flow in.

Italians rightly point out that every country in the world has tax evasion; the difference is that the others don't wash their dirty laundry quite as publicly. Furthermore, no country has a system nearly as complex and far-reaching as the Italian one, making evasion that much more tempting and probable.

This is not to say that Italy has the highest tax levels in Europe. When measured in percent of GDP and by many other standards, in 2012, the Danes, Swedes, and Finns saw higher tax rates than the Italians. This has been the case for decades. What is likely, though, is that Italians have to contend with more individual taxes than anyone else does. Only accountants can understand them all, and self-employed people and business owners would do well to find a good *commercialista* (accountant) before opening shop. With the help of these accountants, taxpayers keep the number of tariffs they pay to a more manageable level, and in doing so, they reach a certain equilibrium: In terms of actual revenues collected per GDP, Italy's taxation rate was closer to the European Union average than any other member nation.

Below is an abridged list of the taxes from which to choose. They are all known by their acronyms, sometimes even a nickname:

- IRPEF: personal income tax; essentially Italy's answer to the 1040 in the United States. As an employee, this will be deducted from your paycheck. Ranges from 12 percent to more than 60 percent.
- IVA: value-added sales tax, which you pay every time you buy something like a cell phone or a car. If you are self-employed in Italy, say as a freelance writer, you must register for an IVA number as well—some people print it right on their business cards. Unlike sales tax in the United States, it is for both goods and services and not limited to retail items. It is charged every step of the way until it is ultimately passed on to the end user. About 20 percent.
- IRPEG: the most common corporate tax. A flat rate, just below 40 percent.
- INVIM: capital gains tax.
- ILOR and IRAP: two regional taxes, the latter of which has been on the rise in recent years.

Then there is a slew of smaller taxes on such things as owning a moped, motorcycle, or car (the annual *bollo,* paid at the post office), on manufacturing, registering land, etc. Anytime you buy or register anything, be prepared to pay a tax.

Indeed the whole landscape is in a continual state of flux, especially with the political seesaw of fortune of late between the center-left and center-right. Only an accountant will be able to keep you up to date.

Tax time comes twice a year in Italy: November and July. Pay your anticipated taxes in the fall, and file for a refund in July. Employees whose taxes, social security, and

DAILY LIFE

health care payments have already been taken out need to file form 740. Self-employed workers fill out form 730, and corporations fill out form 760.

As e-government becomes more popular, many Italians prefer to fill out their taxes online at www.italia.gov.it. You will obviously need to be fairly proficient in Italian to do this by yourself. It is worth the money to hire an English-speaking accountant, at least to get you started.

Finally, those who plan to live off their investments should be aware that there is a 12.5 percent tax on income from foreign bonds. It is the lowest of its kind in Europe. But the best tax deal in Italy for retirees is the northern enclave of Campione d'Italia, which is actually surrounded by Switzerland. Foreigners who can claim residency there—accomplished merely by buying local property—enjoy a special tax status.

U.S. TAXES

Living in Italy may exempt you from a lot of responsibilities at home, but you can never escape the IRS. Whether you earn money in Italy or not, you will have to notify them, too, of your financial situation come April.

This does not necessarily mean you will have to pay any money. If you earn less than the equivalent of US$80,000 in Italy and pay Italian taxes on that income, you will not be subject to U.S. taxes on it, too. All you have to do is fill out form 2555 to file for an exclusion. But if you have retained any holdings in the United States—an interest-yielding savings account, stocks, bonds, money market account, etc.—you will need to file on those earnings, just as if you were living at home.

The IRS has made it easier in recent years to file from abroad, and the local U.S. Embassy or Consulate will also lend a hand. All of the forms you need can be picked up at the embassy or consulate. Staff are available for questions on your particular status and, come tax time, usually have a consultant on hand for more complicated matters. Additional help can be found at the mission's website, www.embassy.it/irs.

The deadline for foreign filers is extended from April 15 to June 15. On the envelope, write "filing from abroad" to make sure your forms are sorted into the right pile. The envelope must be postmarked before June 15. An alternative is to pay online. The website www.irs.gov has a list of private registered companies that offer the "e-file" service, where you can pay with your credit card. It is advisable to pick up all the schedules and worksheets from the embassy beforehand. It can be hard to download certain obscure forms from those sites.

Investing

A LOOK AT THE MARKETS

In Milan's Piazza Affari stands a Fascist-era building called Palazzo Mezzanotte. For almost a century, the captains of industry and their underlings bayed for money there in the so-called Room of Shouts, where a handful of companies were publicly traded. It was a select group of people who understood the stock market in those days. Many of them lived close to the building and whispered buyout rumors in cozy restaurants nearby. The insider atmosphere remains, but the Room of Shouts is no more. It was vacated just before the market went fully electronic in 1994. Italy no longer had a trading floor, only a room full of computers fielding orders on the outskirts of Milan. In 2009, those listings then moved to the new parent board, the London Stock Exchange.

Italians have always been assiduous savers, but the automation of the market coincided with the first real surge of popular investing. Before the 1990s, when large state monopolies were cut up and privatized, Italians with significant savings typically kept the money in real estate or else poured it into a family business. By now, Italians have become more or less seasoned investors in securities. Many of them, despite their state-administered pensions, have taken to the markets when planning their retirements, and they've since experienced the dramatic ups and downs. Mostly the downs.

European markets burned about €1 trillion in the days following the September 11, 2001 attacks. Italy's now-defunct blue chip index, the Mib 30, lost some 25 percent, or €150 billion. The high-tech Nuovo Mercato index—whose total market value had inflated to around €20 billion in the boom years—lost almost all of that when the speculative Internet bubble burst. (Note that all of those indices have changed names since the Borsa Italiana was acquired by the London Stock Exchange in 2009.)

After the drastic start to the new century and a mildly reassuring recovery, another, much bigger storm was on the horizon. The global financial crisis that started in the United States soon reached Milan and the rest of the continent. Between 2007 and 2012, it wiped out about two-thirds of the Italian stock market's value altogether.

HOW TO INVEST

Anyone in the United States can buy Italian stocks, as long as that person's broker is licensed to deal in European markets. Trading stocks and bonds in Italy is equally straightforward. Even nonresidents can buy and sell them through an Italian bank or broker. Most brokers work in what is called a *società d'intermediazione mobiliari* (SIM). Just as in the United States, you have your choice of trading online or doing business over the phone. Commissions generally cost about €10 per transaction.

When you open an account, first you will be asked for an identity card and some form of tax ID. Those with residency in Italy will need to show a *codice fiscale,* as they will be paying Italian taxes, while nonresident Americans, who will pay U.S. taxes, need to show a Social Security number. They also need to sign a document that declares them immune from Italian taxes. The United States is on Italy's "white list" of countries whose citizens are protected from double taxation.

Finally, brokers and banks may ask you to fill out a questionnaire, ensuring that you're a responsible investor, and ask you to sign a waiver. This is meant to weed out those who tend to overexpose themselves to risk. For those who prefer a more hands-off approach to their personal finances, there are hundreds of managed funds that deal in Italian stocks and bonds.

THE COMPANIES

The following (in alphabetical order) are a few of the more intriguing companies listed on the Italian exchanges. By no means does this list represent picks from an analyst or an adviser; they are merely commonly known facts about some of the biggest names in Italian business.

© GIUSEPPE ANELLO/123RF

Milan's Stock Exchange building, Palazzo della Borsa

Autogrill

Controlled by the Benetton family and headquartered in the Veneto, Autogrill is the world's leader in providing quick, quality food to travelers. You'll see the trademark red "A" all over airports in Italy and other parts of Europe, and ubiquitously on Italian autostrade. It helps that the Benettons also operate two-thirds of those highways.

Campari

The Piedmont-based maker of this famously bitter aperitif went public in 2001 but is still family-controlled. The little red bottles first appeared in 1860 and have grown steadily in popularity since. In addition to its own brand and its sister bitter, Aperol, Campari also owns Wild Turkey, Cinzano, Skyy Vodka, and Tullamore Dew.

Eni

Italy's energy giant regularly makes headlines by forging inroads into the East, buying large stakes in Russian upstream assets and jointly building pipelines across Europe to get that natural gas to Italy. Aside from its oil and gas components, Eni is also involved in power generation, engineering, and oil field services.

Fiat

Founded in 1899 and still overseen by the Agnelli family, this is the country's largest employer and a national symbol. Fiat turned its fortunes around under CEO Sergio Marchionne, switching to a cadre of smaller cars and its successful revival of Chrysler. It can also rely on its host of sportier brands: Alfa Romeo, Maserati, and, of course, Ferrari.

EXPAT PROFILE: JEFFERSON SLACK

The man who is supposed to make Italian soccer more profitable should be arriving any minute now at the Four Seasons hotel in Milan. There are a lot of Americans in business suits milling about with cocktails, but Jefferson Slack is recognizable as he glides past the doormen into the piano lounge. He has the sporty look and trim build of a former Ivy League athlete, with the sort of genteel corporate attire one would expect to find at the lavish headquarters of the soccer club Inter, where he works. As he orders a Beck's, starts a chat about licensing, and drops terms like "securitization," it appears that he has little in common conversationally with most of his colleagues on Milan's Via Durini.

Slack was brought in as the president of Inter-Active, a subsidiary of F.C. Internazionale created in 2001 to handle all aspects of the company's operations apart from player contracts. In short, he is responsible for making Inter more profitable without exerting any control over its single largest expenditure. That control is left to Inter president Massimo Moratti. The nitty-gritty details of how to make the money are left to the American.

Slack shows a youthful optimism, a characteristic native to his line of work. "Sports as an industry is less than 20 years old in the way it is managed," he says. "Until the 1980s, the Olympic Committee didn't have a lot of money. In 1984, Los Angeles was a watershed; the Olym-

pics were approached as a marketing platform?.... There is emotion in sports. It has an appeal that other products around the world would kill for."

Slack has spent his entire adult life capitalizing on that appeal. From his high school years at Roxbury Latin in Boston, well into his postgraduate studies at Johns Hopkins University in Bologna, he was a player-manager for his cycling team, signing sponsors and making deals.

After a stint as a sports marketing director in Washington, he worked as right-hand man to David Faulk, the agent who represented such breadwinners as Michael Jordan, Patrick Ewing, Alonzo Mourning, and Boomer Esiason. In 1998, he introduced U.S. investment bank Merrill Lynch to a number of European soccer teams, starting their march toward merchandising—that is, putting team names on wristwatches, coffee mugs, etc.–something Americans know very well. It was in those years that he made important contacts with Italian clubs, and soon landed the job at Inter.

These days, Slack has just enough time to settle in comfortably at his apartment on the famed Via della Spiga and spend free hours with his American girlfriend. The perks of his job have allowed him to take his father—the owner of one of the largest cycling stores in the Boston area—to see the Giro d'Italia from a helicopter.

Generali

This is Italy's largest insurer, based in Trieste. Like most insurers, there's nothing too sexy about it except its sheer size—it is the fourth-largest in Europe—and that it has long been the subject of a tug-of-war between banking rivals. Mediobanca is the biggest of those rivals with a 13 percent stake. The bank's leadership exerted its influence and ousted Generali's longstanding CEO in 2012 after the stock plummeted to a 26-year low.

Geox

Company lore has it that the founder of this shoe manufacturer, Mario Moretti Polegato, got the idea for his first design while jogging in the hot deserts of Nevada and needing to cut holes in the bottom of his shoes. Formed in 1995, this relatively small company grew to sales of about €850 million by 2010.

Lottomatica

Again, I'm the furthest thing from a financial expert but there's something intriguing to me about gambling holdings in tough economic times, and Lottomatica is the largest operator of lotteries in the world. The Rome-based company runs Italy's Lotto and lots of other gaming technologies. In 2006 it purchased GTECH, a Rhode Island–based corporation in the slot machine, lottery, and casino management business.

Luxottica

The world's largest maker of luxury eyeglass frames—founded by Milan native Leonardo Del Vecchio—has had a ticker on the NYSE since the 1980s, but Del Vecchio also listed it on Milan's big board in 2000. The company is best known for its Ray Ban sunglasses and Oakleys (which it acquired in 2007), though it has a lucrative business crafting frames for such brands as Versace, Polo, and Donna Karan.

Mediobanca

The country's largest investment bank keeps itself shrouded in mystery. (Adding to the mystique, the body of its fabled chairman was snatched from its grave eight months after he died in 2000.) Owned largely by other lenders, the bank has significant stakes in most of the nation's principal firms, many of them listed here. It remains the pièce de résistance of any power broker's portfolio.

Pininfarina

This publicly owned, family-run design company represents the artistic genius behind some of the sleekest lines on cars around the world. A small selection of designs born on their sketch pads: the 1984 Ferrari Testarossa, the 1978 Jaguar XJ6, the 2006 Volvo C70. Beyond cars, Pininfarina designers work on everything from bicycles to telephones to many of the high-speed trains around Europe, including the Eurostar.

Telecom Italia

Telecom Italia is the number-one phone utility in the country, and the owner of the leading cellular operator, Telecom Italia Mobile (TIM). It has a significant presence in the South American market with a TIM subsidiary in Brazil and a 50 percent stake in Telecom Argentina, and is a major media presence through its television channels La7 and MTV Italia.

DAILY LIFE

COMMUNICATIONS

The Internet revolution has made just about everything easier these days, but not enough can be said about what it has done for living abroad. You can video conference with loved ones anytime you want, anywhere in the world, practically for free. You can virtually run businesses both in your new home country and your old one. You can watch the Red Sox from your sofa in Rome. In short, if you spend your whole day online, it's like you never left home.

There are now about 36 million Internet users in Italy. Some 20 million of them are on Facebook. That makes them the fifth-most populous online community in Europe, but it should be pointed out that, as a percentage of the population, Italy is one of the least connected nations in the European Union. The relatively advanced age of the population surely plays some part.

In terms of mobile phones, Italy has been ahead of the United States for a long time. Their love affair with their *telefonini* is legendary. The number of cell phones has long since surpassed the number of people, and in fact there are now roughly three Italian cell phone numbers for every two Italians, which is just about the highest percentage on the planet.

Suffice it to say, you'll have no trouble staying in touch in Italy. The rest of the world is just a quick click away.

Of course, if you plan to stay in Italy for a while, a better bet would just be to buy

a phone and accompanying SIM card once you're there. You can buy new phones for as little as €30, and a SIM card for as little as US$10. Just add as much calling time as you want on a prepaid plan.

The huge perk to using an Italian phone or an Italian SIM card is that there are no roaming charges anywhere inside Italy. But remember, even though you can use the same phone and number in, say, Slovenia, you will pay more to make and receive calls with most Italian plans. If you are in France and someone calls you from Italy, the caller pays for a normal Italy-to-Italy cell phone call, but you will pay for the cost of the call from Italy to France.

Telephone Service

TELEFONI AND TELEFONINI

For mobile phones and smart phones, Italy and the rest of Europe are on the GSM system. Conveniently, this is the same system used by AT&T and by T-Mobile (a German company). If you are using a phone issued by Verizon or Sprint, which use the more North American CDMA, you'll need to make sure you have a phone that is GSM-ready. (Verizon will send you a loaner for a trip to Europe, if not.)

Roaming charges can be absolutely exorbitant, so unless you have a very good international plan with your carrier, the best solution is to buy an Italian SIM card and replace the one in your phone. At press time, only certain phones and handheld devices allowed that capability, and only certain carriers allowed you to unlock your phone.

© RADU RAZVAN/123RF

A gondolier in Venice checks his mobile phone.

Be sure to check with you carrier about the fine print. I can tell you from experience that Verizon, for example, made it extremely difficult for me to unlock one of their iPhones, even though that capability was promised up front. I suspect this will be made much easier in the future.

To sign up for a cell phone number—this requires a copy of your passport, for security reasons—you first need to choose a company. There are four national carriers:

- Telecom Italia Mobile (TIM)
- Vodafone
- Wind
- Three

You should wait until you know which company most of your friends are using before declaring your own brand loyalty. This will save you money. If you

DAILY LIFE

PER-MINUTE COST FOR CALLS FROM LANDLINES AND MOBILE PHONES

**NATIONAL CALLS
FROM A LANDLINE**

- Local: €0.02 per minute
- Within 15 km: €0.06 per minute
- Beyond 15 km: €0.11 per minute

**CALLING FROM
MOBILE PHONES**

- TIM customers: €0.12 per minute
- Vodafone customers: €0.15 per minute

- Wind customers: €0.19 per minute
- Three customers: €0.10 per minute

**INTERNATIONAL CALLS
FROM A LANDLINE**

- Western Europe: €0.18 per minute, about €0.40 for cell phones
- U.S. and Canada: €0.18 per minute, about €0.50 for cell phones
- Mexico and South America: €1 per minute, including cell phones

are a Vodafone customer, for example, it is cheaper to call another Vodafone customer than it is to contact a TIM, Wind, or Three user.

You also need to decide between a contract and a pay-as-you-go arrangement. In the first case, you'll pay a base rate every month. As a pay-as-you-go customer, which is most common for transient types, you can buy credit at the local bar, newsstand, tobacconist, etc. Dial in the code anytime you want to boost your minutes. The latter is a slightly more expensive option per minute but offers much more flexibility.

Companies offer various discount programs, so do some homework on the services before signing up. For example, there are programs that give you discounts on calling a certain number most of the time. To compare rates and services, visit www.tim.it, www.vodafone.com, www.wind.it, and www.three.com. Each site has a version in English.

LANDLINES

Italy's public phones, given a futuristic look by designer George Sowden, are inviting but largely unused, and already disappearing. The sleek line of Telecom Italia phones, designed by Ferrari-crafter Sergio Pininfarina, now sit like dinosaurs in the office. In general, cell phone rates are low enough that few people bother to make calls from a public phone, and some don't even bother getting a landline these days, though in both cases they're spending more than they could be.

Many apartments do not come with a phone, and if you don't plan to make a lot of calls, it may not make sense for you to pay €120 to have one installed. Customers pay a base rate of about €15 per month, plus additional charges for an answering service and call waiting, and elevated rates for calling a cell phone. But for those who plan to spend a lot of time chatting, it might pay off to get a landline. (There is a €0.30 connection fee for all international calls.)

At any newsstand or tobacco shop you can purchase individual calling cards for Greece, Estonia, Australia, etc. But if you're calling from a home landline in Italy, you should look into services that route calls through the Internet instead. For example, there's one called I Minuti (www.iminuti.com), with which you can pay pennies per minute on calls abroad. Of course, if you are happy with calling from your computer with a service like Skype, you may not need anything else.

Email and Postal Service

INTERNET ACCESS

Broadband is quite widely available in Italy, partly due to the urban nature of its demographics. Prepare for a world of problems, though, as there are always glitches in the system in these ancient streets and buildings. Getting a technician to properly repair the problem is, in my experience and that of my friends, darn near impossible.

There are a number of broadband providers, and with start-ups and consolidations not infrequent, the field is always changing. Some of the more popular providers in Italy include FastWeb, Tiscali, Wind, BT Italia, and TIM. Budget about €30 per month for a high-speed connection.

If you're only traveling through, you can always rely on wireless hotspots and Internet cafés. T-Mobile's ubiquitous hot spot services can cost around €10 for one hour. You will find dozens of Internet cafés in every major city, a few in most medium-sized cities, and at least one or two in small towns with some kind of tourist attraction.

POST OFFICES AND COURIERS

In the end, anything is better than relying on the Italian mail, which perhaps needs no introduction. To be fair, the postal service has made huge strides since 2010. Its priority mail, which costs €0.62 for a standard letter, really does deliver nationally in fewer than three days—most of the time, at least. Sending a standard letter to the United States through the postal system costs €0.77, though it's still anyone's guess as to when it will arrive. Prices reach €16 for a four-pound package.

That same package will cost about €70 using DHL or €95 with Federal Express, the two most widely used international couriers in Italy, though they are certainly much quicker and more reliable than the regular mail. Both will pick up and deliver to your door. One important thing to remember when shipping packages to Italy—and declaring the value—is the 20 percent import duty. That adds up to a lot on a US$2,000 computer, for example. To avoid any misunderstandings with customs, it's best to bring expensive items on the plane.

a mailbox in Vatican City

Media

NEWSPAPERS AND MAGAZINES

Italians are masters of communication in the sense that they barely need to utter a word in order to be understood. Much communication, be it in a store or on the highway, is done without a sound. This was probably very helpful in the days before television and radio created a national language, when dialects differed greatly from one valley to the next. Italians are well known for their broad vocabulary of gestures, where the slightest change of a hand's direction can alter the syntax entirely.

At the same time, Italy's political disarray suggests that, when it comes to agreeing on historical facts, communication has broken down somewhere along the way. Italy has the lowest newspaper readership in the European Union, and for those who have ever tried to make sense of an Italian article, this is hardly surprising. The point of an article is often found at the bottom, beneath thousands of words of florid description and last-name-only references which only insiders will understand.

Then there is the question of which facts are included, which are omitted, and which are given the greatest play. It seems that the U.S. population came to the conclusion about a decade ago that the mass media was biased in one direction or another; Italians have lived this reality for a long time. In theory, there is probably no such thing as an objective newspaper, and in Italy journalism mostly just foments partisan pride and anger.

The country has no fewer than 10 nationally distributed papers. They are as much a symbol of one's political loyalty as a source of news. Bearded intellectuals will defiantly brandish a copy of *Il Manifesto* or *L'Unità* on the subway next to the closely shaven businessperson carrying a copy of *Il Giornale*—published by Silvio Berlusconi's brother, Paolo. Several others represent the extremes of Italy's political spectrum, though they have more of a fringe following.

The newspaper with the highest circulation, aside from sports papers, is *Corriere della Sera,* closely followed by *La Repubblica.* Based in Milan, *Corriere* is said to have represented the voice of morality during the Clean Hands investigation of the 1990s, and it is about as close as Italy comes to a centrist paper. A major shareholder in its parent company is Fiat, which also controls Turin-based *La Stampa. La Stampa,* too, is considered one of the more reasonable voices representing the middle ground.

Rome-based *La Repubblica* began life in the 1970s as an independent voice in Italian politics, raging against the establishment. But when the conservatives lost their grip on power in the 1990s, *La Repubblica* hitched its wagon to what it must have imagined to be a rising star and now has a decidedly progressive bent.

For those who don't speak or read Italian, there is always the English-language press. Many Italians also regularly check the foreign press to see how their country is portrayed, or to get a less biased point of view.

I don't know many people who go to the newsstand these days to read news from home. If only for historical background, it is worth knowing that before the arrival of the Internet, U.S. expatriates in Italy relied heavily on the *International Herald Tribune* for news from home. The *Trib* started out life in 1887 as the European edition of the *New York Herald*. It was partially bought out by the *Washington Post* in the 1960s and later merged with its major European competitor, *The New York Times,* which then bought it outright in 2002. For decades, it provided expatriates and the local elite with an all-star lineup of stories from the two papers. These days, the *Trib* faces much greater competition. The number of English-language publications available in Italy has blossomed to dozens, including the *Wall Street Journal Europe, USA Today, The Financial Times, The Guardian, The Independent,* and a wheelbarrow-full of other British papers, plus the major weeklies and monthlies: *The Economist, Time, Newsweek, BusinessWeek, The New Yorker, Wired,* and so on.

TELEVISION

Variety has finally arrived on Italian television, but quality is something you'll always have to pay for. Free-to-air TV now has hundreds of channels, with everything from local news to the state-run RAI to some Disney channels and the occasional U.S. news, such as MSNBC.

But for good English-language news, a wide selection of live sports, and recent movies, you will need to pay. Rupert Murdoch's monopoly, Sky, has a lock on all the premium sports, from Grand Prix racing to the NBA. Subscriptions cost about €30 per month depending on the package, so many Italians prefer to view such events at the local bar. Currently, Mediaset has a less-expensive option, closer to €10 for a smaller selection.

All of these of course come with the standard Italian fare of variety shows and news, which apart from soccer make up the daily fare of the average viewer. After all, that's about all there was to watch for most adult Italians' lives.

From the days of Mussolini until the 1980s, there was just one major broadcaster: the state-run RAI. No competition was allowed on the national level. One man, Silvio Berlusconi, managed to get around this monopoly by somewhat illegally transmitting the same programs and commercials simultaneously on local stations. He emerged legally unscathed from the affair, and his newly created Mediaset empire set the table for increased television competition. Now, free-to-air TV is of course an open market.

RAI remains a public entity that lives off of tax revenues and a yearly viewer fee called the *canone.* It costs about €100 per year, paid by anyone who has purchased a television. The code from the new TV goes from the store to the state, and you are responsible for the annual fee. If you are a renter, this is of course not your responsibility, and if someone gives you an older TV, well, no one is going to come after you for the TV tax.

DAILY LIFE

TRAVEL AND TRANSPORTATION

In Italy, it's often repeated that under Mussolini, at least the trains ran on time. You may hear old-timers mumbling this adage today when trains are running a few minutes late. It's an unfair assessment of a system that is, for the most part, efficient, cheaper than many of its continental counterparts, and yet close to the European average in terms of safety.

It's hard to say just how well the state railway performed under Mussolini, though it almost certainly had an occasional delay. Even the Swiss railway isn't perfect, and it serves a smaller country. What is more likely is that no one dared complain to the Fascist dictator about the train being a few minutes late, and certainly no one was getting a refund, as they do today.

Similar slander has been thrown at the state airline, Alitalia, over the years. Passengers can decide for themselves what sort of service they are getting for the money. Like any other major carrier, it has been hurt by Internet ticket sales and given a run for its money by upstart discount carriers. British airlines like Ryan Air, Go, and bmibaby have almost taken over the Italy–London route, for example. Smaller domestic rivals such as VolareWeb have also taken a slice of the pie.

© PURESTOCK

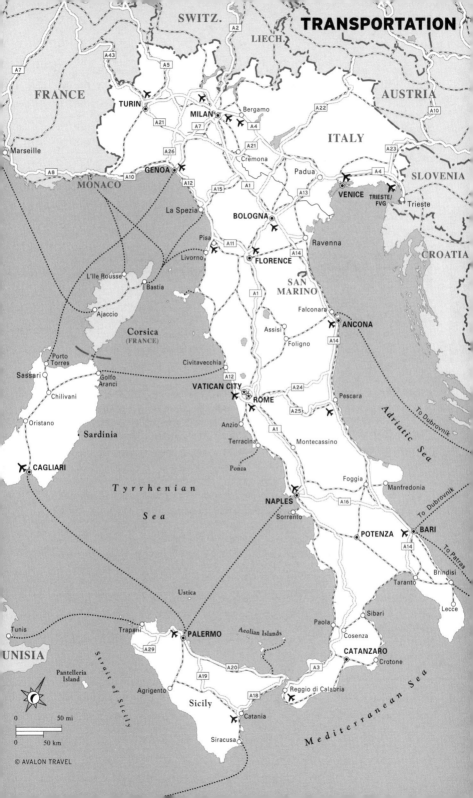

It would be hard to ignore some of the more obvious complaints, however, such as the recurring nightmare that leaves Alitalia passengers stuck at the airport due to a strike, with no airline personnel to be found. While the recently privatized carrier has made an effort to improve its image, Alitalia's customer service sometimes still feels as if it were being managed by the state.

The stereotype about Italian drivers is probably the closest to the truth. Italy is a nation of fine race cars and speed demons, traffic laws that are considered negotiable, fiery tempers behind the wheel, and lots and lots of accidents. The problem is so persistent that Pope John Paul II used to appeal to the faithful to pray for those killed on Italian highways. There are some 8,000–9,000 traffic fatalities reported in Italy every year. Old-timers can say what they will about today's trains, but annual deaths on the railways barely make it out of the single digits.

By Air

Getting to Italy from the United States is a breeze. Alitalia, American, Continental, Delta and U.S. Airways all have direct flights to Italy, while the options multiply greatly when you add in a stop in Northern Europe. I've always found that the cheapest way to fly between North America and Italy is to get a cheap ticket to London or Dublin or another airport that has a low-budget carrier, and switch to Ryan Air, EasyJet, etc., from there.

Besides giving Milan a 20th-century alternative to the tiny Linate airport downtown, one reason that the Malpensa airport, by the Swiss border, was opened was that it was supposed to be less affected by the area's notorious fog. Advertisements at the airport claim that Malpensa has a gleaming record on that front, but ask anybody who has been held up for more than 24 hours there until the fog cleared, and you'll get a picture of just how meteorologically cursed northern Italy can be.

The problem is most urgent at Linate. On one foggy day in November 2001, Linate saw the worst airport accident in the nation's history when a small private plane wandered into the path of a Scandinavian Airlines flight taking off for Denmark, killing more than 100 people. Visibility was partly to blame.

Due to the fog, well-documented baggage thefts, and the interminable strikes by airline and airport staff, flying in and out of Milan can be a headache. Most of the time, though, it really is convenient. Malpensa has a built-in railway station with modern trains leaving for downtown every half hour. It can take as little as an hour between clearing customs and stepping off the train next to Milan's downtown castle. Linate is even better situated, just a 20-minute taxi ride from the city's epicenter, the Duomo. And since the bulk of international traffic has been redirected to Malpensa, Linate is often quite deserted. It makes Milan look more like a provincial outpost than the nation's financial capital.

Rome's airport in Fiumicino, named after Leonardo da Vinci, is also relatively convenient, if slightly outdated. The trains there are not as modern as in Milan, but only take about 40 minutes to reach downtown. Weather is rarely a problem, and except for the crowds that are common in any national capital—especially in late spring and early summer—it is no more chaotic than the city itself.

Several minor airports in Italy have now found a niche market in serving low-cost airlines. If you are flying from within Europe on that sort of carrier, be prepared to make one of the following cities your gateway to Italy: Ancona, Bergamo, Brescia, Pisa, Pescara, or Venice.

Just about every city in Italy has at least a small airport, but most domestic air travel in Italy is concentrated on flights to Sardinia and Sicily, or between the North and the South. The Milan–Rome shuttle is certainly the most popular for business travelers, though many people who work in the North have family in the South, and so flights between Turin and Bari, for example, often sell out over the holidays.

By Train

Considering the low price, train travel in Italy is a deal. The manageable size of the country and the obstacles to driving—high cost, persistent traffic, and highway dangers—make it the default method of transportation for many Italians and almost every foreigner.

The state railway, or Ferrovie dello Stato (FS), offers three major types of trains: the Interregionale, which stops in virtually every town along the way; the Intercity, which connects only the principal stations; and the Eurostar, the high-speed link that stops at the biggest cities.

On the Rome–Milan route, for example, most Eurostars will pick up and drop off passengers only in Florence and Bologna. It costs about €50 for a second-class seat and takes four and a half hours. An Intercity train will make about 10 stops on the same trip, taking six hours and costing about €10 less. Rome to Milan on an Interregionale would require anywhere from eight hours to an eternity, depending on the route it takes, but nobody would voluntarily subject himself or herself to a cross-country voyage on a string of local trains.

If the Italian railways have a bad reputation in Europe, it is due less to delays than to the carriages' decrepit appearance. Switching from a French regional train to an Italian one is like going back 40 years in time. The air-conditioning might very well be turned off when it is needed most—such as when the train is stopped inexplicably in the middle of nowhere for 20 minutes—and yet Italian passengers just shrug their shoulders and bear it. Summer travelers who would describe themselves as impatient people should avoid the Intercity or Interregionale at all costs.

The Eurostar is the most luxurious way to ride. It was developed as an answer to France's TGV, replacing the *pendolino* (tilting train) of the 1980s, and can reach speeds of 300 kilometers per hour. The country is still hoping to open more high-speed links in the North (which in this economy could be an uphill battle.) The Eurostar does break down occasionally—eight times in one recent summer—but it is the most reliable Italian train in terms of getting there on time, mostly because cheaper trains normally give it the right of way. Official estimates say the Eurostar arrives within 15 minutes of schedule 92 percent of the time. If it is more than 25 minutes late, passengers are entitled to a partial refund.

Unlike on the Intercity and Interregionale versions, you won't find people cramming the aisles and gangways on a Eurostar. Reserved seating is required, and spots will be

DAILY LIFE

© PURESTOCK

the slow train to Venice

snatched up by Thursday night for busy Friday afternoon departures. Buying a ticket on any train requires that you pay an extra penalty, so reserving a seat beforehand is recommended. Even with a ticket in hand, you should turn up at the station at least 10 minutes before departure. Jumping onto a train at the last minute can end in disaster.

I remember beginning an Intercity train ride on a steamy summer day in Rome. As I competed for oxygen in the crowded gangway, a man in a suit leapt into the carriage as it was leaving the platform. As he muscled out the last square inch of floor space, he asked if the train was headed to Naples. As it turned out, it was headed for Florence. He was trapped for an hour going in the wrong direction. What followed was a lengthy tutorial in the fine art of Neapolitan cursing.

When planning a trip, start with the FS website (www.trenitalia.it). Punch in your departure station, arrival station, and the date, and it will list all the possible trains in the following 24 hours. This is a lot quicker than running through the timetables or asking at the information office at the station, especially if you're making a series of connections. For many of the routes, you can buy your ticket directly from the website.

Anything is better than going to the ticket window at the train station. There are often huge lines, especially on the weekends, as only a fraction of the available windows are open at any given time. Aside from the website, other alternatives are to buy your ticket at any travel agency or at the machines at the station. The people who usually end up at the ticket windows are those with lengthy questions about connections, discounts, or refunds.

There are numerous ways to save money on train fares. One is by proving you are a student or a senior citizen. Another is to buy a "green card," which is like a frequent-flyer membership that offers massive discounts on weekends.

Finally, before you board the train, remember to stamp your ticket in the little yellow machines on the platform. Otherwise, the conductor will assume you're scheming to use it again.

By Bus

In the circulatory system of Italian public transport, the trains are the arteries and veins, and the buses are the capillaries. They will be the last leg of any journey to an out-of-the way village or neighborhood. Though many small hamlets often have their own train stations, those on top of a hill or otherwise off the railroad grid can be reached only by bus. Italy has more of them than any other European country.

A bus stop is easily recognized by an orange, yellow, or blue sign marked Fermata. Schedules for each bus and a list of stops on the route are usually posted at the stop. Unlike in most other countries, you cannot buy a ticket on board. You need to buy them beforehand at a local bar or tobacco store (marked by a black-and-white sign with the letter "T").

In cities, tickets work much as they do on a train. They need to be stamped by the little yellow or orange machine on board to be valid. But, unlike on a train, the tickets are almost never checked. Rome has cracked down on freeloaders in recent years, but in Milan and less-touristed towns, authorities tend to assume that no one would go through the embarrassment of being ticketless in the rare event that an official were to climb aboard.

Like anywhere else in the world, buses never come as often as you would like them to, and they are not always on time. If you plan to live in a place where a bus is the only connection to the outside world, you should carefully consider buying a car.

By Car

Much has been written about car culture in Italy, little of it flattering, and there's not much that Italians can say in their defense. Actually, they would see nothing to defend. Cars are simply driven faster, and Italians have their own code of conduct on the road.

The pace of Italian life is so relaxed that such an obsession with speed seems illogical. The streets are the only place in the country where people seem to be in a hurry. Put another way, Italians will drive very fast to get somewhere where they can walk very slowly. The same people who casually show up 20 minutes late for dinner will tailgate, pass in the face of oncoming traffic, and lean on the horn the second the light turns green. Motorcyclists routinely use the sidewalk to bypass traffic. On the highway: havoc.

Almost every Monday morning on the news, there is a body count from the weekend on the autostrada. Thousands die every year, and this is likely to continue. There has even been talk in Parliament about raising the highway speed limit from 130 to 160 kilometers per hour (78 to 96 mph). Drunk driving is certainly punishable, but only after a driver is pulled over, which is much less common than in the United States. That said, *carabinieri* (police) have the right to flag you over to the side of the road for no reason other than to check your driver's license and registration.

ROAD RULES

It is easy to be the victim of miscommunication in Italy, but nowhere is it easier, or are the consequences more severe, than on the road. Signage can be as misleading as the indications from drivers themselves.

The first thing you'll notice about city roads is that there are so many signs pointing to the highway or adjacent towns that it seems you don't even need a map. In many cases, this is true, except that the green signs pointing the way to the autostrada or the blue ones to state roads do not necessarily suggest the quickest route, but rather one that will eventually lead there. All roads lead to where you are going, sooner or later.

Italians know this, of course, and so it is common practice to stop a pedestrian to ask for directions. If your Italian is not good enough to understand the response, and you have to rely on the signs, first you need a lesson in the language of arrows. An arrow pointing left for Rome, for example, does not mean turn left for Rome. If the sign is on the right-hand side of the road and the arrow is pointing left—that is, toward the road in front of you—it means go straight ahead. A turn will be signified by a diagonal arrow pointing either up and to the left, or up and to the right. When the arrows disappear, go with the flow. You will have to take a leap of faith between signs and stay on what appears to be the major thoroughfare, even if it makes sharp turns. When there is a legitimate question at an intersection where it joins a large road, there will usually be another sign.

Traffic lights can also be confusing, and remember that many drivers consider a red light to be more of a guideline than a law. Also, when approaching a flashing yellow light at a four-way intersection, do not assume that there will be a flashing red in the other direction. More often than not, it, too, will be a flashing yellow.

Another of the famous *faux amis* is a car flashing its headlights at you when you are signaling to turn into its path. In North America, this usually means, "Go ahead." In Italy, it means, "Don't even think about it," and often will be accompanied by acceleration. A miscommunication could have some unpleasant consequences.

Italians also flash their headlights when there is a speed trap or traffic block ahead. The number of times they flash their lights depends on how high-ranking the authorities are. A triple flash signifies the *carabinieri*, the law enforcers with the broadest powers—and that rare stripe of official with whom you cannot smile your way out of a speeding ticket.

Finally, stay out of the left lane unless you are very serious about passing, or you will become a legitimate target for tailgaters. Some drivers are in perpetual passing mode, and will signal their intention by keeping their left blinkers on. To qualify for this group, you will need to maintain a speed of at least 150 kph (90 mph).

Another reason to avoid the roads is that there are simply too many cars. Italy ranks third in the world for the number of vehicles per capita, after the United States and Australia. Especially on the A-1 thoroughfare that runs the length of the peninsula, traffic jams stretch for miles. Gridlock is sometimes so severe that traffic comes to a complete stop, and people get out of their cars to stretch their legs for 10 minutes, an hour, or sometimes more. Workdays provide little relief. Despite a good public transportation system, millions decide to take their vehicles onto the beltways and avenues of Rome, Florence, Milan, and other cities.

There is an endless list of other arguments against driving. Parking is nearly impossible in downtown areas. Tolls are expensive: about €10 per hour of driving in the North. Insurance policies border on highway robbery. And then there's highway robbery itself: Milan leads Western Europe in the number of cars stolen per year.

Scooters, or *motorini,* are the most practical way to navigate narrow streets in Italian cities.

If all that weren't enough, gasoline costs four times what it does in the United States. Much of that price comes in the form of taxes. The state does what it can to make driving unappealing. Italy, like the rest of Western Europe, is far from sources of oil, and its foreign policy therefore walks a diplomatic tightrope between U.S. allies and the alleged terrorism-sponsoring countries, such as Iran, that hold Italian investments. There are daily Alitalia flights to Tehran, for example, a route you're not likely to catch from the United States.

It is unsurprising, then, that Italy is among the countries leading the push for alternative energy. Hydrogen-powered buses are already in use in Turin, and the world's first public hydrogen fuel pump is set to open near Milan. Both cities sometimes close their downtown streets to all traffic except taxis on Sundays, when smog levels are high. Other times, driving privileges are granted alternatively to cars with odd-numbered and even-numbered plates during the week.

But even Europeans are entitled to drive their cars, and the truth is that Italians have some of the most beautiful roads on the continent. Driving your car along the country's oleander-lined thoroughfares and winding rural roads can be so pleasant that you'll feel as if you're part of a luxury car commercial (perhaps because many of those commercials are in fact filmed in Tuscany and other bucolic landscapes). You truly need a car to visit most of those country roads in the Alps, Tuscan vineyards, and far-flung towns in the South. The question then becomes: Do you need to buy one, or would you be better off renting?

RENTING, LEASING, AND BUYING A CAR

Buying a used car in Italy can be a good deal, especially if you're looking for the kind of model that would cost a fortune in the United States and would be impractical to drive there anyway, because no one could service it.

To buy and drive a car, motorcycle, or moped in Italy, you need several documents. First, you need a *codice fiscale* (see the *Making the Move* chapter) before you make the purchase. The items that need to be tucked in your glove compartment are not much different from those in the United States: registration, proof of insurance, a valid driver's license, and an inspection certificate on the windshield to show that you're not polluting the environment.

Italian regulations on emissions have become much stricter in the 21st century. Every car must have a catalytic converter, and leaded fuel is outlawed. Those with older cars were given a grace period, but any car imported into the country must be up to standards. Still, don't be surprised to see cars or mopeds spewing black smoke. It cannot be stressed enough that, although Italy has some fine laws, few are ever enforced.

For your registration to be valid, it must have a new tax stamp stuck on it every year. The road tax is widely known as *il bollo* and is calculated on the kilowatts of power the engine puts out. For a medium-sized hatchback, it comes out to about €200. It can be paid at the post office.

Driver's licenses from any European Union (EU) member country are automatically valid in Italy. For those from non-EU countries, a current license is good for one year, assuming the driver has not established residency in Italy. Residents need to transfer their licenses into Italian ones, a process that requires no exams for as long as the foreign license is valid.

Besides gas, the greatest annual expense of owning a car is insurance. The cost depends, of course, on the kind of car, the extent of the coverage, where you live, and how long you've been driving. For an eight-year-old Volkswagen Golf in Milan—one of the more expensive places to own a car—a regular policy will cost around €1,000 per year through the offices of a major insurance company. The biggest ones in Italy are Generali, RAS, Winterthur, and Mediolana. But cheaper policies can be found on the Internet. For example, you might want to try out Genial Lloyd, owned by RAS. Insuring the same VW Golf in Milan through their site costs about €400 per year.

The final expense, which is actually one of the first you will incur when buying a car, is an official document of sale. It needs to be signed by a notary.

Renting a car through the largest groups in Italy—Europcar, Avis, Hertz, and National—costs about €60 per day for a compact car, though most of them have a three-day weekend special for about €100. If, on the other hand, you require a car more than a month at a time, leasing will be much cheaper. At Europe By Car (www.europebycar.com), a 60-day lease has a base price of €1,200. The car is straight from the factory. In theory, you are buying the car and then selling it back, but they only ask for a €100 deposit, so that clearly is not the case in practice. For a little extra money, you can lease some pretty sporty numbers as well. They come with full insurance, roadside assistance, etc. Another such company is Auto Europe (www.autoeurope.com).

Although there is no legal reason to use anything other than a U.S. driver's license when renting or leasing a car for that period of time, companies will sometimes ask you to arrange an international driver's license ahead of time. All it requires is sending an Italian translation of your local driver's license, and the company should be able to handle the rest.

Here are some additional tips for renting and leasing a car in Italy: If you plan to go to the mountains in the winter, make sure to ask for chains in advance. The car won't come with snow tires, and many mountain towns require cars to have chains, and police issue fines on the spot for those that don't. Also, since Italy is so close to many non-EU countries in Eastern Europe, it is tempting to take a rental car there. Most Italian rental cars are not insured in those countries, however, and major agencies based in Rome, Milan, and other large cities will put the kibosh on those plans quickly. You can always take a train and then rent a car once you're in Eastern Europe, but another option is to call rental agents in Trieste, most of whom are less skittish about letting their cars travel eastward.

DAILY LIFE

PRIME LIVING LOCATIONS

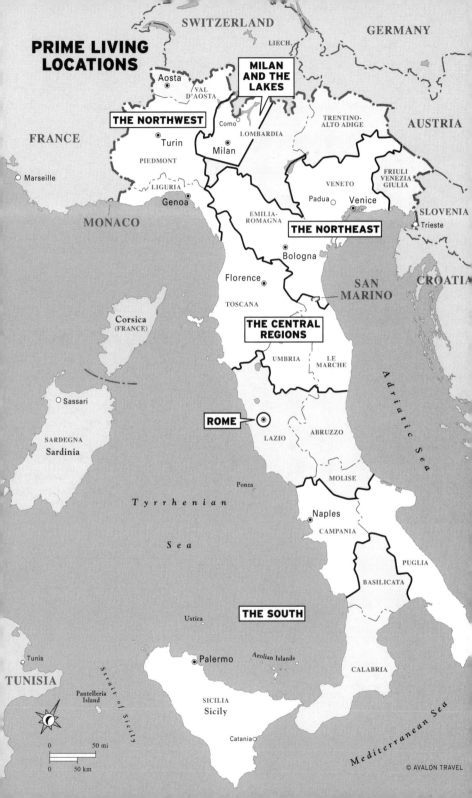

OVERVIEW

Choosing the right place to live in Italy is like surveying a dessert cart. Everything looks too good to pass up. A waiter might suggest a few specialties, but you're always going to wonder what you missed.

There are no bad choices among Italy's cities and regions, though some are more practical than others. If you're a career person, for instance, remote southern locations should probably be scratched off your list. Other places, like the choicest towns in Tuscany, will be financially out of reach for the average homeowner.

The following two chapters highlight Italy's two largest cities, Rome and Milan, each of which offers greater numbers of job opportunities for foreigners. Then there are four chapters dedicated to the best of rural and small-town Italy: the northeastern-central regions of Veneto and Emilia-Romagna, the northwestern regions of Piedmont and Liguria, the center regions of Tuscany, Umbria, and Le Marche, and three regions from the South: Campania, Puglia, and Sicily.

Venice and Florence are not covered. Though they are two of the most popular places to visit in Italy—and for good reason—they are not, in my opinion, the best places to live. Tourist season itself is one major reason to steer clear. The streets in both places are so crowded with English-speakers in the warmer months that it hardly feels like you ever left home. You'll have to battle the crowds on the streets just to get

a bottle of milk. (Disgruntled locals in Venice will tell you that even milk is hard to find, now that the tourist shops have overtaken the corner grocery stores). You'll have to struggle with long lines at the train station. Veneto and Tuscany have so much to offer outside of their famous capitals that you might as well take advantage of these lesser-known places and live like a local, saving the tourism in Florence and Venice for weekends in the off-season.

ROME

Rome has been a magnet for foreigners ever since the Goths sacked the city and moved in. Its featured attractions need little introduction. Millions of Americans come to this hub of Western civilization every year, and many of them refuse to leave.

The weather in Rome is superb. Though it lies on roughly the same latitude as New York City, palm trees lazily grow out of ancient ruins, and the most you'll need to wear in winter is a lightweight jacket. That alone is reason enough to move in, but Rome's history is its greatest asset. The aura of the ancients is present in every little act of modern life in Rome, whether it is setting an appointment to meet friends in front of the Pantheon, driving to work on the Appian Way, or coming home late at night to your apartment behind the Colosseum. The eternal monuments are a constant reminder of the greatness of this city and the wisdom its people have attained through the centuries.

Indeed, while the monuments are what initially attract foreigners to Rome, the Roman way of life is what makes it so hard to leave. These people have spent millennia identifying the essential and enduring elements of life, and the answers almost never include work. On any given afternoon, well-dressed Romans will let the hours roll by at lunch, then glide off on their *motorini* to their next appointment with pleasure. Few seem bothered with such banausic preoccupations as a paycheck. This feature of daily life will be off-putting to those who demand efficiency, but for those armed with sufficient patience and seeking a relaxed lifestyle, there really is no other place to be.

MILAN AND THE LAKES

For many foreigners, Milan is defined as a fashion capital, where models rush between sleek office buildings for photo shoots and others shop frantically to catch up with the trends. This definition isn't altogether off the mark. In the late 1960s and early 1970s, Milan stole the fashion-capital title from Florence, and it is now the home of the big-name labels and all the catwalk shows that count.

Milan is also the hub of financial services and the headquarters of the country's biggest businesses. For that reason, it is known to Italians as a place to make money and a career, and that's about it. Yes, it looks a little drearier than the nearby Riviera or the Alpine scenery just to the north, but the indoors lifestyle contributes to the city's mystique. If the Milanese aren't at the office, they're hanging out in nice bars and restaurants or entertaining at home; then they escape on the weekends to Europe's renowned playgrounds, just an hour or two away.

Especially close to the city is Italy's lakes district, Lake Como in particular. This Alpine lake is so well connected to the city, in fact, that many locals enjoy the best of both worlds by residing near paradise and working downtown. The suburbs of Brianza, which stretch from the city limits to the lakeshore, are attractive in their own right.

THE NORTHEAST: EMILIA-ROMAGNA AND VENETO

The northeast corner of the country, bound on the north by the Dolomites, on the south by the Apennines, and on the east by the Adriatic Sea, has produced some of Italy's most prosperous cities, which enjoy a very high standard of living. Emilia-Romagna, traditionally the wealthiest regions in Italy, and the Veneto, once upon a time among the poorest, have little in common historically or culturally, but foreigners will find a similar style of life in these two regions today. Both are composed of comfortable, medium-sized cities boasting world-class universities and hospitals, with fertile farms and vineyards surrounding them.

Verona, for example, is small and picturesque, a fitting setting for Shakespeare's *Romeo and Juliet,* which may be a reason that many foreign couples, especially from Britain, have begun to call it home. Expatriates have also flocked to Bassano del Grappa and other northern towns, especially since the provinces of Treviso and Vicenza house important military installations. Some of the country's choicest rural living is found there, most notably in the vineyards that produce the grapes used in Prosecco, Italy's answer to Champagne.

Emilia-Romagna's wealth shows up in its homegrown luxuries. Ferrari, Maserati, and Lamborghini cars are from here, as are a number of their owners. If you choose to live in Emilia-Romagna, the greatest hardship you're likely to face is picking the city itself. Bologna, Ferrara, Modena, and Parma are all very comfortable places to live, with blossoming industry and a transportation infrastructure that is second to none. Each can lay credible claims to the finest cuisine in the country. Those with discerning taste and a penchant for epicurean pleasures need look no further than Emilia-Romagna.

THE NORTHWEST: PIEDMONT AND LIGURIA

Piedmont and Liguria contain the best that Europe has to offer, condensed into a mountainous corner. The region starts at the Alps' tallest peaks, rolls through foothills that produce truffles and Barolo, and then melts into the Italian Riviera. In late spring, you can ski snowy slopes in the morning and bask by the Mediterranean in the afternoon, stopping off for some excellent wine and cheese in between.

The two regional capitals of Turin and Genoa don't draw many tourists, but they do produce jobs. Turin is home to the nation's largest private employer, Fiat, which has fallen on hard times in recent years as car sales have sagged, but will always hold a place in history as a driving force behind the Italian economy in the 20th century. It and the region's high-tech industry ensure that Piedmont will never be just another pretty place to visit.

It is little wonder, then, that surveys regularly name Piedmont towns as offering the best quality of life, while the region of Liguria has an equally convincing claim to fame as home to the oldest inhabitants in the world. The secret to longevity, its centenarians say, is a relaxed lifestyle and one glass of wine per day.

THE CENTRAL REGIONS: TUSCANY, UMBRIA, AND LE MARCHE

Picture this for a lifestyle change: You're driving back from the beach in a red Alfa Romeo convertible, winding your way through aromatic Tuscan vineyards at dusk. You round the corner, marked by a hilltop castle, and pass a field of sunflowers. Turning onto a dirt road, you see your house come into view: a stone-walled villa with a large garden and a vista over the hills.

Unfortunately, many others have already bought into that dream. The hills just north of Siena—playfully known as 'Chiantishire' for the number of English home-owners there—have become exceedingly expensive. The same is true around Todi, in Umbria, also studded with million-dollar homes. But other areas of Umbria still offer up bargains. Terni, for example, is an oft-overlooked corner of Umbria, which is sur-prising when you consider that it is only 40 minutes from Rome by train. It's also not too far from Perugia, a mecca for foreigners, thanks to its university.

As Tuscany and Umbria outprice themselves, Le Marche has become the next fron-tier for foreign homeowners. There are loads of bargains in this mountainous region by the sea, although admittedly it is farther away from international airports than its famous neighbors.

THE SOUTH: NAPLES, PUGLIA, AND SICILY

While the entire South may seem like a foreign country to the rest of Italy, there is something familiar about it for Americans. This is the Italy the rest of the world came to know when mass emigration emptied out its rural towns at the turn of the 20th century. In many cases, it seems that little has changed since then. The hospitality is still legendary; even families that don't have much money will spend a small fortune to accommodate visitors. Family values are still very strong, and old traditions like chivalry have never disappeared.

Unfortunately, things haven't improved much in terms of the economy. Campania, Puglia, and Sicily have still failed to catch up with the rest of Italy, if they care to do so at all. There has been some progress in cleaning up organized crime (without which, the National Statistics Institute likes to point out, the South would be on financial par with the North). But southerners don't seem to be in any hurry to reverse their fortunes if it means changing their pace of life. Spend just one week there, and you'll understand why.

ROME

It's lunchtime in Rome, and you wander into a pizzeria by the Pantheon. The *pizzaiolo* cuts you a slice with zucchini and eggplant, you plunk down your €2 and walk back into the balmy air to find a place to sit down. Munching away, you look down to find that this round piece of stone where you have planted yourself is not exactly a bench. It is the big toe of an erstwhile colossus that loomed large above this street some 2,000 years ago.

This sort of thing happens every day in Rome. The alleyways and thoroughfares are so thickly sprinkled with the remains of ancient history that you couldn't possibly notice them all. Anywhere else, this marble appendage would have been carted off to a museum, but in the Eternal City, it's merely part of the landscape. There are buildings that fell apart centuries ago, and no one has bothered to fix them. Flowers, ivy, and graffiti crawl over the remnants and fill history's void with beauty, showing that, in Rome at least, time heals all wounds.

The cradle of Western civilization is a paradise for history buffs and people who enjoy life in the slow lane. With fine weather and smiling faces everywhere you turn, it is easy to sit around and wait out any hardships that present themselves. If patience is a virtue, Rome must be the most virtuous city of all.

For everyone else, the city is a grueling test. Rome suffers from—or, some would

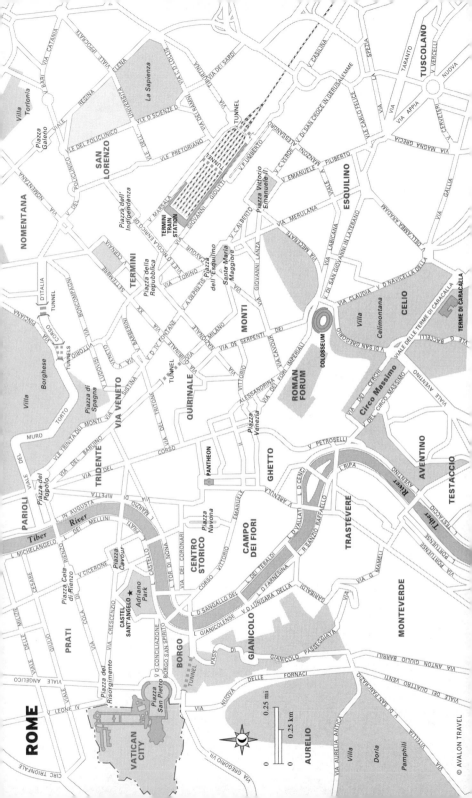

say, enjoys—a syndrome called *menefreghismo*. This is the attitude that the present matters little, that problems like ringing telephones will eventually go away, and that nothing, ever, is urgent.

The city doesn't bat an eyelash at new ideas. It has seen them all: democracies, emperors, popes, conquering hordes, dark ages, rebirths, more conquerors, monarchists, fascists, communists, and the sunrise and sunset of the Internet millionaire. Despite this, or more likely because of it, nothing ever truly changes. The city still has its popes, fascists, communists, and Internet entrepreneurs, all of them only slightly reformed. Even Italy's exiled royals have been allowed to return. In Rome, a scandal today is forgotten tomorrow, and you will always be forgiven.

Rome's live-and-let-live attitude has attracted admirers from all corners of the globe, and it has long had a lively English-speaking contingent, going back to the days of Byron and Shelley (now buried in the city's Protestant Cemetery). They were followed in the 1950s by the café-dwellers of Via Veneto, and later by crowds of tourists from the United States when air travel became affordable to the middle class.

Though it hosts millions of religious pilgrims and thousands of regular tourists, Rome has never been considered a cosmopolitan capital on par with the likes of Paris or London. When in Rome, outsiders were expected to eat and behave like the Romans, and they did so enthusiastically. Over the past decade, this has changed a little, thanks to the forces of globalization and growth in immigration. Where once there were modest trattorie, now there are Irish pubs. Corner stores in the historic center have become McDonald's, and even a handful of sushi and African restaurants have sprung up. For cautious expats, this all means a gentle introduction to a foreign land.

It's also a good place for them to find a job, since a number of English-speaking institutions are headquartered here: universities, international organizations, media groups, etc. Some U.S. companies operate out of Rome, though many prefer to locate themselves in Italy's financial and business capital, Milan. (Jealous northerners will often remind their fellow citizens that modern Rome—much like Washington, D.C.—would be little more than a southern backwater had it not been for its fortunate political status and the jobs that this created.) Rome is therefore a good place for those fresh off the plane to land a short-term lease and try out their luck in the job market before planning a longer-term move.

The Lay of the Land

Entire university courses are devoted to studying Rome's cityscape, which may seem chaotic at first, but in fact was a masterpiece of urban planning, perfectly laid out to make the most of each approach to a monument. Don't expect the geography of Italy's medieval cities, where everything revolves around a central cathedral. Rome is a mosaic of ancient, medieval, Renaissance, and Baroque structures dotting either side of the Tiber River, and each neighborhood has its own particular importance.

The oldest and most orthodox way to refer to Roman geography is by its seven hills: the Aventine, Capitoline, Celium, Esquiline, Palatine, Quirinal, and Viminal. Romans still use these names to refer to an institution now located there: Il Quirinale is the president's offices, Il Viminale is the Ministry of the Interior, Il Campidoglio

REGIONAL DIALECTS: ROME

Roman dialect, known as *romanesco*, or pejoratively as *romanaccio*, has hundreds of colorful expressions. Here are a few of the more polite ones, what they sound like they might mean, and what they really mean.

Parla come magni.
Sounds like: Talk like you eat.
Means: What are you trying to tell me?

Semo a cavallo.
Sounds like: We're on horseback.
Means: We're in good shape.

Nun stamo a venne li fiori 'n cima a la collina.
Sounds like: We're not selling flowers on the hilltop.
Means: Let's stop wasting time.

Te stai a allarga'.
Sounds like: You're extending yourself.
Means: Stick to things you know.

Stai popo a sgrava'.
Sounds like: You're giving birth.
Means: You're exaggerating.

Sta 'n campana./Stai manzo.
Sounds like: Stay by the bell./Stay beef.
Means: Stay on your toes.

Nun c'e trippa pe' gatti.
Sounds like: There's no tripe for the cats.
Means: We're broke./There's nothing left.

Stai a guarda' er capello.
Sounds like: You're looking at the hair.
Means: You're being too picky.

(Capitoline) is City Hall, and so on. Referring to the hill will usually work if you're describing a general area of the city center, but it will only get you so far when flipping through the classified ads for apartments.

Officially, the city is divided into 22 *rioni* (districts), which can be found on government maps and in erudite city guides. They were imposed upon the city about a century ago, after Rome became the capital, and they never gained the name recognition of, say, Paris's *arrondissements*. Sometimes, they can sound downright awkward. For instance, if someone were advertising an apartment on Via della Croce, they would much sooner refer to the area as "della Croce" or even "Piazza di Spagna" than use the official *rione,* "Campo Marzio." Some official *rioni* names, however, are very commonly used, especially Prati, Trastevere, Testaccio, and Monti.

Instead, classified ads and the average Roman will mention the closest subway station, if there happens to be one nearby, or else the closest square—such as Popolo, Navona, or Bologna—or, in some cases, an ancient road, such as Appia, Cassia, or Flaminia.

Housing

The capital is an expensive place to live. It's still not quite at the level of London, or even Paris, but it's close. Citywide, the average rent for 100 square meters (which would be a large two-bedroom apartment, is about €1,600. Downtown, that's closer to the rate for a one-bedroom apartment. However, the most recent economic crisis has created a noticeable uptick in vacancies, and even if rates aren't exactly plummeting, that's always a good time to negotiate.

Prices vary widely depending on standard measurements such as location, size, and amenities, but also on more Rome-specific considerations, such as the presence of an ancient column or some other artistic treasure buried in the walls.

The greatest factor, of course, is location. Rent for apartments inside the city's Aurelian walls is almost always more expensive than for those outside them. The following descriptions of neighborhoods give an indication of what you might expect to pay in rent per square meter, the measurement used in all classified ads. For a single-bedroom apartment, multiply by 50 or 60 square meters. For a two-bedroom place, multiply by 70 or 80.

For buyers, prices will vary even more widely than rents. As a rough indication, the average home downtown sells for €10,000 per square meter. Add on the 3 percent tax for first-time property owners (or 7 percent for those who already own), and the average two-bedroom apartment downtown will cost about a million dollars.

That's for the choicest area of Rome. Farther out from the center, prices drop dramatically. Parioli, for example, costs about two-thirds of that, while suburban real estate averages about €2,500 per square meter.

WHERE TO LIVE
Downtown

The first on any list of Roman neighborhoods is the *centro storico* (downtown), which in Rome's case means the part that holds the major monuments and squares. This vaguely defined "historic center" is bound on the western side by a sharp curve in the Tiber, and more or less contained on the eastern side by the Colosseum, Santa Maria Maggiore, the Baths of Diocletian, and the city's ornate park, the Villa Borghese. If you had an apartment here, you could walk to a dozen of the Western world's most photographed monuments in just a few minutes, plus most of the government buildings. The prices reflect this. If a map of downtown Rome were a Monopoly board, the Spanish Steps would be Boardwalk and the Via Veneto would be Park Place. Rents there are highest, at about €25 or €30 per square meter. Apartments near the Pantheon, Piazza Navona, and Piazza del Popolo will come close to that price, as will any address directly across the river in the *rioni* of **Borgo** and **Castel Sant'Angelo.** There, you can wake up in the morning and walk over the Tiber on your way to work as flocks of pigeons flap into the pink, hazy sunrise.

The southeastern limits of the downtown are marked by the *rione* of **Monti,** a cozy corner of alleyways between the Termini train station and the Colosseum. It is an excellent choice if you have the means. In my opinion Monti has a more neighborly feel than some of the posher districts described above, but because it has become

PAJATA: THE "INSIDES" STORY

The menu at Checchino dal 1887 is bound to raise some eyebrows. Just a stone's throw from Rome's former slaughter-house in Testaccio, the restaurant's posted list of brains, intestines, tails, and feet looks, to the uninitiated, more like a recipe for a witch's brew than an array of local specialties.

Many a tourist and even some locals would rather not see, let alone eat, a plate of animal innards. Yet no other dish can claim to be as Roman, and what some might consider a macabre meal can be found in every quarter of the capital.

Coda alla vaccinara, il cervello, and es-pecially a *pajata–vaccinari* (workers) were allowed to bring home to their families.

Pajata was for centuries the staple meat dish in Rome's historically poorer districts, like Testaccio and Trastevere. These days, at restaurants from the up-scale Checchino to the more modest Ostaria da Edmondo–not far from the Olympic stadium–*pajata* is served as a fanfare for the common man.

"*Pajata* is the most important dish at my restaurant," says Checchino owner Elio Mariani. "It is the most representative of the *quinto quarto*"–*pajata* is a common re-frain among Testacco restaurateurs, but an odd claim for a kitchen that purports to have invented a rival Roman favorite.

Legend has it that the daughter of Checchino's founders took an oxtail and some cheek meat from the slaugh-terhouse across the street and added it to a celery stew usually reserved for pricier cuts of beef. Thus, *coda alla vac-cinara* was born.

Pajata, also spelled *paiata* or, less com-monly, *pagliata*, is made from the upper intestines of a yearling calf. Animals that young still feed from their mothers, and it is important that their intestines con-tain the mother's milk. Only a fraction of the very upper section of the intestine is used, so that the bits of grass–called *paja* in dialect–the calf has grazed on are only partially digested. Any further along the digestive tract becomes something that not even the poorest of Romans could bear to stomach.

extremely popular with the expatriate crowd, especially, prices have crested to €25 per square meter.

On either side of the Vatican are two of the more comfortable, upper-middle-class quarters of Rome, called **Prati** and **Trastevere.** They each attract slightly different crowds. Trastevere is a dream for students, artists, and other bookstore-browsing types who have a bit of extra cash to spend on an apartment with character. It may be a stretch to call it Rome's answer to Greenwich Village, but there are some good hole-in-the-wall bars and restaurants with a rustic flavor. There is even a small English-language movie theater, the Pasquino. If you're single and in your 20s or 30s, or even middle-aged with an appreciation for hip venues, this would be an ideal place to live. Rent here has also risen to €25 per square meter in many cases. Prati is more staid and quiet, the home of the national broadcaster RAI and a number of law offices, and is generally a serene place to raise a family. There are some very good restaurants in the area and a few decent shops, but mostly it is a modern residential zone with wide, relatively uninteresting boulevards. It is just slightly cheaper than spicier Trastevere.

Across the river from Prati is a similarly conservative, family-oriented neighborhood that's even better-known for its yuppies. **Parioli** is so stately, in fact, that many national governments have set up their embassies here. Cafés and shops play to the whims of cautious diplomats looking to make a good impression. If you see a group of young

Victor Emmanuel Monument at Piazza Venezia, Rome

men with neatly ironed slacks driving expensive mopeds, you may safely assume that they are *pariolini*. All snickering aside, Parioli is a very clean neighborhood with some elegant apartments, and if that's your cup of espresso, it's well worth the price: about €23 per square meter.

Outside the Center

The *centro storico,* Monti, Borgo, Prati, Parioli, and Trastevere, are about as good as it gets, geographically. If you can't walk to where you are going, it's only a short moped or bus ride away. But as real estate prices in Rome move out of reach even for moneyed foreigners, you will probably want to look a little further afield for the bargains, and Rome has a number of well-connected neighborhoods outside downtown.

Monteverde has long been a popular option for U.S. expats looking for a nicer-priced apartment. Although it is tucked back on Janiculum Hill behind Trastevere, it might as well be downtown if you consider the convenient public transportation along Viale Trastevere. Modern, air-conditioned trams run from the heart of Monteverde to Largo Argentina, just steps from the Pantheon, in about 15 or 20 minutes. Monteverde Vecchio, as the name might suggest, has older and more interesting architecture than its younger sibling, Monteverde Nuovo, and is therefore a tad more expensive. With the exception of the district's more luxurious buildings, both are still cheaper than downtown. You can find an apartment in Monteverde Vecchio for as little as €15 per square meter, and even slightly less in Monteverde Nuovo.

A similarly priced neighborhood can be found on the opposite side of Janiculum Hill from Monteverde, directly behind the Vatican. It takes its name from the avenue that runs through it, **Gregorio VII,** but it's also known as Pio XI after the square where the

© ANTHONY MARAGOU/123RF

colorful houses in Trastevere, a typical Roman neighborhood

street ends up. (Streets and squares around here are often named after popes.) This is a modern and comfortable neighborhood, but relatively short on charm.

Another middle-of-the-road option is **Testaccio,** just south and across the river from Trastevere. The general area is also known as Ostiense. This is the old butchers' district, which today holds meat markets of a different kind: discos and singles bars. There are also some excellent restaurants in the area, serving true Roman specialties. Plan on about €17 per square meter.

Farther south down Via Ostiense, you'll reach **EUR,** Mussolini's ambitious, sprawling exposition center. The architecture is Fascist, naturally, and the apartments surrounding it house mostly middle-class couples and families. For the same €1,500 that you could spend for a one-bedroom apartment downtown, you could find a three-bedroom, two-bath apartment, maybe even with a garage, in EUR. The price is right, but the commute can be tedious.

Closer to the center are a few other affordable areas. Two behind the Termini train station are worth noting: **San Lorenzo,** the stronghold of Rome's student population, at about €15 per square meter; and **Piazza Vittorio,** once an immigrants' neighborhood that is quickly becoming gentrified. Depending on the size and frills, apartments in this part of the Esquilino cost around €17 per square meter. Indeed, many neighborhoods just outside the historic center started off as low-income housing and are now some of the most preferred properties in the city. In the southern neighborhoods of **San Saba and Garbatella,** there are single-family houses with unusual architecture so appealing to families that they are very rarely up for grabs. There are some rentals on par in price with Trastevere.

St. Peter's Basilica, Vatican City

The Suburbs

In relation to Milan, suburban options in Rome are not quite as appealing. For one thing, the towns immediately outside of Rome are mostly examples of urban sprawl, whereas Lombard cities like Monza and Bergamo have a history in their own right. Also, the public transportation to the outskirts of Rome leaves a little to be desired, comparatively speaking, and you will almost certainly need a car.

One good suburban option, however, is **Olgiata,** off the Via Cassia, where many U.S. expatriates have set up house. It is a gated community with modern villas and swimming pools, the sort of place where you might expect to see more satellite dishes and SUVs, because Olgiata is more about New World comfort than Old World charms. Its appeal for expats is the proximity of the Overseas School of Rome, one of the more famous English-speaking schools in the country. The largest drawback is that you really need a car.

Owning a car also opens the doors to one last, and very good, alternative to urban living in Rome. The lakes district has dozens of quaint villages with prices to match. South of the city are towns on **Lake Albano** and **Lake Nemi** where apartments go for as little as €6 per square meter. Similar prices can be found on **Lake Bracciano,** north of the city, which has already drawn a foreign crowd, thanks to ads in English-language publications like *Wanted in Rome.*

LIVING THE FOODIE DREAM

So you have a pretty good job, do you? Nice office with a view, a few weeks' vacation? Boss is cool, casual dress on Friday? Check out this one: getting paid to eat the world's best gelato, all around Rome, every day. Kind of makes that office look a little smaller, doesn't it?

This job actually exists. And that is only because Elizabeth Minchilli dreamed it up and starting doing it recently, as part of her overall pursuit to eat the most delicious foods Rome has to offer and make a living in the process.

Elizabeth really does take the concept of dream jobs to a whole new level. She manages to do this because she knows Italy well, she stays on top of technology, and is bullish on the idea that when it comes to tourists in search of fine food and wine, Italy will always sell.

Elizabeth's route to her life in Rome will sound familiar to many. She spent a year abroad in Italy during college, earned a master's degree in art history in graduate school, and soon fell in love with a handsome Italian. But while most stories like this make a turn back to the United States, leaving only fond memories of Italy behind, Elizabeth was here to stay.

The St. Louis native explains, "I decided that maybe I didn't really want to go back to the States and teach undergraduate art history somewhere in the Midwest. So I changed gears and very soon had a husband, babies, dogs, and a brand-new career writing for magazines like *Architectural Digest, World of Interiors, Art & Antiques* and *Bon Appetit.*"

Like many magazine writers, Elizabeth one day realized that she had become a blogger, too. These days, she posts regularly about the tempting cheeses, enticing vegetables, and extraordinary meats she has comes across in the Eternal City, the recipes that contain them, and the hidden restaurants that serve them.

In turn, her blog became a great tool to attract readers who might want Elizabeth to take them around on eating tours. After munching her way across Rome for 20 years, she has a mental database of all the places to find the tastiest pastries, freshest mozzarella, or whatever it is you're craving. Most recently she has created two mobile apps, called Eat Rome and Eat Florence, that put her personal recommendations at the fingertips of hungry tourists on the move.

One sunny June day in Rome, she had just completed one of her first ice cream tours and sort of marveled aloud at the turns her career had taken. She never dreamed she'd be doing this sort of thing back when she was poring through archives for information about the 16th-century garden grottoes designed by Bernardo Buontalenti.

Then again, no one really knows what career turns lie ahead. Take Buontalenti himself for example. It turns out that he too liked to think about food a little more than architecture, and in the end he made a pretty important contribution to the Italian culinary scene. You guessed it: the invention of gelato.

Getting Around

Choosing a place somewhere near where you work is important, because the city streets are crowded and public transportation is not the best in the country. This has a lot to do with Rome's ancient past; it's hard to build a subway when you bump into a buried archaeological treasure every few feet. Planning the simplest tunnel or parking garage is a constant struggle against the remnants of Roman history.

The subway has just two lines. The first, the red line, starts near the Vatican, crosses the river, skirts the northern edge of the historic center, passes the Termini train station,

© PURESTOCK

un motorino

and finishes in the southeastern outskirts. The second, the blue line, starts in the eastern suburbs, runs through Termini, the Colosseum, and Testaccio, then ends near EUR in the southwest. If you have the luck or the foresight to live and work near one of those lines, getting around won't be too hard. The subway is fairly efficient, though packed at rush hour.

The great majority of Romans live outside walking distance of a subway stop, and so public-transport commuters rely on buses and trams. Both are reliable in the sense that they exist and will come eventually (except during strikes). They are not famous for their punctuality. Bus tickets are valid for 90 minutes, which starts the moment you punch the ticket in the on-board machines. If you don't punch the ticket, you'll get a fine in the off-chance that an inspector steps on.

No discussion of Roman buses would be complete without a brief mention of old No. 64. This route cuts through the heart of the city, from Termini to the Vatican. As you might expect, it's loaded with pilgrims, priests, tourists, and some very crafty pickpockets. If you do ride No. 64, and chances are you often will, make sure to keep an eye on your bags and pockets.

Like anywhere else in the world, it takes a certain type to enjoy riding the bus. They're particularly hot and stuffy in Rome, and every time you board and look out the window, you start dreaming about getting a scooter. The classified ads are full of used mopeds, and they come pretty cheap—as low as a few hundred euros. They are the ideal form of transportation in a city that certainly wasn't designed around the automobile, and where downtown is off-limits to most cars except taxis.

If you don't want to deal with the paperwork of getting a license plate and the other necessary permits, there are loads of agencies around that lend out mopeds by the hour or by the day. You might even be able to strike a deal where you can rent one for a month at a substantial discount.

If you prefer pedal power to motors, by all means, bring your bike along, but don't expect smooth riding in Rome. In Italy's northern cities, getting around town by bike is a way of life; in Rome, it can be a shortcut to death. And inline skating is out of the question, except in the leafy Villa Borghese, where skates can be rented. There's no better way to spend a lazy Sunday afternoon.

PRIME LIVING LOCATIONS

MILAN AND THE LAKES

At first blush, Milan is a bland European metropolis where the quality of life pales in comparison to other, more pleasant Italian settings. Small talk at the dinner table invariably begins by stacking up Milan against Rome. The capital always comes out looking good in the comparison.

But as the dinner progresses, some of Milan's finer points are brought to light—its proximity to popular vacation spots, its ethnic diversity and nightlife, its relative orderliness, its high profile in the worlds of design, media, and finance, and its curious subtleties—all of which Rome lacks to varying degrees. In the end, many of those around the table will confess that they now find Milan hard to leave.

The capital of Lombardy is not only the obvious choice for those interested in working hard and enjoying a cosmopolitan setting, it is also a great springboard for road trips out of the city, located about 90 minutes by car from the Riviera and less than an hour from the Alps. France, Switzerland, and Austria are all just around the corner. The surrounding cities of Como, Pavia, Cremona, and Bergamo are each national treasures in their own right. At first, you will find it tempting to head out of town every weekend. Then, as you start to move to the city's rhythms and turn up its hidden offerings, you may find it hard to tear yourself away.

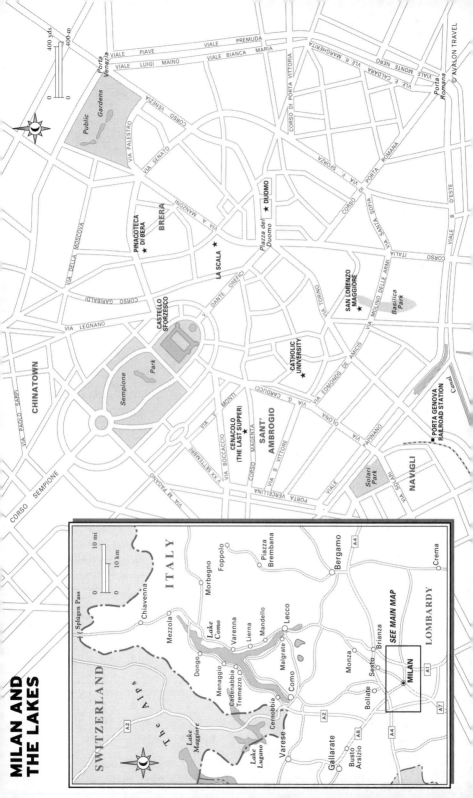

MILAN AND THE LAKES

© AVALON TRAVEL

Main Map Labels

Viale Premuda
Viale Piave
Viale Bianca Maria
Viale Luigi Maino
Porta Venezia
Viale E. Caldara
Viale R. Margherita
Via Monte Nero
Viale B. D'Este
Porta Romana
Corso di Porta Vittoria
Viale Monte Santo
Via A. Manzoni
Corso Venezia
Via Palestro
Via Senato
Via Sforza
Public Gardens
Corso di Porta Romana
BRERA
PINACOTECA DI BRERA ★
DUOMO ★
Piazza del Duomo
LA SCALA ★
Dante Orefici
Corso di Porta Romana
Via F. Sforza
Via Italia
Corso Italia
Via Santa Sofia
Via Molino delle Armi
Corso di Porta Ticinese
SAN LORENZO MAGGIORE ★
Basilica Park
Corso Garibaldi
Via della Moscova
Via Legnano
CASTELLO SFORZESCO
Via Dante
Via Torino
CHINATOWN
Via Paolo Sarpi
Corso Sempione
Sempione Park
Via M. Pagano
Via XX Settembre
Via Boccaccio
Via Monti
Via G. Carducci
CATHOLIC UNIVERSITY ★
Via Edmondo de Amicis
Via San Vittore
Corso Magenta
CENACOLO (THE LAST SUPPER) ★
SANT' AMBROGIO ★
Porta Vercellina
Viale
Via Olona
Via Papiniano
Solari Park
Via Solari
NAVIGLI
PORTA GENOVA RAILROAD STATION ■
Canal

400 yds
400 m

Inset Map — Milan and the Lakes

SWITZERLAND
ITALY
LOMBARDY
The Alps
Splügen Pass
A2
Chiavenna
Mezzola
Dongo
Menaggio
Cadenabbia
Tremezzo
Lake Como
Varenna
Lierna
Mandello
Morbegno
Foppolo
Piazza Brembana
Lecco
Bergamo
A4
Crema
Malgrate
Certobbia
Como
Lake Lugano
Lake Maggiore
Varese
Gallarate
Busto Arsizio
A8
Bollate
Sesto
Brianza
Monza
Brianza
Sesto
A1
MILAN
SEE MAIN MAP
A7
A4
A2

10 mi
10 km

Milan

Milan has been known as the nation's fashion capital ever since Giorgio Armani and Gianni Versace showed up on the scene in the 1980s. Now home to dozens of labels on every fashionista's shopping list, Milan is a mainstay on the circuit that runs from New York to London to Paris. Be sure to visit during the *settimana della moda* (fashion week) to get the full picture.

More broadly, Milan is a design center. We're not talking about just clothes, but also cars, furniture, and cutting-edge household goods. The lines that define Fiat, Alfa Romeo, and the sort of kitchenware you'd like to show off were drawn by such local names as Pininfarina and Alessi. In April, the city's exposition center holds the Salone del Mobile, the world's premier design show. It attracts artists and architects from around the world, yet anyone who needs to be near the vanguard of the industry already lives here.

Italy's stock market is based in Milan—no actual trading floor, mind you, as it is completely electronic—and most of Italy's financial services are firmly rooted here. If you're coming to Italy on a business trip, chances are you'll be spending a few days in Lombardy.

Finally, the city holds a self-conferred title as the nation's moral capital. This is a reference to the Clean Hands investigations, whose prosecutors worked out of Milan's high court. Consequently, the local newspaper and Italy's leading daily, *Corriere della Sera,* became a symbol of the transparency that brought the "Bribesville" days to an end.

The journalists, lawyers, judges, bankers, and others who make up this busy city have a different social life than many of their Italian peers, but it is contemporary and cosmopolitan in a way that Rome is only now becoming. The mosaic of nationalities reveals itself in Milan's restaurants: Japanese, Turkish, Eritrean, Chinese, Moroccan, Sri Lankan, Korean. It does not yet have the selection of, say, Chicago, but you will be hard-pressed to find anything but Italian food elsewhere in the country. The city's multiethnic population also reveals itself in the religious community. Milan has the largest mosque in the country, at least a couple of synagogues, and more churches than it will ever need.

Diversity is one reason that Milan draws parallels with U.S. cities. On top of that, it is sprawling, busy, and bordering on stressful. If you're making the move for relaxation or an excuse to underachieve, this is not the Italy you are looking for. Milan is inhabited by professionals who dream of success in the boardroom, or else moving back to a quainter part of the country as soon as they have the money to do so.

THE LAY OF THE LAND

When Italians visit cities in the United States, they often have a hard time finding the "center" of town. That's because it doesn't exist—at least not in the way they imagine it, with a cathedral at its epicenter and major streets leading directly to it or in concentric circles around it.

Milan is a classic example of the medieval European planning that U.S. cities lack. It is a bull's-eye, with the cathedral at the center. It and the castle sit inside the city's innermost circle, the neighborhood Italians like to refer to as the *centro storico*. About a half kilometer farther out along the radius is a loop road, called the *bastioni,* which

a Liberty-style *palazzo* in Porta Venezia, Milan

© JOHN MORETTI

demarcates what an North American might call "downtown." Here are the proverbial city walls, each with a gate named after the destination of that road: Porta Romana, Porta Venezia, Porta Ticinese, etc. The next ring road is the major thoroughfare in town, called the *circonvallazione.* Outside that road, the rent gets cheaper, the architecture generally less inspired, and all of it is encompassed by the *tangenziale* (beltway).

Some of the nicest areas to live in without paying extraordinary sums are near the city walls. The most popular of these residential areas are Porta Venezia, Porta Romana, and the up-and-coming neighborhoods in Chinatown, which is near Porta Garibaldi. Then there are the city's two best-known nightlife districts, Brera and the Navigli. The latter is named after the canals that run through it. (Milan used to be covered with such waterways, much like Venice, until almost all of them were paved over to fight waterborne diseases.) Prices in the Navigli can be slightly higher, because this is an attractive location for young people.

Of course, choosing an apartment for rent or sale will depend mostly on availability. There are a number of nice places in the city to live, but you will really have to shop around for yourself to see what you like and what's actually there for the taking.

Milan remains among the most expensive places to live in Italy, although the slowdown in the economy has made for easier negotiations in this business-minded city. If you demand a place within the loop road, expect to pay at least €700 a month for a small one-room apartment, and at least €1,200 for two bedrooms. The prices go up from there. The average monthly rent for an apartment sits at about €1,200, which takes into consideration every size, location, and level of luxury. A nice alternative for young people is to scour the universities for postings, which can sometimes turn up a room in a student-held apartment for about €500 per month.

WHERE TO LIVE

Chinatown is one of the more attractive neighborhoods for its exotic flavor and wide selection of restaurants, and above all, reasonable prices. Purchase prices for single-bedroom apartments (about 55 square meters) start at €150,000. Two-bedroom apartments (about 80 square meters) start at nearly €250,000. The neighborhood also has a high ratio of studios (each about 30 square meters), which run in the €60,000–80,000 range and are usually advertised as "investments," so as not to suggest that the owners might subject themselves to living in such cramped quarters.

The **Navigli** and especially the adjacent **Sant'Ambrogio** neighborhood are two of

REGIONAL DIALECTS: MILAN

Zucch e melon a la soa stagion.
Literally, "Pumpkins and melons have their seasons," this refers to middle-aged people who want to appear younger than they really are–e.g., a balding man who wears a hairpiece or an older woman with an exceedingly short skirt.

Và a Bagg a sona l'òrghen.
Literally, "He's going to Baggio to play the organ," this refers to slackers who like to waste their time. Baggio, now part of the downtown, was once a suburb of Milan whose parish was too poor to afford an organ, so the pastor painted one on the walls.

Taccàsù el capell.
Literally, "He's hung up his hat," this refers to a man who has married a wealthy woman and no longer has to work.

Va a ciapà I rat.
Literally, "Go catch the rats," this means "Get out of here."

the most comfortable residential areas for foreigners. Many of the apartments have been restructured by budding architects and may be on split levels. Expect to pay about €250,000 for a small one-bedroom apartment. A place to house the whole family, although in luxurious surroundings, will cost at least €500,000 and will often run past €1 million. Sant'Ambrogio is certainly the most convenient location in town, well-connected by all kinds of public transport, and even the cathedral is a short walk away—a good thing, because you won't find anywhere to park a car there.

Brera is a Cinderella story in the annals of real estate, an example of how a neighborhood can be gentrified in a single generation. In the early postwar years, it was home to the city's brothels. It was, coincidentally, also home to some very stately buildings just steps from the cathedral. In the 1960s, artists moved into Brera, and it became what might be called Milan's *rive gauche.* The roaring '80s— termed *"Milano da bere,"* (owing the phrase to a Ramazzotti liquor ad and loosely translating to "Milan in a glass") brought a boom of more mainstream nightspots. By the 1990s, it was already among the most expensive neighborhoods in town. It is common to see apartments advertised for €30 per square meter, or about a half million for a one-bedroom apartment. On the whole, expect prices to be about 20 percent higher in Brera than in the other neighborhoods, though you never know what you might find.

There is a lot of cheaper stuff to be had, especially well outside the city. One extreme example is in the fairly industrial suburb of **Busto Arsizio,** in the outskirts near Malpensa airport. You might find a two-bedroom apartment there for €75,000 or an entire penthouse floor for €200,000 in a sparkling new building.

GETTING AROUND

Getting around Milan is easier than in many major European cities. Since it is much more compact than, say, London, a subway ride from one end of the line to the other takes only about 30 minutes and costs only €1. Milan's subway network is the largest in Italy, which is not saying much, but it takes you almost everywhere you need to go. Despite its frequent strikes, when the city is thrown into a chaotic traffic jam, the subway is reliable because the trains generally show up on time. The last ones run at 12:30 A.M.

© OLENA BUYSKYKH/123RF

Milan's old orange tram

Trams are also largely trustworthy and certainly the most characteristic of all public transport. Alas, some of the old cars have been sold off to San Francisco and replaced by pan-European-looking green units. They are air-conditioned but lack the charm of the orange trams with their wooden benches, fin-de-siècle light fixtures, and the sound of old wheels rattling on steel.

Then there are the buses. As in any other part of the country, they almost show up on a whim. If you're going to an appointment with that rare person who appreciates punctuality, you're better off in a taxi. Bear in mind that after 9 P.M., taxis start their meters at €6—it's not a tourist scam, just an added cost for a night on the town. Taxis also have a certain snob appeal. The Milanese always prefer driving to public transportation. Italy has the third highest rate of car ownership in the world, and it seems like every single one of them is on Milan's streets during rush hour. But driving is a luxury in which you do not need to indulge yourself, unless you live off the beaten path and beyond the reach of the buses.

Monza and Brianza

Like most Italian cities, Milan has its share of commuters. They come from neighborhoods in the east, west, and south, but at the end of the workday, most of the trains head north, toward the lakes. At 6 P.M., there is an all-out stampede for the city's northern stations, Cadorna and Garibaldi. There, the trains leave for the provinces of Lecco, Como, and Varese, all of them hosting bedroom communities (though that term in Italy suggests something more interesting than it might back home).

The highest concentration of commuters comes from a loosely defined area called Brianza, with Monza as its imagined capital. The suburbs are so densely populated there that just a few years ago Monza was awarded a provincial status of its own. It already has an enlarged train station, its own dialect, and a distinct flavor, combined with a noble beauty that makes it worth considering as a home base while working out of the big city.

As an alternative to commuting, entrepreneurial-minded expats might consider buying a small business in Brianza. The area is brimming with everything from travel agencies to boutiques to small factories that serve industrial clients. In Italy, it can be difficult to buy an existing business because most of them are privately held family firms, where the shareholders' number-one priority is the future of the

REGIONAL DIALECTS: BRIANZA

El Poo el sarav minga Poo se Ada e Tesin no ghe mettessen coo.
Literally, "The Po wouldn't be the Po if the Adda and Ticino didn't flow into it." That is, behind every great and powerful person is an army of helpers.

Chi ha danee fa danee, chi pioeucc fa lenden.
"People with money make more money, people with lice make lice eggs." The concept is the same the world over: It takes money to make money, and poverty breeds poverty.

O gent o argent.
"Either people or money." That is, in order to build a house, work the land, and so on, either you have friends to help you, or you're going to spend a lot of money.

next generation. That said, there are businesses for sale all the time in the outskirts of Milan, which suggests the next generation has plans of its own.

WHERE TO LIVE

Real estate prices in **Brianza** vary greatly depending on the town, ranging from the blue-collar Sesto San Giovanni, termed "the Stalingrad of Italy," to the haughty addresses of the rich and powerful. The most famous resident of nearby Arcore, for example, is media baron Silvio Berlusconi, the nation's wealthiest man and occasionally its prime minister.

Many foreigners choose **Monza** because it is well connected to the city via public transportation and yet offers the relative peace of a residential town. It is known for its good public education, though many English-speakers prefer to send their children to a British academy in town or to another of the myriad such schools in Milan.

Monza, now a suburb, once had a strong identity of its own. Americans may recognize the name from the old Chevrolet Monza. The inspiration for that model is thought to have come from the Ferrari Monza or the Alfa Romeo Monza, both of which reflect the city's fame as home to the Italian Grand Prix.

The racetrack sits inside the massive Parco di Monza, Europe's largest public park and originally the garden of the Villa Reale. The villa is the city's centerpiece, a neoclassical palace that served as the summer home for Italy's Turin-based royal family in the 19th century. The grand boulevard that leads to the palace is lined with the stately abodes of the royal court.

The Monzese cling dearly to the days of aristocracy. Many of the older generation will tell you how their grandparents were florists or tailors to the king and queen, giving the city a bourgeois flavor in the historic sense of the word. The Milanese and Monzese share a term for the modern version of such wealthy burghers, *bauscia,* which can be applied to virtually anyone who drives the latest BMW and generally espouses nouveau-riche values.

The stores and restaurants in Monza are as upscale as you can expect to see just outside the big city. The real estate prices reflect this, although you can still get much more space for the money here than in Milan. A one-bedroom apartment for a couple, roughly 70 square meters, costs in the vicinity of €120,000. The majority of the apartments were built for families, however. A three- or four-bedroom place, with lush balconies and floor space ranging from 90 to 150 square meters, costs between €160,000 and €250,000.

Rents in Monza, which has become more and more popular among young professionals, have almost reached the levels of Milan, but not quite. For example, if €800 per month affords you a small one-bedroom apartment in Milan with a kitchen tucked in a corner, in Monza it can land you a full kitchen and a larger living room. In general, you won't find the same number of tiny living quarters in Monza as you will in Milan. Most of the apartments here were designed for more comfortable suburban living.

Real estate near the park or in one of the alleys near the cathedral is the most expensive. It is also the most elegant. Many three-story buildings near the park were built for friends of the royal family. Nearer the cathedral, there are classic split-beam houses with new copper tubing and an alpine flavor. Outside that, it's the same old 1960s-era sprawl of high-rises of mediocre construction.

From Monza, Brianza extends northward through the foothills of the Alps before giving way to the towns around Lake Como. There are hilltop castles along the way, winding roads with wisteria-laced brick walls and bubbling brooks that only become polluted rivers once they've passed through Monza and Milan. Here, the real estate is a mix of apartments and villas, depending on the size of the town. Keep in mind that this is a growing suburban area, not altogether a bucolic medieval paradise like Tuscany. The beauty is the convenience of having a modern and cosmopolitan city next door, while still bordering on some of the best alpine scenery and recreation in Italy.

One of the most scenic towns is **Montevecchia,** a hilltop village with such pleasant curvy roads and leafy parks that it is on the regular Sunday circuit for cyclists from Milan. Real estate there is in the middle to high range for Brianza. A two-apartment villa costs about €400,000. Other towns in the area—**Giussano, Lissone, Carate Brianza, and Sovico,** to name a few—have a more suburban feel. Space here has become tight, ever since a housing boom kicked off in Brianza in the 1970s; apartment buildings are still going up at a clip. In a past generation, you might have expected a nice country villa for cheap. Now, much of what you will find are *palazzi,* with 10 to 20 apartments for families, ranging in price from €150,000 to €250,000 each. Rents in some of the smaller towns in Brianza are slightly lower than in Monza.

Keep in mind that Brianza is just one wedge of Milan's sprawling northern suburbs. The province of **Lecco** to the east and the province of **Varese** to the west have quiet, well-connected towns with character and history. The small and picturesque village of **Gorgonzola,** for example—where the famous cheese was born—is on the green line of Milan's subway and only about a 40-minute ride from the center. On the western side of Brianza is **Saronno,** which food buffs may recognize as the home of *amaretti* (almond cookies). The modern and reliable Malpensa Airport Express makes one of its four stops in Saronno, bringing it to within 30 minutes from downtown.

Lake Como

Stendahl, D. H. Lawrence, and other writers have heaped all sorts of praise on the lakes region, and on Lake Como in particular. Italy's best-known tour guide, Virgil, labeled it succinctly as "our greatest lake." At 416 meters, or about 1,200 feet, it is unquestionably the deepest. Alpine foothills tumble vertically into the water. The roads are lined with the kind of trees and flowers you might expect in the tropics, framed by snowcapped peaks in the near distance. It is a mystical garden suspended between the austerity of Switzerland and the relative hedonism of Italy below.

Its shape, famously described in Alessandro Manzoni's novel *The Betrothed,* is an upside-down "Y," with the southeastern leg called Lake Lecco. The most prominent villas cling to the steep banks of the opposite leg, which stretches up from Como, continues first to Tremezzo and Menaggio, where the two legs join, and then onward to the tip of the lake and the beginning of the mountainous Valtellina valley.

Once a hilly redoubt for wandering authors and a haven for tennis-playing aristocracy, Lake Como has become a home for Hollywood stars. They retreat here from the flashbulbs of Milan's catwalks, where they often show up to give designers that extra pinch of publicity. Giorgio Armani's poster boy, George Clooney, recently purchased a villa here, and Madonna often visits her friend Donatella Versace at the designer's lakeshore mansion.

Other villas have a bit more history behind them. The Villa d'Este, just outside of Como in Cernobbio, started life as the private residence of Tolomeo Gallio, the local cardinal. Throughout its 400-plus-year existence, it has been owned by a ballerina, a Napoleonic general, a queen, and a Russian empress. Today, it houses minor aristocracy as a luxury hotel. Italian and international business leaders hold their gala conferences in Cernobbio, which even today exudes a princely air.

The Villa Carlotta, farther up the lake, was built in 1690 by a family of wealthy textile merchants. It was then bought and sold by an aristocratic family before being purchased in 1843 by Princess Marianne of the Netherlands. She gave it to her daughter Charlotte, for whom it is now named. The highlight of the villa is the exotic garden that runs along the lakeshore. The towns around those two historic properties have arguably the most beautiful real estate on the lake and, as a matter of record, the highest prices.

Around the Villa d'Este, it is difficult to find any hidden jewels for sale. They've been

REGIONAL DIALECTS: THE LAKES

Cent cò, cent crap'.
"One hundred heads, one hundred opinions."

Quell che fa ciapà la cioca l'e sémper l'ûltem bicér.
"The last glass is always the one that makes you drunk."

Quii de Valtulina: scarpa grossa, crapa fina.
"People from Valtellina: big shoes, sharp minds." (That is, they may be peasants from the mountains, but they're not dummies.)

© JOHN MORETTI

rooftops near Lake Como

snatched up by very well-to-do Italians and foreigners. There are, however, still a few deals to be had near the Villa Carlotta, in the area around Menaggio and Tremezzo, the series of towns known as the Tremezzina. When people tell you they're going to visit Lake Como, this is generally where they mean. Tremezzo and Menaggio are packed with German, English, and North American tourists in the summertime, more often than not in their late 60s or 70s, enjoying lengthy meals at hotel gardens and waltzing the night away.

The best time to enjoy the lake is in the spring, before the crowds arrive. The shores explode in color, as wisteria covers the villas' iron gates and petunias hang off Roman-era walls. (The inhabitants of Lake Como, or "Lario," as the locals once called it, were Roman citizens starting in 59 B.C.) Early fall is also an excellent time to take on the hiking trails, before the cold November rain arrives. Several trails lead to mountain refuges that serve polenta and wine as a reward for the climb. Winters are deathly quiet. Rental prices in the off-season are a half or a third of what they are during June, July, and August.

WHERE TO LIVE

Real estate agents here will tell you it's too difficult to give a general price range of what is for sale, because the selection is so wide. Anything on the lakeshore itself, if a place even goes on the market, will be in the €3–4 million range. Farther inland, there are more approachable prices, at about €300,000–600,000 for a house. One item recently for sale in the town just above Menaggio was a rustic stone house with 150 square meters, a large front yard, and a lake view for €350,000.

For that same price, there are family-sized apartments for sale in large villas and castles. Since most of the villas have attained prices out of reach for the average homeowner looking to live on the lake, many large properties have been subdivided. Again, the range is vast, comprising everything from the somewhat modest €300,000 apartment to the luxurious one that runs in the millions.

A humbler option, with similarly beautiful scenery—and, more importantly, a train station within walking distance—is the eastern leg of the lake between Lecco and Varenna. The towns to watch out for in the classified ads are **Lierna, Malgrate, Mandello, and Varenna** itself.

It is common to find two-apartment villas for sale, or single-apartment villas in a cluster of others. Land isn't cheap in this part of the world, and to keep at least some open space along the lake, local governments have developers create what are known as *ville a scheira* (cluster-villas). A two-bedroom villa of this sort with a nice terrace, wine cellar, and lake view sells for about €200,000. As might be expected, a two-apartment villa sells for about twice that.

Those intent on working in Milan while living on the lake should probably consider living in Como or Lecco proper. So many people drive into Milan that it makes sense to take a train, and both cities are well connected in that regard.

In **Lecco,** a nice two-bedroom apartment with a balcony, garden, and garage by the lake will cost about €140,000. Demand there has surged in recent years, with the supply holding steady, but prices are not quite as high as in **Como,** where you can expect to pay slightly more for the same sort of apartment. Incidentally, Como is a popular spot for professional soccer players and coaches, as it is relatively close to the stadium but still far enough away from the pressures of being a celebrity in the big city.

Because the lake is a popular holiday destination, rental prices vary according to season. For a one-bedroom apartment in Menaggio, for example, expect to pay about €300 per month in winter, and twice that in the summer months.

THE NORTHEAST

It's a little unorthodox to group Veneto and Emilia-Romagna in the same chapter. The Veneto is described in weather reports and history books as the northeast, a traditionally impoverished land of boreal forests and goose farms whose underdog entrepreneurs only brought prosperity to the region in the latter half of the 20th century. Emilia-Romagna, on the other hand, described as the center-north, prides itself on a long tradition of wealth and nobility. It is a mainstay of the so-called Red Belt of left-leaning voters that includes Tuscany and Umbria, while the Veneto is a power base for the formerly separatist, anti-immigration Northern League, and friendly turf for conservatives. The two regions may share the Adriatic coast and have a common border on the Po, but the river divides centuries of cultural history. The Veneto was shaped by the Venetian Republic and the subsequent occupation by the Austrians, while the duchies of Emilia-Romagna swore loyalty to the pope, temporarily hosting the capital of the Roman Empire at Ravenna.

But Emilia-Romagna and Veneto have much more in common when you start talking about a style of living. They have some of the nation's most affluent and comfortable towns, and they contain a disproportionate share of Italy's fine art and culture. Parma, Modena, Bologna, Ferrara, Verona, and Padua are all midsized cities—large enough for a top-flight soccer team, but too small for a subway. Public transportation

THE
NORTHEAST

SLOVENIA

CROATIA

Adriatic Sea

25 mi
25 km

SWITZERLAND

Sorico
Lake Maggiore
Varese
Novara

LOMBARDIA

Lake Lecco
Bergamo
Milan
A4
A7
Tortona
Ovada
A26

Capo di Ponte
Iseo Lake
Vestone
Ghedi
A21
Cremona
A4

LIGURIA

GENOA

Gulf of Genoa

Tolmezzo
FRIULI VENEZIA GIULIA
Udine
A23
Gorizia

TRENTINO-ALTO ADIGE
TRENTO
Belluno
Piave
Valdobbiadene
Conegliano
Piave River
Treviso
Bassano del Grappa
Marostica
Cittadella
Vicenza
Verona
Lake Garda
Vestone
Mantova
Po
Parma
A14
A15
Salsomaggiore Terme
Castelnovo ne' Monti
Fivizzano
Pietrasanta
Sestri Levante
La Spezia

VENETO
Padua
Battaglia Terme
Monsélice
Montagnana
Adige River
A13
Ferrara
Modena
A22
BOLOGNA

Portogruaro
Caorle
A4
VENICE
Chioggia
Gulf of Venice
Mouths of the Po

TRIESTE
Piran

Pula

EMILIA-ROMAGNA

Comacchio Valley
Idice Reno River
Ravenna
Forlì
Rocca
Imola
A14

SAN MARINO

TOSCANA
A11

© AVALON TRAVEL

A2

N

25 mi
25 km

is still very good—in Emilia-Romagna's downtowns, for example, digital readouts at bus stops tell you how many minutes you need to wait—and with a smallish number of expats living in each of the cities, you'll never feel entirely isolated. Overall, there is a sense of community here that some may find stifling, but others will find reassuring.

For English-speakers, Bologna, Padua, Parma, and Verona are the most cosmopolitan spots, and may even feel like home, as they tend to attract the most ethnic diversity. On the flip side of the coin, non-English-speaking immigrants, especially those of Arabic or African descent, may encounter some unfriendliness in the northeast. Though local mayors have tried to brush off this reputation, racism is an unfortunate reality in parts of the Veneto.

Emilia-Romagna

WHERE TO LIVE
Bologna

Bologna's train station is the busiest in Italy, but that's mostly because passengers are passing through on their way to somewhere else. The city can't claim an art gallery on par with those in Florence and doesn't have the name-brand recognition of Venice or Pisa; Bologna's canals are all underground, and its towers don't seem to lean far enough to draw a crowd. Centuries ago, the city tried to build a cathedral larger than St. Peter's, but those plans were swiftly nixed by the Vatican.

Bologna's appeal is less obvious than that of Rome, Pisa, or Venice, but every bit as urbane. It makes fine machinery and has done so for hundreds of years. Bricks, engines, machines—before Turin started churning out cars at the turn of the 20th century, Bologna was the nation's mechanical capital. Today, the city's Ducati motorcycle factory is just one example of that legacy, and a look around any downtown parking lot shows that the industrial complex is still spitting out its profits.

Marching hand in hand with Bologna's wealth is its reputation for good living—it regularly sits in the top ten list for best places to live in Italy—and its appetite for refined cuisine. Only here can you join the Learned Order of the Tortellini, dedicated to the preservation of the city's native pasta. Tagliatelle is its younger brother, typically smothered in a ragu or sprinkled with the most luxurious of extras: truffles from the nearby mountains. Sausages are its other specialty. The term "Bologna" was borrowed by such food giants as Oscar

© JOHN MORETTI
the central square in Bologna

PRIME LIVING LOCATIONS

Meyer, but the cold cut in its hometown is no baloney. Generically called *mortadella,* it is a very respectable meat and not something to be thrown away on a cheap sandwich.

Bologna is home to Europe's oldest university, founded in 1088. The University of Bologna and its associated business and medical schools—and its highly regarded program in Art, Music, and Show (known as DAMS)—make up one of two very prestigious schools here. The other is the Bologna campus of SAIS, the Johns Hopkins University's School of Advanced International Studies. For international policy wonks, it represents the pinnacle of studying abroad in Italy.

The university atmosphere adds to a left-leaning environment, but the cost of living is anything but proletarian. Rents are on par with Milan, and the demand is steep in such a student-dominated city with a high turnover rate. A small two-bedroom apartment in the city, for example, runs about €800 per month (about €200,000 to buy it), and even those can be hard to find. Just outside the city, however, it is a different story. While the polls show that Bologna itself is one of the tightest markets for real estate, local agents seem to offer lots of comfortable suburban and country homes at reasonable prices. A nice small house in the outskirts, if uncharmingly modern, can be had for about €150,000. For €200,000 and up, you can find a country farmhouse in decent shape.

Hiking and cycling in the Bologna hills are the best way to keep in shape. It's no coincidence that several cycling champions throughout history hailed from Emilia-Romagna. Those who like to take their sports sitting down can always head out to the Stadio Comunale soccer stadium to see the red and blue take on their Emilian neighbors.

Modena

Modena is what Bologna might look like if it were boiled down to its essentials. It is smaller, but boasts a university and a soccer team, plus an extraordinary level of wealth—specifically, the highest per-capita income in Italy.

Modena's showmanship and culture can be summed up in two last names: Pavarotti and Ferrari. Both the tenor, Luciano, and the race-car pioneer, Enzo, called Modena their home. (For tax reasons, Pavarotti sometimes preferred to name Monte Carlo as his home, a subtle distinction that met with a poor reception at the Finance Ministry.) Ferrari still has its headquarters in the suburb of Maranello, and Pavarotti often did winter concerts at the city's Teatro Comunale.

The food is also world-class. Aside from its tortellini and prosciutto—Emilian staples produced in each of its cities—Modena's best-known product is balsamic vinegar, which carries a DOC label so it's not confused with inferior imitations. Less haughty is its sparkling red Lambrusco wine, present at any simple country picnic along with a *piadina* (roll-up) sandwich.

Deciding between the countryside and the downtown will be difficult. The central square and its 11th-century cathedral make for an idyllic meeting place and cultural venue, often hosting pop and rock concerts. I saw an unforgettable Bob Dylan show there, his stage sandwiched between the Duomo and the medieval clock tower.

Farther afield, the architecture becomes more modern. Modena was bombed considerably in World War II, and much of what was built afterward clearly had a more contemporary look, though perhaps more tasteful and thought-out than the postwar constructions in Milan, for example.

THE WORLD'S OLDEST WINE BAR

Osteria al Brindisi, located in a brick building next to Ferrara's cathedral, is not just any old wine bar. According to the *Guinness Book of World Records*, it is the oldest one on Earth. That's a hard record to beat. Unlike challengers to the world's largest lollipop (a peppermint-flavored structure in Denmark), al Brindisi's competitors have more than 550 years of history to reckon with.

The first documentation of Ferrara's premier drinking establishment dates back to 1435, and some of the illustrious guests to belly up to its wooden bar include the Renaissance master Titian, sculptor Benvenuto Cellini, and poets Ludovico Arisoto and Torquato Tasso. In those days, it was known as the "Hostaria del Chiuchiolino," taking its name from *ciuc*, a handy term in dialect that means "three sheets to the wind." A few decades later, a fun-loving science student by the name of Copernicus moved into a strategically located apartment in the same building. (Nonetheless, he managed to graduate from Ferrara's university at a still-collegiate 26 years old.)

It should come as no surprise that this corner of Emilia-Romagna has an enological claim to fame. The sandy fields between Ferrara and the Po River are spotted with vines. The *vini delle sabbie* are full-bodied and aromatic when they come from higher ground. When they come from the more frequently flooded land closer to the river, they become smoother and more velvety.

Federico Pellegrini, whose family runs Osteria al Brindisi, can tell you everything you ever wanted to know about the local vineyards. He's been a sommelier for 12 years. "Now I will show you a stupendous wine," he says, a black scarf tied around his neck. With a flourish that would make even Titian himself look artless and sober, he unleashes a stream of red from Mantua into a large, wine-coated glass.

A pleasant house or villa just a few kilometers outside the city can cost anywhere from €150,000 to €300,000. Around Modena, for whatever reason, the rustic houses sell for considerably less than you might expect from such a wealthy city. Attractive brick farmhouses, in need of restructuring but still inhabitable, are on the market for as little as €100,000, reaching €400,000 for a true gem. The average rent in Modena for a two-bedroom apartment is about €650 per month.

Ferrara

Once upon a time—namely, from the 13th to the 17th centuries—small and unassuming Ferrara was one of the peninsula's most important cultural centers. Its university and wealthy dukes attracted such sought-after minds as Petrarch, Tasso, and Titian. Ferrara was one of the only cities in Emilia with independence from the Florentine nobility in the Middle Ages, and it lays important claims to the development of urban planning and theater.

But in the late 1600s, the Este dynasty fell apart, and Ferrara and its dukes were all but forgotten. It spent the next few centuries as the ugly stepbrother of the wealthier neighboring states, and its poorer inhabitants developed a taste for eels from the Po River delta.

Even these days, Ferrara's enological and gastronomic delights rarely draw a crowd. Much of that has to do with geography. In the powerful triangle that comprises Emilia-Romagna's three major cities, Ferrara occupies the lonely corner. Unlike its

© JOHN MORETTI

Bikes are a must in Modena.

twin siblings, it does not share the A-1 autostrada, the country's backbone, or the parallel railway that handles most of the nation's traffic.

This anonymity can only be a good thing for anyone in search of Italian pleasures without the tourists. Ferrara is a quiet place, clean and livable. Slowly pedaling around on a bicycle seems to be the preferred mode of transportation in this city best known for its Lamborghini cars. It has a network of bike paths that leads from the medieval castle to expansive, leafy parks and stretches eight kilometers north to the banks of the mighty Po. When imagining the downtown, don't assume that the city has lost its grandeur. Its center is dominated by a bona fide castle, with turrets, a moat, and drawbridges. From there, the main pedestrian artery leads to one of the most peculiar cathedrals in Italy, crafted of pink marble and flanked by an arcade of merchants.

The moral of this fable is, if you're in search of fairy-tale Europe, where princesses and knights live among moated castles, Ferrara is the first place you should look—mostly because it won't cost a king's ransom. Real estate here goes for noticeably less than in Bologna: a modest two-bedroom apartment can be purchased for €100,000 or rented for about €550 per month. Or, for about twice that, you can move your family into a large suburban house. If your budget is healthy and your timing is right, €500,000 will land you a wonderfully restructured villa from the 19th century and a nice plot of land, a miniature fiefdom for the 21st century. Keep in mind that Ferrara lies in a floodplain, not in the hills, so the views can be pedestrian. Stately villas and estates don't appear to be as common here as elsewhere in central Italy—for example, Parma—and if you do find one, it may be difficult to convince the wealthy duchess or farmer to move out.

Parma

Parma's food requires little introduction. Parmesan, prosciutto di Parma, and its cousin, *culatello,* are among the peninsula's most important exports, and are treated as national treasures. Travelers on the Rome–Milan train will find it tempting to jump off at Parma come lunchtime, and in fact many of them do. Those who live here are particularly proud of their gastronomic heritage, but also of their art and music. Giuseppe Verdi, for example, was born just down the road, as was Arturo Toscanini.

The *parmigiani* will tell you that there is no better place in Italy to live. Public transportation is punctual, the streets are immaculate (uncluttered with cars, because many prefer to take their bikes to work), and their community spirit is known nationwide. Prices are also quite reasonable—the average two-bedroom apartment rents for €650 per month.

Indeed, the close-knit nature of its neighborhoods is one reason why some people are not keen to move to Parma. They say that gossip flies around this city as fast as it does in a small town, and as a foreigner, you may find that people know more about your life than you'd care to share.

Those in search of more privacy may be tempted to find a place in the surrounding countryside. The low-lying hills between Parma and Piacenza are famous for their dozens of medieval castles, revealing the Lombard influences of the Milanese Visconti and Sforza families, who once controlled the city. Gallic flavors are also strong, due to the French connections of Parma's subsequent rulers, the Farnese family. The picturesque burgs themselves attract many tourists today, especially Castell'Arquato and Salsomaggiore Terme. The latter is famous for its natural springs and their allegedly curative waters.

Veneto

WHERE TO LIVE
Verona

One of the selling points of Milan and Turin is that the cities have mountains, sea, and wine just a short trip way. The same can be said about a lot of Italian cities, but none of them can claim to be as centrally located as Verona. It's an ideal spot for those who don't need to work in a major city but like to have one nearby. It sits halfway between Venice and Milan, about 90 minutes in either direction. Due north are some of the most beautiful mountains in Europe, the Dolomites, and due south is the cultural and culinary haven of Emilia-Romagna. The respective homes of two extraordinary wines are just outside the city: Soave and Franciacorta. And if a 90-minute drive to the Adriatic is too long for you in the summer heat, you can cool off just next door in Lake Garda, a land of both U.S.-style amusement parks and exclusive villas of the European elite.

Then again, you may want to spend all of your time in Verona itself. You will want for little in Shakespeare's setting for *Romeo and Juliet,* even if these temptations lie outside the city walls. Verona has top-notch culture on its doorstep every year, when opera and concerts come to its coliseum, the second largest in Italy. The food is very good, though not world-renowned, and there are even two good soccer teams in town, Hellas Verona and Chievo. All in all, not bad for a community of just 250,000.

Those who want to take maximum advantage of small-city living, where you can

the fictional home of Juliet (Romeo's star-crossed lover) in Verona

ride your bicycle to work and walk around the corner to a grocery store, should consider a family apartment in the historic center. Verona can be an elegant city when it wants to be, the sort of place where even a Sunday afternoon walk around the shops calls for a suit and tie, so don't expect rock-bottom real estate prices. Then again, don't expect to pay what you would in Venice or Milan. An average two-bedroom apartment of about 60 square meters near the city center will cost about €150,000, or will rent for about €600 per month. A three-bedroom place of about 90 square meters, not far from the Arena, should cost about €250,000.

Others might prefer the suburban life, and Verona is surrounded by nice homes on vineyards and olive groves, or else steps from the shore of Lake Garda. A one-family villa with at least 200 square meters will start at €120,000 for a rather ordinary suburban home, while a large architectural wonder with an olive garden and panoramic views will cost closer to €500,000. To live like a country baron or baroness in a historic rustic estate, prepare to spend at least €250,000 for the land and the structure, and possibly just as much to turn it into something livable and attractive.

Padua

Despite its history, few tourists come to Padua except as a launching point for Venice. Those who spend the most time here are usually students assigned to programs in the city's 13th-century university, the second-oldest in Europe.

The university testifies to the city's cultural and scientific importance. Padua is a cradle of the arts, exemplified by the Scrovegni Chapel and its recently restored frescoes by Giotto. The artist Tasso once studied here, and Galileo was employed as a professor. To this day, the science program often makes headlines in newspapers and academic journals.

Modern-day Padua, population 210,000, is very industrial-looking, and many of its buildings are less than inspiring architecturally. Like Milan, Padua is now a place where people come to study or to find jobs, rather than to tour historic sites and museums. The industrial complex has lured thousands of immigrants, especially from North Africa, adding to the northeast's racial tension.

Considering the economic health of the place, housing in Padua is reasonably priced. For €80,000, you can find a fully furnished mini-apartment smack downtown. Prices vary, of course, depending on the exact location. Two-bedroom apartments in the city start at about €60,000 for purchase (or about €650 per month for rental) and reach €300,000 for a lovely three-bedroom unit measuring 100 square meters.

If the threat of encountering urban blight doesn't dovetail with your idea of living in Italy, the suburbs might be a better option, as the countryside here is dotted with fortified cities. The most noteworthy towns are found to the southwest, toward Verona: **Battaglia Terme,** with its 16th-century fortress; **Monsèlice,** with an 18th-century castle; and **Montagnana,** a citadel entirely encompassed by a turreted wall. This last town is an excellent compromise between Verona and Padua, with several cheap fixer-uppers for sale.

Here's one of them: A 150-square-meter house shaded by trees, with a dilapidated vineyard, two floors, and a classic red tile roof that costs just €60,000, but is literally falling apart at the seams. You'll have to build from scratch, but at least you'll have a nice plot of land and the frame of a house to start with. Alternatively, you could land a less charming but more healthy one-family villa in the same area for about €250,000. Not bad, when you consider it's just a 30-minute drive to Venice.

Prosecco and Grappa Country

Though small-city living has its advantages, many North Americans who come to Italy aren't looking to socialize much, and tend to settle down in the country. Veneto, more so than Emilia-Romagna, has lots of isolated hills and relaxing vineyards, extending northeast from Verona and Padua toward the border with the Friuli region. This is the land of Prosecco, Italy's answer to Champagne. The gateways to this hilly region, along the Brenta River and wedged between the Dolomites and the Adriatic, are the small towns of **Cittadella, Castelfranco, Bassano del Grappa, and Marostica.**

Like Ferrara, these villages seem cut from the pages of a storybook about knights and princesses. Both Cittadella and Castelfranco are surrounded by moats. Marostica's castle has a giant chessboard where actors in medieval costume play a human-sized version of the game. Bassano del Grappa is the architectural gem of them all, perched around a covered bridge designed by Palladio. Though the area is rustic, it has been discovered by outsiders, and the prices for an old home can reflect this. For a crumbling stone farmhouse near Marostica and Bassano del Grappa, expect to pay about €200,000.

Better deals can be had farther north, into wine country. In the **Valdobbiadene Valley,** close to Vittorio Veneto, old farmhouses with stone wine cellars sit in fields, shaded by patches of forest overlooking the Prosecco vineyards. Here, a

150-square-meter farmhouse, with the walls, roof, and floors in good shape and sitting on five square kilometers of land, sold recently for about €150,000. The facade is loaded with windows and newly fitted with wooden shutters, and the property is bordered by a waterfall.

On the lower end of the price scale is a €70,000 hilltop house of the same dimensions, with solid walls and a decent roof, but sketchy floors. Dozens of others are in the €150,000 to €200,000 range, and massive estates in decent condition can be had for less than €300,000, small vineyard included.

THE NORTHWEST

Penned in by the Alps and the Mediterranean on one end and spilling into the Po River plain on the other, Italy's northwestern corner is one of its most diverse. It boasts cobalt-blue seas and snowy peaks, birch and chestnut forests, and misty rolling vineyards, plus a wide swath of foggy rice paddies (Italy is Europe's number-one producer of rice), where locals stir their famous risotto with frogs' legs.

If this is starting to sound a bit like France, it should. Not only do Piedmont and Liguria fit snugly against the border, but much of modern-day Alpes Maritimes and the Haute Savoie once flew the Italian flag as well—or at least the flag of Piedmont's kings, who once controlled Genoa and Sardinia as well. Turin was the capital of this spacious kingdom, and later of all Italy, when Garibaldi and his men unified the country under the Savoys.

The Turinese were then, and continue to be, among the wealthiest and most progressive of their compatriots. The bespectacled liberals were the ones who came up with the idea of a united Italy in the first place, with the blessing of the king. And after their royal family was exiled, another Piedmont clan soon took their place: the Agnelli family, founders of the Fiat dynasty. Heavy industry drove the local economy throughout the 20th century, though telecommunications and other high-tech industries in and around Turin are changing that now. With high technology, a

progressive reputation, and a bounty of sea and snow, Piedmont has a lot in common with Northern California. One big difference is that outsiders haven't flooded in. Why they haven't done so is anyone's guess.

The Ligurian coast has a more international reputation, thanks to its wealthy resort towns. Glitzy San Remo, opulent Portofino, and the newly famous fishing villages of the Cinque Terre are responsible for attracting homeowner hopefuls. Parts of Liguria are expensive, and others are downright elitist, resembling the poshest enclaves of the Côte d'Azur. Much of Liguria, though, is approachable and friendly, especially the family-oriented towns around San Remo and the tucked-away villages on the mountainous inland. There is not much land, but Liguria still manages to offer something for everyone who's seeking a little slice of the Italian Riviera.

Piedmont

Turin and Lake Maggiore are two hot spots for tourists, but Piedmont's most prized territory really lies at its heart, starting south of the city and extending southeast toward the mountainous French border. Le Langhe, as the hilly area is known, is dominated by Alba, Asti, and Bra, three small cities each with separate claims to gastronomic fame. Alba is home to the white truffle. The province around Asti produces the *spumante* (sparkling wine) that bears its name. Bra's newfound identity comes in the form of Slow Food, a local nonprofit organization dedicated to the art and science of eating well. The group has attracted tens of thousands of members and fans around the world. Slow Food's cheese festival, held on odd years in Bra and host to thousands of cheesemakers, is a widely anticipated event, as is the Salone del Gusto, held in the even years and dedicated to organically grown products and local dishes and wines.

The people who come to these sorts of events look forward to a tour of Bra and its environs, which produce some of the country's most prestigious wine. You may already have heard of Piedmont's two most elite growing areas, Barolo and Barbaresco, just around the corner. The hilltop villages recall those in Tuscany, except that there are no camera shops and really no tourist infrastructure to speak of, except the local family-run *agriturismi* (rural bed-and-breakfasts) that cater to a mostly Italian-speaking public. In fact, there are few signs at all pointing to Barbaresco, making it difficult for the accidental tourist to find.

WHERE TO LIVE

The trouble for prospective homeowners is that the vineyards themselves are so pristine and priceless that there are very few houses available. Those that do go on the market from time to time are considered too valuable to be used for any other purpose than winemaking. Part of the appeal of Barolo, and one of the reasons it costs more than almost any other wine in Italy, is because the territory where it can be produced is restricted to very few acres. All the space is devoted to growing, and no new construction is allowed. The best place to start looking for a house nearby is in **Asti** and the area around **Nizza Monferrato,** also an important growing region.

In the center of Asti, a 130-square-meter home with three bedrooms, surrounded by greenery, sells for about €250,000. Prices decrease from there as you go out from the

the castle of Count Cavour in Piedmont

city, as long as you're not right in the vineyards. About 10 miles out of Asti, you can expect to pay as little as €70,000 for a 150-square-meter house. A vineyard in Nizza Monferrato, though a smallish one, can sell for about €600,000. An antique home there, in good shape, sells for about €120,000.

Lesser-known wine country lies just a few miles to the east, around **Tortona.** Up-and-coming vintners produce what they call Oltrepò Tortonese, a play on the more famous hills just over the border in Lombardy, near Pavia, called Oltrepò Pavese (see the sidebar *A Forgotten Wine is Reborn*). Aside from the wine, Tortona's cuisine draws day-trippers from Milan and Turin. Both cities are about an hour away by car, making Tortona a good option for commuters as well. Houses here cost just a fraction of what they would in Milan or Turin and are surrounded by misty vines, rather than smoggy streets.

In Tortona, a nice, two-floor walk-up in an older building with a wine cellar and a garden costs about €160,000, or as little as €30,000 if it needs a lot of work. A classic commuter home for young couples—a newly built, two-bedroom house with balconies and a garden—goes for about €120,000 in the small towns around Tortona. For those who prefer something in the countryside, a beautiful new villa, with about 400 square meters of floor space and a stable, surrounded by greenery, was selling recently for €300,000. Period farmhouses with some kind of vineyard attached will cost more.

South of Cuneo, sitting on the peaks of the French border, is the ski area of **Limone.** To call it a resort would be deceiving. It's a quiet place, far from the crowds that inhabit the rest of Piedmont's periphery—Sestriere, Courmayeur, the Matterhorn—and the prices that reflect their international acclaim. Limone, instead, is Piedmont for the recluse and anyone else looking for peace and scenery, with the option of trotting downhill to Nice or Turin for some excitement. There is even an alpine train connecting them.

A FORGOTTEN WINE IS REBORN

For wine amateurs, Oltrepò Pavese is relatively easily defined: It's known as a wine with a decent price tag at the supermarket, a red spumante that isn't always the best choice for a dinner but passes muster at a cocktail party. The area has more sophisticated wines as well, but the fizzy stuff is its trademark.

For the same wine amateurs, the name Oltrepò Tortonese means nothing at all. Although this part of Piedmont near the Lombardy border grows most of the same grapes as its cousin in the province of Pavia, few casual wine customers have ever heard of it.

At the 2002 Salone del Gusto food and wine exhibit in Turin, local producers featured the Timorasso, a naughty white grape from the Oltrepò Tortonese wine family that once covered these hills in abundance but was only rediscovered in the 1990s. The grape's flaws are many. The fruit is sparse, and picking it is a delicate operation. It's often called "the grape that rolls on the ground." Worse, the plant has several layers of leaves that are notorious for shading the fruit, and so it has to be spread far and wide—eating up lots of valuable land. It has been historically vulnerable to *Botrytis*, a parasitic mold that is harmful to grapes.

But the clay-based soil in southeastern Piedmont is perfect for Timorasso, says vintner Elisa Semino, and its enthusiastic reception by the public has made the resurrection effort worthwhile. Her family vineyard, La Colombera, based in the hillside town of Vho, has grown the grape for five years. It is a small harvest, cultivated on only about an acre of land, resulting in an exclusive label the vineyard calls "Derthona."

Another local producer, Walter Massa, says the renaissance of Timorasso was "a stroke of good luck in my life." Massa is considered the first to start growing the historic grape some 10 years ago, and he had what he says was tremendous success with his 2000 vintage of the Costa del Vento label. He has since petitioned authorities for Timorasso to be awarded the DOC (*Denominazione di Origine Controllata*) label, a decision ultimately made by the European Union. A third producer, Franco Martinetti, sold 2,000 bottles of it that same year, calling the light, pear-scented varietal "Martin."

Wine merchants around Tortona report that customers are now starting to ask for Timorasso by name. Laura Forlino, who owns a wine store in the center of town, says she has sold some 1,200 bottles of it in recent years, whereas in previous seasons, "people didn't even know what it was." Some of the North's most exclusive restaurants are also serving Timorasso: for example, the highbrow Aimo e Nadia in Milan. So are top restaurants around the rest of Europe—at Convivio in London, a bottle of Timorasso sells for the equivalent of about €50.

Timorasso remains a rarity, however. The Colli Tortonesi area is still better known for its reds. In discussions about Italian wine, it often gets a brief mention as a neighbor to the Alessandria province, boasting a handful of Barbera producers. There are some 30 vintners in the Colli Tortonesi producing a wide range of DOC wines, including Cortese, Dolcetto, and especially Barbera, plus various blends with Pinot Nero, Croatina, Riesling, and Cabernet Sauvignon.

PRIME LIVING LOCATIONS

On these mountain slopes, plumes of smoke rise from chimneys on stone houses, the silence interrupted only by the occasional clanging of cowbells. Near the ski lifts and in the tiny villages spread around Limone is an array of housing possibilities, ranging from rustic stone houses to wooden chalets to more modern condominiums.

Compared to houses in the more famous ski resorts of the Alps, some prices here are reasonable enough that you might even consider the property a second home. For example, a simple but cozy and well-built cottage made of fieldstone, with about 70 square meters spread over two floors, can be had for about €50,000. Next up on the price scale are condominiums, which often come fully furnished and are equipped with a communal pool and a large garden. They range in price from €120,000 to €200,000. Finally, individual chalets with terraces overlooking breathtaking panoramas fall into the €200,000 to €250,000 range.

As for rentals, the towns around Alba offer some very inexpensive places. In **Alba** itself, you might find a spacious four-bedroom apartment for less than €350 per month. In **Nizza Monferrato**, in the heart of wine country, you will likely not pay more than €450 per month for a nice two-bedroom apartment.

Liguria

Just before Piedmont reaches the sea, Liguria steps in its way. The name is synonymous with the Italian Riviera, a thin, mountainous coastline of fishing villages–turned–tourist attractions that extend from the French border to Tuscany. Vacationers and retirees alike have come here for more than a century to enjoy its seafood, pesto, white wine, and sunshine.

Its capital, Genoa, was once a proud seafaring republic and is now a gritty port city trying to regain its medieval title of "La Superba." While it dusts itself and its image off, tourists head for either side of the region that Genoa cuts in half: To the southeast is the *riviera di levante* (land of the rising sun), while the northwest is *riviera di ponente,* where it sets. Both have famous resorts, but different points of view.

Driving into Italy from Monaco and the French border town of Menton, you know something has changed once you pass over the line. There is no longer a customs house here—the Schengen agreement wiped them away—but the difference is immediately palpable all the same. The tunnels that cut through the cliff-lined coast get a little grayer, their rocks rougher-hewn. The hillsides are dotted with greenhouses that grow Liguria's famous flowers, and to the west, the sea is tracked by fishing boats hauling in squid. The first visible traces of civilization show up about 20 minutes from the border: the clifftop town of Imperia, followed by San Remo.

WHERE TO LIVE

Anyone who has seen or read *The Talented Mr. Ripley* has some idea of **San Remo**'s jet-set reputation in decades past. These days, the resort is best known for its annual music festival, where Italian pop stars are made. The festival was started in the Fascist era as a way to build a pan-Italian cultural identity, and that popular spirit pervades to this day. Unlike Portofino and other swanky centers of the Levante, San Remo is unpretentious and hosts hundreds of summer homes for the Milanese middle class. Even its casino has a casual atmosphere when compared to nearby Monte Carlo.

The downtowns of San Remo, and especially Imperia, hold little appeal for homeowners looking for the best of the Riviera. At times, they can be grim. The better real estate lies in the small beach towns on either side of the cities, or in the mountains farther inland. In the surrounding villages, you should be able to find a smallish stone home, without much land around it, for less than €100,000. A well-restored, three-bedroom country home in the hills just behind San Remo, with a view of the sea,

© BLUEDARKAT/123RF

harbor in the fishing village of Camogli

should sell for between €200,000 and €250,000. These kinds of stone houses often sit on olive groves and almost always have an ample garden where you can grow fresh basil to make pesto. Prices per square meter become much more expensive when you move down to the waterfront. There, villas are generally divided into apartments, as there is little space for new construction on the steep slopes. Expect to hear prices between €300,000 and €500,000 for a nicely furnished family apartment.

Or, you may decide to do what many bargain-hunting Europeans started to do in the early 1990s, and explore the mountain valleys farther inland, where local traditions are strongest and the real estate relatively cheap. The hottest spot these days is the group of valleys running from Liguria's highest peak, Monte Saccarello, along Route 548 past Badalucco to the coast near San Remo. The tight alleys of **Andagna, Triora,** and **Agaggio** are surrounded by oleander and rhododendron, the refinished houses painted pink and ocher, others awaiting final touches of their new owners' choosing. The valley has dozens of characteristic stone homes in need of serious work but selling for less than €20,000, 12th-century mills for less than €50,000, and fully restored cottages, complete with horse stables, for less than €100,000. These are true mountain hideouts, where small trattorie serve pasta with walnut sauce, and yet the towns also hold festivals dedicated to stockfish—after all, the beach is just 20 minutes away.

Rents are not cheap on the Ligurian seaside, especially in the Levante. Lots of foreign services offer weekly rates for tourists, and the monthly rentals, which are slightly harder to come by, reflect the scarcity. Still, in **Rapallo,** for example, you can find a large four-bedroom apartment with an expansive terrace overlooking the sea for about €1,000 per month. Renters will have more luck on the Ponente side. **San Remo,** in particular, has lots of options for short-term rentals, and some great deals—as little as €10 per square meter. For example, you could find a three-bedroom apartment measuring approximately 80 square meters for about €800 per month.

The Levante

The Levante is a spectacular place to visit, but good values for homes are few and far between. Portofino is its most elite port of call, a de rigueur stopover for well-equipped yachts and their passengers. Some not-so-famous people have managed to afford homes in the two cities that flank Portofino, Santa Margherita and Rapallo, but there is scant room or tolerance for new construction on the steep rocky coast, and so prices there, too, are very high. South of Rapallo, you'll find the **Cinque Terre**—five small fishing villages hugging their respective inlets. U.S. guidebooks have given the towns a mythical reputation that eludes most Italians, and so tourists come every year to walk the hilly hiking trails and ponder this pristine scenery.

In my opinion, the nicest two towns in the Levante are at its extremes: **Camogli** in the north and **Portovenere** in the south. The first is a more down-to-earth Portofino, with the same pastel buildings but more palatable prices. Camogli's finest hour is when the townspeople put on a giant fish fry, preparing the day's catch in pans that are at least 10 feet wide. Portovenere is a little more upscale.

With some exceptions, the available property on the coastline consists of apartments in three- or four-family villas, or else in a larger apartment building. In **Rapallo,** a nice three-bedroom apartment geared toward foreigners sells in the €300,000 range. Alternatively, you might look a little farther inland. Just 20 minutes into the hills from Portofino, around **Fivizzano,** rustic stone houses sell for as little as €50,000, though they would need thorough restructuring.

THE CENTRAL REGIONS

Well, this ist it. The promised land for well-to-do foreigners who have always dreamed of owning a house in Italy. It's no mystery why thousands of North Americans and Northern Europeans have chosen the subtle curves of the Apennines as their new home. Tuscany, Umbria, and Le Marche represent the quintessential Italian retreat, evoking daydreams of cloudless mornings in the garden and homegrown picnic lunches among olive groves. An afternoon outing might include a trip to the thermal spas near Arezzo, wine-tasting in Montepulciano, or a walking tour of some of Florence's Renaissance art and architecture. Even the drive between these cities is an experience that other tourists travel thousands of miles to enjoy on vacation.

From Lucca and the Mediterranean beaches of Versilia to the quiet Adriatic solitude of Le Marche, there are lots of options for prospective homeowners spread across the breadth of the peninsula. The trick is to find an area that hasn't been too "discovered" yet, then determine if there's a good reason why it hasn't. You need to hone in on the regional peculiarities that fit your personality and the housing prices that fit your budget.

Tuscany

Tuscany requires little introduction, as it has become the hottest real estate market for Anglos since the rush to southern France in the 1980s. The ocher-colored house on the hill with the cypress-lined drive is now faded by camera flashes, and anyone that hasn't been there need only read the deluge of literature expounding on the pleasures of living in this Italian paradise.

The pictures don't lie, and every praising word is true, though it is hard to express in words the unique appeal of Tuscany without coming off as trite, if I haven't already. It is a subtle landscape of olive groves and vineyards, with forests spilling out chestnuts, white truffles, hares, and wild boar, just as they did centuries ago.

Tuscans turn to the Renaissance for their identity. This golden period not only produced the region's beautiful art and architecture, but it also gave the rest of the peninsula Dante, whose Florentine dialect would become the national standard. The scent of the era is so strong here, you get the impression that the average Tuscan would prefer to be living in the 15th century. Annual medieval festivals here are greatly anticipated events of high pageantry; feudal flags are unfurled, while men in tights and silly hats proclaim the local lore with period music, food, and contests.

Ancient rivalries between the region's major cities endure to this day. Livorno and Pisa still avenge centuries-old grudges on the soccer field and in the grandstands; a Florentine license plate in Arezzo still elicits a snarl. But the feuding doesn't stop at the town line. Within the cities, neighborhoods have a go at each other each year in such anticipated events as the Palio of Siena and the Giostra del Saracino in Arezzo. And then, within the neighborhoods themselves, battles between families and even family members can be dragged out for decades. This region that claims to have united the country linguistically is actually about as fractious as they come.

Rural Tuscany remains a fiefdom of country barons—politically progressive but culturally conservative—and their elected leaders reflect this dichotomy. This is the Red Belt of Italy, a historically left-leaning community that can claim the first legal codes in the world outlawing the death penalty. At the same time, local entities make sure that nothing ever changes here aesthetically, demanding that even factories have a characteristic red tile roof. Altering the color of a window shutter can give rise to a protracted battle with the town authorities.

The architectural intactness of the landscape and the aroma of old money

© LUCIE ERICKSEN

The Arno River winds through Florence.

have helped lure legions of foreigners—all eager to drive vintage cars on roads winding through sunflower fields to turreted hilltop villas—to Tuscany's real estate agencies. These days, if you stop by an agent's office in Lucca or Siena, be prepared to see a long list of properties selling for well over €1 million.

WHERE TO LIVE
The High End

The best-known market for foreigners is **Chianti,** often dubbed "Chiantishire" for the overwhelming number of English homeowners that have moved into the vineyards between Florence and Siena. Since the 1960s, the primary appeal of this region has been its wine—it's been exported to Britain for hundreds of years. In the 1980s, the Dutch, the Germans, and the Swiss arrived, giving the entire region a Northern European accent and bringing the prices of real estate to stratospheric levels. Some of the more noteworthy neighbors include the rock star Sting, who has a home in the town of Montevarchi.

Chianti's expats have long experimented with making the local wine. More recently, expats in other important growing regions, such as the one between **Montalcino** and **Montepulciano,** have begun producing wine. This crescent of vineyards is flatter than the rolling sagebrush of Chianti but spiked with hilltop medieval towns. Its wealth of monasteries, Renaissance monuments, and thermal springs make it quintessentially Tuscan, and so it should come as no surprise that real estate prices have gone through the roof here, too. The swath of million-euro properties extends from the outskirts of Pienza, a Renaissance jewel, northeast to Cortona, where Frances Mayes wrote her best seller, *Under the Tuscan Sun.* If you meet other North Americans in Cortona, they're likely to be students in the local language program for foreigners, real estate shoppers, or here to catch a glimpse of Ms. Mayes's home.

the Arezzo home depicted in Roberto Benigni's film *Life Is Beautiful*

The area between Cortona and Arezzo, the **Valdichiana,** is far from undiscovered, but for some reason it has been spared the full colonization of Tuscany's other scenic venues. Its villages are quaint and authentic, braced by medieval walls and towers, but skipping the fanfare for tourists. And while the architecture is nothing special in Chianti, near Arezzo you'll find elaborately finished *palazzi nobili* (noble palaces) with imposing gates and driveways.

Arezzo is a particularly well-preserved medieval city, although the Florentines worked hard during the Guelf and Ghibelline wars to ensure that it would never rise to the prominence of Florence.

WHOLESALING THE TUSCAN DREAM

Don't bother asking in the local tourist office in Cortona where Frances Mayes lives. The American author, whose best-selling *Under the Tuscan Sun* portrays her part-time life there, doesn't seek publicity, and has apparently asked the tourist office to ward off the curious. "It's outside of town, in the hills over there," came the vague response from the functionary at the tourist board. When asked for more specific directions, I was told, "The house is not on our map, I can't help you."

Ms. Mayes's well-worn formula for success? Buy a gorgeous villa in a spectacularly beautiful location somewhere in Europe, set out to fix it up, and confront the usual predicaments that accompany any housing renovation. Meanwhile, get to know some of the locals and their folklore, imbibe the regional wines, learn at least one ancient art—such as the pruning of olive trees—and write a fabulously successful book about the experience.

As Peter Mayle did in the 1980s with his *A Year in Provence* and its sequels, Ms. Mayes tills the soil of the travel memoir—*Under the Tuscan Sun* was on the *New York Times* best-seller list for well over a year. Like Mr. Mayle, she has spawned a merchandising machine with *Under the Tuscan Sun* date books and calendars.

"The town spends a lot of money each year for advertising, but this simple book brings more people to our town than any government initiative," says Marco Molinese, a grocer in Cortona who, like most traders in town, considers Ms. Mayes a friend. "But the locals, they don't know her or the book," he adds. Making further inquiries about the author on a stroll down Via Nazionale, Cortona's main street, I find out that a local bookstore has sold out of her book. Giulio Nocentini, who has run the store for 45 years, says he has read it and thinks it's a suitable primer for tourists visiting the area. "But no Italian would want to read it. We're quite accustomed to having foreigners try to interpret our lives," he says. Mr. Nocentini says the book is selling the Tuscan dream. He has seen a lot more North American tourists arrive at his door as a result, in search of that dream or the next closest thing—a glimpse of the author and her house.

(Contributed by Paul French, a Canadian travel writer who lived in Tuscany for two years.)

The beige buildings are so characteristically Tuscan that filmmaker Roberto Benigni chose Arezzo as the backdrop for *Life Is Beautiful.* Locals take much less pride in this silver screen claim to fame than in the city's splendid works by Renaissance painter Piero della Francesca, or even in their renowned antiques market. Another perk to this area is that it is next to Italy's major north–south highway and a stop on the high-speed Rome–Milan train line.

In the more remote corners of this countryside especially, there are still some reasonably priced old homes. For example, Arezzo-based real estate firm Tagete (www.tagete. agenzie.casa.it) recently advertised a rustic stone farmhouse, six miles outside Arezzo, with a dominating hilltop view for just €250,000. That probably represents the lower end of the price spectrum in the area (at least for something that is well-built.) Further up the scale, the same real estate company proposed a beautifully restored 17th-century mill, with fountains and period fireplaces, for €650,000.

Bargain-Hunting

Driving south of Montalcino along Route 323, you'll arrive in the **Val d'Orcia,** a more sparsely inhabited area unmarked on many tourist itineraries. The Val d'Orcia produces some wine, but it is more famous for Tuscany's other agricultural products: olive oil, pecorino cheese, honey, and saffron. One of the many high points of life in this rural area is picking chestnuts in the forested hills and bringing them home to prepare flour for bread or even pasta. There is a wealth of hiking trails nearby, especially on Monte Amiata, a modest ski area in the winter. Much of the land is protected, as it is home to such rare species as the European wolf, and this also means that there are relatively few houses. Luckily, the ones for sale aren't very expensive—within the €300,000 range for something in good shape.

The biggest challenge to living here is its remoteness. The largest towns around Monte Amiata have only about 5,000 inhabitants, which means there aren't very many services nearby. Those who plan to settle here should be dedicated to country living. It is a long, albeit scenic, drive to any city.

Farther south are the valleys and pastures that make up the **Maremma.** This is cowboy country, complete with rodeos and a beef-heavy diet. It, too, is remote, well off most guidebook itineraries, and yet full of Etruscan monuments and natural wonders. One of my favorite spots in Italy is here, in Saturnia—thermal springs just off a country road. They are semicircular white pools, formed by the calcium in the volcanically heated water. Romans come up for the weekend to smear themselves with the warm, white mud.

This ancient homeland of the Etruscans extends all the way north to the town of Volterra, known for its mining. This whole corner of Tuscany offers reasonable prices on homes, as long as you steer clear of the Argentario peninsula (the takeoff point for ferries bound for the isle of Elba), which is quickly gaining appeal among foreigners.

There are other hidden niches in Tuscany, which, after all, is a pretty big place. You really never know what might turn up. Maybe someone in Chianti needs cash in a hurry. Who knows? You could even see an entire Tuscan village go up for sale. In 2002, the regional government put a 1.4-square-kilometer medieval burg on the auction block, starting at €300,000. (Don't feel too bad if you missed it—it was described as a real fixer-upper.) Not long before that, all 18 houses in the town of Toiano, near San Gimignano, were placed simultaneously on the market, each priced at about €500 per square meter. The island of Pianosa was put on the auction block in the fall of 2003, along with its own police station, for €8 million. If you can't afford an entire Tuscan island, maybe you'd settle for a slice of Tuscan beach? The bidding for one in the town of Portoferraio started at just €5,000.

Rentals

Arezzo is a very stately city with relatively high rents. Downtown, expect to pay €600–800 per month for a two-bedroom apartment. But just a few kilometers outside the city, near Cortona, a one-bedroom apartment with a garden can be found for about €350 per month. Family villas in the area can rent for as little as €650 per month for something very small in an uninteresting town, to nearly €10,000 per month for the lap of luxury. On average, though, expect to see prices closer to €2,000 per month for family villas in the heart of Tuscany.

Most of the nicer villas in Tuscany are rented out to foreigners on a weekly basis.

Websites such as www.tuscandream.com offer a week's stay in gorgeous villas for €2,000–4,000 per week for a place that sleeps 6–8 people. Couples can rent a single-bedroom residence for closer to €500 per week.

Umbria

If real estate agents blindfolded you, drove you to Umbria, and told you it was Tuscany, you'd have little reason to doubt them when the blindfold came off. Just about everything in Umbria looks, feels, and tastes like Tuscany, at least at first glance. There are fortified hilltop villages with Renaissance frescoes, rolling hills, fertile valleys, good local wines, and tasteful stone houses. Even the bread and prosciutto are made without salt, just like in Tuscany. This is a throwback to the days when the popes in Rome denied the central regions their salt to break their independent streak. That was in 1540. Like the Tuscans, the Umbrians don't forget their past.

Aside from the distinct Umbrian accent, the biggest difference between the two regions is in their people's respective characters. While the Tuscans are known for their sarcastic wit and appetite for a good, foul-mouthed debate, the Umbrians are more inward-looking and gentle people who prefer candid statements and shy from confrontation. After all, the region produced both St. Francis of Assisi and St. Valentine, from Terni, universal symbols of peace and love and all that warm, fuzzy stuff that would be mocked in Machiavelli's Tuscany.

They say that this quiet introspection and humility come from the region's landlocked hills and the agricultural lifestyle that they breed. Umbria is called the "green heart of Italy," thanks to its position in the very center of the peninsula and its endless shades of green, from the tobacco plants of the Tiber Valley to the grassy hills dotted with olive groves. The painter Pietro Perugino was inspired by this idyllic countryside to produce *The Adoration of the Magi* (1504), considered the precursor of modern landscape painting. It is a lot more lush and fertile than the Middle Eastern shepherds might have remembered it.

WHERE TO LIVE

Running down a list of Umbria's cities, you'll see a lot of familiar names, but they're not necessarily the best places to look for a house. Assisi, for example, is a marvel of a city and a major stop on any religious pilgrimage because of the Basilica of San Francesco, but the ultra peaceful, almost lunar landscape around it is practically uninhabited. Perugia is another stunning hilltop city, renowned for its university for foreigners, but locals grumble that it has become crime-ridden in recent years. Terni, the home of St. Valentine, is not in itself a very lovable city, though the countryside nearby deserves some attention.

From a homeowner's perspective, the number-one place to settle in Umbria has long been **Todi,** situated halfway between Perugia and Terni. Expat homeowners and those looking to join the club have already pushed the selling price of attractive houses there beyond the half-million-euro mark.

Not far away, however, there are still intriguing stone farmhouses, with four

© JOHN MORETTI

Pigeons flock to a fountain in Narni.

bedrooms and set on a few square kilometers of land, for about €200,000, though you will probably have to invest that same amount to get them into livable shape. Alternatively, there are finished homes of similar dimensions and character for €400,000 to €500,000 if you want to spare yourself the effort. If your heart is set on living very close to Todi, but you are looking to spend about €200,000 or less for something in good shape, you should steer away from rustic farmhouses and look at one-family villas, something that might be called a cottage in the United States.

Farther south, along the border with Lazio, is an even better option in the towns between **Terni** and **Orvieto.** It's amazing this area isn't more densely populated, the towns of **Narni** and **Amelia** in particular. Both are stunning fortified hill towns, surrounded by olive trees in the low-lying hills west of Terni. They started off life as Etruscan settlements, became important Roman strongholds, and later were medieval fortress towns. The flavor of the Middle Ages is everywhere here, especially when Narni holds its annual medieval celebration, La Corsa all'Anello. The municipally owned, underground taverns in each of the town's quarters open their doors to the public, and the pasta and wine flow freely.

Best of all, this seemingly isolated corner of pastoral paradise, teeming with herds of sheep, is just 40 minutes by car from Rome. The prices hardly reflect this. Like anywhere else in Italy, the options range from a €500,000 architectural wonder to a pile of rocks, but there are some real bargains in between. A real estate agent from the Gabetti franchise in Terni told me a story of a Scottish couple who showed up in 2002 looking to spend less than €75,000, and found a nearly inhabitable farmhouse for €30,000. For that price, don't expect anything too fancy, but at least the place will have charm. Houses in this corner of Umbria are often warm and uncomplicated—much like the reputed character of Umbrians themselves. Many are built of rough fieldstones, approached by driveways that are little more than wheel tracks in the grass at the side of a white, limestone pebble road. Inside, the dominant feature will probably be a stone hearth where you can bake bread like the locals, sticking it on a grate over the coals and finishing the crust by covering it with ashes.

In Terni and the outlying towns, such as Narni, rents are low. The monthly rent for a three-bedroom place there, even a massive one, will rarely crest €400 per month. Rents in **Perugia,** however, are quite a bit higher. A three-bedroom apartment near the University for Foreigners should run at least €750 per month.

Le Marche

When American homeowners in Le Marche tell you how they ended up in this mountainous region on the Adriatic, the story often starts out with a dream about Tuscany. A couple plans to buy their dream home near Chianti or Montepulciano. They start clicking through postings on the Internet, and soon come to the conclusion that Tuscany is too expensive for their budget. Then they move on to their fallback, Umbria. Back in the late 1990s, this was a feasible alternative, and English and U.S. newspapers heralded Umbria as the new frontier. But even by the turn of the millennium, much of Umbria had outpriced itself as well.

"Prices in Tuscany can be prohibitive, and Umbria, though a little cheaper, is not miles away," said Mike Braunholt of Britain-based Prestige Properties, one of many foreign real estate firms active in central Italy. "Le Marche is the third wave." When I spoke to him, his group was listing an unfinished three-bedroom country home in Umbria, sitting on a few acres of olive grove, for about €280,000. At the same time, they were offering a similar three-bedroom house in Le Marche, also in need of renovation, for about €20,000. "Keep in mind," Braunholt said, "that many of these places aren't much more than bundles of rocks." Both houses needed big-ticket items like a new roof and floor, which might add an additional €300,000 to the investment.

While you can never judge the price of a home by the region alone, it's usually a safe bet to say that a property in Le Marche is going to be cheaper than a comparable one in Tuscany or Umbria. Le Marche is the younger, harder-working sibling of the two noble regions, and it bends over backward to market itself as a vacation destination, plastering posters all over Italian airports and train stations, and even on the trains themselves.

It shouldn't be a hard sell. Mountains make up 30 percent of its territory—and real mountains, too, the kind with snow at the top and rocky faces. It has vineyards, some notable art and architecture, and beaches—something you won't find in Umbria. It also happens to be the accordion capital of the world; the town of Castelfidardo is famous for the handcrafted instruments.

Le Marche takes its name from "borderland," as it was commonly the battleground for the Papal States' expansionist plans. But nature lovers will get more pristine beauty for their money in Le Marche than anywhere else in central Italy. Those restoring old homes can expect fewer bureaucratic battles. The *marchigiani* are eager to please.

One issue has stifled mass investment by foreigners thus far: Le Marche is not very close to the country's two major international airports, in Rome and Milan. In fact, it is about as distant from them as you can get in Italy. This may become less of a problem in the future. The fast rise of budget carriers in Italy means that the country's smaller airports are gaining European routes, and Le Marche's airport in Ancona has emerged as a front-runner for that business—along with Pisa and Bologna, which aren't too far away.

WHERE TO LIVE

For all the snide comments painting the *marchigiani* as backward sheep farmers, their region has made some impressive contributions to Italy's cultural heritage. The cities of **Urbino, Ascoli Piceno,** and **Jesi** aren't on the standard tourist itinerary, though they

STARTING AN *AGRITURISMO*

Lori Cintioli and her family used to live in Castelfidardo, a small town in Le Marche. Cintioli ran a clothing store, while her husband was a craftsperson. Then came the big decision: They sold their apartment and moved to the countryside. "With the money from the apartment's sale and from a bank loan, we bought four and a half hectares (11 acres) of land and an old farmhouse that we started to restore," Cintioli says.

A 1985 law gave farmers the chance to offer accommodation, food, and drink, and to organize activities for tourists. Essentially, it made applying for hotel and restaurant licenses easier. The only conditions were that farming had to remain their main business, and the products served had to be mostly homemade, in order to set up such an *agriturismo*.

That proved to be a sticking point for New York native Nora Kravis, who started renting rooms on her Tuscan farm in 1988. She applied for an agritourism permit in her town of Radda, in the Chianti area, but the authorities turned her down. That was because Kravis was a veterinarian, and she earned more money from that profession than from farming itself. To run an *agriturismo*, farming has to be your major source of income. It took her seven years to get the municipal government to change its mind. After she passed an exam for her license, she started serving local produce and selling the goat milk, cashmere, and related skin care products that she makes on the farm.

Despite the potential obstacles that Italians like the Cintioli family and foreigners like Kravis face, the trend of starting

an *agriturismo* is catching on. In 2001, the number of employees working in agriculture saw its first increase since World War II, and there are now more than 10,000 *agriturismi* operating across the country. In an average year, more than two million visitors, 25 percent of whom are foreigners, stay in them.

"When I started my business in 1990, the *agriturismi* of this valley offered accommodation for 50 people only," says Vittorio Cipolla, who manages his own farm resort in Val d'Orcia, Tuscany. "Now there are some 150 *agriturismi* with an average of 10 beds each."

One of the premier success stories is located just down the road from Kravis, where, incidentally, her skin care products are proudly offered to guests: at La Petraia, owned and operated by a Canadian couple. There, Susan McKenna Grant and her husband, Michael, have built the quintessential *agriturismo*, complete with a Noah's Ark of native livestock and game surrounding the beautiful stone house. A Europe-trained chef, Susan draws eggs from her chicken coops, aromatic greens from her sprawling fields of herbs, fresh peas from her terraced vegetable garden, and fruit from medieval orchards to produce some of the most gratifying dinners in Chianti. Michael, meanwhile, travels between his finance job in Toronto and his mountain of administrative duties at the farm. Together, they have proved that with the right skills, patience, and, of course, capital, these flighty Tuscan fantasies can be etched, in fact, in stone.

should be, and they probably will be once travelers start looking to Le Marche to find some of Italy's undiscovered treasures. They are good places to start searching for homes.

Though it won't stun you with its size, the way Brunelleschi's dome in Florence does, Urbino's Palazzo Ducale is considered by many art critics to be the pinnacle of Renaissance architecture. And if that's a surprise, this probably will be as well: The artist Raphael was born here, and a modest local museum holds some of his works. This all may seem unexpected for such an out-of-the-way city, but Urbino is known among Italians as a *città d'arte* and a cultural center, and indeed, its university is respected nationwide. Its students make up half of the population and give the otherwise quiet and somber area a steady nightlife and a decadent edge.

The other cultural hot spot in Le Marche is at the region's southern end, in the province of Ascoli Piceno. Even Urbino fails to gather very much international attention, so you can't be blamed if you've never heard of Ascoli Piceno, though if you lived in Roman times, you certainly would have. Ascoli was an important ally of the Latin tribes, and one of the protagonists of the Social Wars that aimed to overthrow Rome's privileged class. The remains of those days can be seen in the city's gates, its ruined temple, and the Roman amphitheater just outside town, in Ricci.

The city itself can be dirty and noisy, but the countryside around it is peppered with isolated towns and historic real estate at reasonable prices. Fixer-uppers with some land and a lot of charm start as low as €60,000, or €100,000 for something in better shape.

One of the more historically significant towns in the area is **Fermo,** once a Roman stronghold and later a university town. Its undisturbed beauty and its hilltop position about five miles from the sea give it everything a homeowner could ask for. About €130,000 in Fermo can buy you a historic villa with handsome columns, boasting ornate details but awaiting quite a lot of work, on several acres of forested land.

The disadvantage of this southern corner, and Urbino, too, is that they are both far away from the main city, Ancona. Then again, some people might consider that a blessing. Ancona is a busy port with an interesting walled center, but other than that, it's a pretty dreary-looking place. While the *New York Times* called it a "city of revelations" in a recent travel article, James Joyce put it down as a "filthy hole," and that was before it was bombed during World War II, flooded, and destroyed by an earthquake. It's hard to believe that some of the nicest real estate in Le Marche is less than 10 miles away.

On the hills just inland of the city, the town of Jesi attracts a lot of foreign attention these days, not so much for its elegant theater and churches and 14th-century walls as for the stately homes dotting the countryside around them. A good case study is the stretch of vineyards between Jesi and Osimo, which grows a potent white wine, Verdicchio. This varietal was forgotten for many years in Italy, as were many of the vineyards that grew it. The result is a community of rustic houses in need of repair, sitting on lots of cultivated land. Recently, a survey of a dozen of them pegged asking prices at between €60,000 and €120,000 for those most in need of repair. Those that have already been restructured were selling for about twice that amount.

This still seems like a bargain once you take a look inside the refinished properties. A unique farmhouse that recently was selling for about €130,000 boasted 500 square meters on two floors and an annex, and sat on several square kilometers of panoramic vineyards. The ground floor had two large storage rooms and stables fitted with wooden beams. On the exterior were twin stone staircases leading to the second floor, comprising a kitchen, a central fireplace, and six rooms. The catch: You'll need to hook up the water and electricity, as well as rebuild the roof and floors.

THE SOUTH

If you've never been to Italy before, you might envision a seaside land of spaghetti and mandolins, where families gather at the cemetery on Sunday. You might imagine a lunch with lots of mozzarella, arguments, and gesticulations, until the red wine engenders a spontaneous outburst of Neapolitan song. You've heard about the tradition of women bringing out the coffee as their dark and handsome husbands, named Mario and Salvatore, discuss politics over a game of cards.

In fact, many travelers come to Italy expecting these kinds of stereotypes and instead find something very different. These vacationers never venture south of Rome. The regions of Campania, Sicily, Calabria, Basilicata, and Puglia, collectively called the Mezzogiorno (Midday), represent the Italy of popular imagination, since so many southerners emigrated overseas and brought their customs with them.

The area is still poorer than the North, and joblessness persists, but many expatriates choose the Mezzogiorno for its soul, which is concentrated on such human affairs as the family.

The region has an ideal climate for a life of leisure. Temperatures rarely reach freezing, the land is dotted with almond and lemon trees, and some of its beaches are the sandiest and most isolated in all of Italy. It offers all of Italy's renowned recreation but serves it up with a southern twist. For example, other regions may be better known

© PERSEOMEDUSA/123RF

THE SOUTH

Adriatic Sea

Vieste

A14

Vasto

Termoli

Gargano Promontory

Manfredonia

MOLISE

Barletta

BARI

Polignano
a Mare

Fasano

Foggia

Molfetta

Cisternino

Monopoli

Brindisi

Bojano

Candela

PUGLIA

Alberobello

Ostuni

Martina
Franca

A14

Lecce

SALENTO

A16

BASILICATA

Matera

Maglie

Benevento

Tricase

A1

CAMPANIA

POTENZA

Pisticci

Taranto

NAPLES

Eboli

Gulf of

Amalfi

Policoro

Taranto

Sorrento

Amalfi Coast

A1

Capri

*Gulf of
Salerno*

Agropoli

Laurito

Cariati

*Gulf of
Policastro*

*Pollino
National
Park*

Corigliano
Calabro

Tyrrhenian

Cosenza

Crotone

CALABRIA

Sea

CATANZARO

*Gulf of Santa
Eufemia*

*Gulf of
Squillace*

A3

Guardavalle

Aeolian Islands

Rosarno

Lipari Island

Bovalino
Marina

*Vulcano
Island*

Messina

Milazzo

Reggio di
Calabria

Ionian

*Ustica
Island*

A18

Melito di
Porto Salvo

Sea

Patti

Taormina

PALERMO

Cefalu

A20

Mt Etna
10,902ft ▲

Catania

Erice

SICILIA
Sicily

A19

Alcamo

Corleone

Enna

rapani

Caltanissetta

Siracusa

A29

Caltagirone

Marsala

Gela

Modica

Porto
Empedocle

*Gulf of
Gela*

Vittoria

0   25 mi

© AVALON TRAVEL

Mediterranean Sea

0   25 km

for their skiing, but you can still make turns down Mount Etna's volcanic cone and some snowy peaks in Calabria. The rest of what made Italy famous—food, wine, and history—the South pulls out in spades.

Most of the *primi piatti* (first courses) and *dolci* (desserts) that inhabit North America's Little Italy menus (spaghetti alla marinara, orecchiette, cannoli, granita, pizza, etc.) are southern creations. Greco di Tufo is a prized wine from Campania; Sicily provides the world with Malvasia and Nero d'Avola grapes and their associated labels, and Puglia is known for its Primitivo. In fact, any enological tour is a good way to discover the South's ancient roots. Italy was Oenotria (Land of Wine) to the Greeks—and they weren't referring to Tuscany. The colonies of Magna Graecia comprised everything from Puglia west to Sicily, and its cities were legendary: Syracuse (modern-day Siracusa), in Sicily; Croton (Crotone), the home of Pythagoras, in Calabria; and Neapolis, the "new city," which now seems an odd way to describe Naples.

The South offers everything a tourist could want, but above all, it represents a good real estate investment. There are few foreigners here, even at a time when local governments and the European Union are offering money and low-interest loans to cities to make them more welcoming for tourists. This means that the Mezzogiorno could be pay dirt for pioneers. Old farmhouses are still relatively cheap in Puglia and Sicily, both of which are up-and-coming travel destinations. Naples itself is an attractive place for adventurers because of its undiluted Italian flavor and vibrant atmosphere, all for a cost of living that is relatively low.

Naples

"See Naples and die," they say, a nod to one of the most captivating urban landscapes in Italy. The city is spread out before Mount Vesuvius and embraces an azure bay. If the proverb sounds a little melodramatic, that should be your first hint about the character of this city and its inhabitants. Life is drama in Naples, a city that gave the world the crooner Enrico Caruso, the comedian Toto, and the eternal diva Sophia Loren. Every little triumph and trial evokes an outpouring of emotions, coming hot and fast like an erupting volcano.

The city's tempo is just as chaotic. While the southern drawl is as drawn out as a typical Neapolitan lunch break, mopeds buzz through the streets at breakneck speeds, and red lights are considered suggestions. Laws are written for someone else as far as the Neapolitans are concerned, and only the smartest people, the logic continues, will find a way to get around them. When legislation went into effect requiring all Italians to buckle up in their cars, someone made a great deal of money selling T-shirts in Naples with a seatbelt printed across the front.

The crime rate has improved in the past decade, and Naples is no longer the pit of petty pilfering it once was, but purse snatchers do still exist. The Baroque palaces have been cleaned up for tourists, but make no mistake: Naples is still a gritty town. You still have the occasional garbage-collectors' strike, which is about as unpleasant a strike as any, plenty of drug deals in the bad neighborhoods of town, and other nuisances caused by organized crime and general corruption. Naples is edgy and unpredictable but really only dangerous for those who go looking for trouble.

Restaurants here set the standard for a cuisine that is termed "Italian" abroad. Real *mozzarella di bufala* can only be found in Campania; seafood dishes are simple and excellent; and Naples's historic pizzerias serve what is, no discussion allowed, the best pizza in the world. (Warning: Living here can be hazardous to your waistline.)

Again, only adventurous and patient people should consider making downtown Naples their home, but those who do will find reasonable prices for living quarters. For about €200,000, you can find a four-bedroom, 150-square-meter apartment in the city center. Renters can find small places for as low as €400 per month, while the €700 per month you would pay for a studio apartment in Rome or Milan can land you a three-bedroom, 100-square-meter apartment in Naples.

WHERE TO LIVE
The Amalfi Coast and the Islands

Neapolitan music is known around the world, in particular, *"Torna a Surriento,"* or "Come Back to Sorrento." The song tries to lure a lover back to the Amalfi coast, a stretch of spectacular shoreline south of Naples where the scent of oranges lingers in the air and medieval villages cling to cliffs that precipitate into turquoise waters. It's hard to imagine a woman packing up and leaving. (Indeed, the song is about a politician, not a lover.)

Aside from the obvious attraction of Positano and its Moorish domes, the rest of the craggy coastline possesses extraordinary beauty in its blue grottoes and smaller towns that once belonged only to fishers and pirates. Now it is mostly a holiday resort for couples.

The lack of flat, developable land on the cliffs makes real estate expensive, exacerbated by the huge demand for houses from anyone who has visited. Furthermore, the disinclination of Neapolitan and Roman families to sell their older homes makes it almost impossible to buy the best ones. There are just a few Vendesi (For Sale) signs along the coast. You might be lucky enough to find a three-bedroom home perched on a cliff with a large backyard for €450,000, such as one recently advertised near the town of Amalfi.

It's just as difficult to find real estate on Capri, which families guard jealously (but happily rent out for a week or two). On the island of Ponza, the houses are built into caves, so there is a short supply, and new development is rarely allowed. The one island off of Naples that has a regular turnover of real estate is **Ischia,** perhaps less attractive than Capri (most of the world is), and certainly more developed than Ponza. Still, it is a

the Amalfi coast

hopping summer destination for Neapolitans and Romans, which allows homeowners to ask anywhere from €350,000 to €1 million for a single-family villa. One-bedroom apartments start at roughly €100,000.

Renting an apartment on a monthly basis on the Amalfi coast is difficult—most of the rentals are for tourists who come for a week at a time and pay top euro. In some of the less frequented towns, however, such as **Vietri sul Mare** (which produces most of the coast's famous ceramics), you can find a two-bedroom apartment for as little as €450 per month.

Puglia

From the spectacular coastline of the Gargano promontory to the mesmerizing Baroque architecture of the Salento, Puglia possesses a beauty that rivals that of the Amalfi coast. But aside from that comparison, Puglia, on the other side of the peninsula, may as well be a world apart from the South. Campania is mountainous, Puglia is mostly flat, and the two peoples are just as dissimilar. Neapolitans are compulsive extroverts and wear their emotions on their sleeves, while the Pugliese seem quiet by comparison, as if they were holding back a secret.

The land casts an enigmatic, Eastern charm, and it does hold its share of secrets. Puglia thrives on the inexplicable, as anyone who has seen a rendition of the *tarantella* can tell you. The name comes from the city of Taranto, as does the word tarantula, and folklore dictated that anyone bitten by one of the region's brown spiders (don't worry—the local variety is much smaller than the big furry ones that now carry the name) was supposed to dance out the venom until he or she dropped from exhaustion. Popular festivals reenact the dance to the beat of tambourines.

Perhaps the greatest example of Puglian mysticism is the late Franciscan monk, Padre Pio, recently canonized by Pope John Paul II. Padre Pio's body showed the stigmata, the five bleeding wounds on the palms, feet, and rib cage that Christ is said to have developed when he was crucified. In addition to that unexplained occurrence, Padre Pio was deemed responsible for at least two miracles, and he became a cult figure throughout the Catholic world. His followers believed he could be in two places at one time, and he was known for his ability to cast out demons. More than seven million pilgrims come every year to Padre Pio's shrine in San Giovanni Rotondo (twice the number of visitors to Rome's Colosseum), snatching up pins, mugs, and key chains adorned with the suffering saint's likeness.

Even Puglia's architecture has its own inexplicable miracles. One good example is the Castel del Monte, a puzzling castle built by Holy Roman Emperor Frederick II, and now featured on the back of Italy's one-cent coins. Frederick was a lover of octagons. Almost every town in northern Puglia has an eight-sided tower, and the Castel del Monte was the granddaddy of them all: an eight-sided building with eight octagonal towers. Frederick based its floor plan on the Golden Ratio, coined by his friend, Leonardo Fibonacci, a kindred spirit and a fellow admirer of the Arabic world. The building is perfectly aligned with each of Puglia's other sacred monuments. No one knows why, but it was not likely a coincidence, since Puglia's early surveyors were attentive to these kinds of details. But what is most unusual about

© GABRIELA INSURATELU/123RF

Castel del Monte in the Puglia region

the building is that no one can explain its purpose. It was too sparse to be a hunting lodge and too indefensible to be a fortress, so people have stopped guessing and just call it a fine work of art.

Finally, there are Puglia's domed *trulli,* stone houses with cone-shaped roofs and adorned with strange symbols—a crescent, a plain orb, a star, and the like—that may or may not have indicated the profession of the owner. Historians have made guesses about who might have built the *trulli*—even the druids have been mentioned—but no one is quite sure.

WHERE TO LIVE
The Land of the *Trulli*

One of the most picturesque parts of Puglia, and the one that some foreigners have already discovered, is the **Valley of Itria.** This, in the northern reaches of the Brindisi and Taranto provinces, is the land of the *trulli.* They are concentrated in or near the towns of **Martina Franca, Cisternino, Ostuni, Fasano,** and **Alberobello.**

The last is considered the *trullo* capital of Puglia, with more than 1,000 specimens, as well as the oldest ones, most notably the Trullo Sovrano (Supreme Trullo), which was built on two stories. Most of the structures are only one story high, perhaps because the stone domes act as a sort of natural air-conditioning. The conical roofs are still built today using the same sort of fieldstones, because there is a certain local pride associated with owning a piece of Puglian culture. Newly built *trulli* are, of course, less expensive, and can be had for as little as €40,000. You might pay about the same for one that has fallen apart at the seams. Then there are the real gems: huge, 14-room estates in an olive grove, featuring a swimming pool with an

MOVE OVER CHIANTI, HERE COMES PUGLIASHIRE

When Giovanni Veronesi, a paper and pulp business consultant from Milan, went to Puglia on holiday a few years ago with his wife, he was quickly entranced by the Valley of Itria. Between Bari and Brindisi, this lush inland valley is home to *trulli*, the region's famous cone-shaped buildings, as well as olive groves, vineyards, and the whitewashed hilltop town of Ostuni.

"It's just like Tuscany was 30 years ago," says Mr. Veronesi. He speaks with some experience here, as he is also the owner of a home in Tuscany, though he said he virtually "abandoned" that property. Within six months of his Puglia vacation, he purchased Le Taverne, a 17th-century *masseria* (farmhouse) three kilometers from Ostuni. "It was love at first sight," he says.

He bought the *masseria* from a 90-something-year-old aristocrat who had moved to Rome many years before. Surrounded by 75 acres of knotted olive trees, the stone building with colorful Baroque-era carved trimmings has an ancient olive mill in its vaulted basement and some 20 rooms that Mr. Veronesi and his wife are currently remodeling to convert into an exclusive hotel.

"Our plan is to one day settle down and retire there," he says. Mr. Veronesi is one of many clients who have employed Milan-based architects Ado Franchini and Giovannella Bianchi di Donnasibilla to make their dream of living under the Puglia sun come true. The husband-and-wife architect team regularly travel to Italy's heel to track down *trulli, masserie*, and other historic buildings with market potential from Foggia to Lecce. They recently unveiled a website (www.sitidoltremare.it) designed to match sellers and buyers and win the ensuing remodeling contracts. What sets them apart from other real estate brokers is that they are the first to focus firmly on a brand of clientele relatively new to Puglia, a region often dismissed as backward and too far off the beaten track.

"The investors attracted by Puglia have an entrepreneurial spirit," says Mr. Franchini. "That's what gives that region such enormous potential." Indeed, real estate prices are 30-50 percent lower than in regions like Lazio and Umbria. In Puglia, some €250,000 can buy a *masseria* with a sizable chunk of surrounding farmland.

More relaxed building regulations are also attracting investors. The forward-thinking town hall of Ostuni allows buyers to add as much as 20 percent in volume to an existing structure. That kind of flexibility is unheard of in conservative zoning farther north, where even updating a bathroom involves a tedious wrestle with red tape.

(Contributed by Monica Larner, author and Italian correspondent for Wine Enthusiast *magazine.)*

adjacent *trullo*-style cabana, for just north of €1 million. These big country estates are called *masserie*. The word comes from *mas,* the Celtic term for house. There are other palaces with nearly that level of luxury at about half the price, which would be a steal anywhere north of Naples. In general, expect to pay about €200,000 for a large, rustic estate, and as little as €60,000 for a villa in an olive grove, though the building will at the very least need some cosmetic work.

It is counterintuitive that Puglia should have so many bargains. Prospective homeowners in Italy tend to look for exactly what this part of the country has to offer: old stone walls surrounding olive groves and their respective ancient mills, just 10 minutes by car from the sea. They also look for signs of history, and the scent of the past in the Valley of Itria is overwhelming. It is a kaleidoscope image of whitewashed

© ARKANOIDE/123RF

the domed *trulli* in Alberobello

homes on hilltops, reminiscent of the Greek settlements from which the first inhabitants came; the names Gallipoli and Monopoli speak to their ancient Hellenic origin, and the ubiquitous Byzantine cathedrals are reminders that those ties remained close for centuries.

Bari

Bari is the hub of Puglia, the South's second-largest city, boasting a major airport and an even busier seaport. Today, ferries from Bari carry tourists to Greece and to the Balkans, while immigrants make the opposite journey across the Adriatic and land on Bari's shores. The city serves much the same purpose as it did hundreds of years ago, when it was considered Italy's gateway to and from Byzantium.

Bari still thrives on commerce, some of it illegal—such as smuggled cigarettes and immigrants—and the result is an unfortunate reputation for crime. But, like most reputations soiled by a few teenaged, cocaine-sniffing mobsters, Bari hides a fascinating side that few dare to discover. For example, the modest-looking Basilica of St. Nicholas (the saint known as Santa Claus to the rest of us) holds the relics of the saint from modern-day Turkey and is an oft-cited example of Romanesque architecture.

For prospective homeowners, Bari is a good place to fly in and out of, do some shopping on Via Sparano, check out the sites near Piazza San Nicola, eat a fantastic dinner of orecchiette and raw sea urchins in fishers' trattorie by the port, and then make your way south to more tranquil waters. Some of Italy's most pleasant beach resorts are found on the coast between Bari and Brindisi, an ideal place for homeowners to set up shop and unwind. If you're the adventurous type and want to give living in downtown Bari a try, you can rent a three-bedroom apartment for about €650 per month.

Polignano a Mare and **Monopoli** are gleaming white coastal towns perched on the blue Adriatic. They were settled by the Greeks before seeing a renaissance under the Byzantine Empire, and later the Normans. If your idea of paradise is eating at a restaurant on a rocky beach with blue water seeping into limestone caves, this part of Puglia is Caput Mundi.

And the prices, again, are affordable. In Polignano—which, incidentally, claims to have more ice cream shops per capita than any other Italian town—you can find a rustic, 100-square-meter, pink-stone *masseria* on an olive grove, with an arcaded veranda, for some €200,000. There are countless such fixer-uppers in this area, some in pastoral surroundings and some not, but all just a short bicycle ride from the sea. Another option in the area, especially for those in search of a simple summer home, would be a similar-sized but more modern villa with the same red tile roof, for less than €100,000 and with less work required.

Lecce and the Salento

You'll have to drive to the southernmost tip of the boot to find it, but Lecce stands out as truly one of the most beautiful cities in southern Italy—even from a plane, you can see its curious cluster of all-white buildings near a blue sea. A center of Southern Baroque, Lecce has a collection of architectural marvels, all built of the aptly named *pietra di Lecce,* a soft, easily carved stone. Much of it has been eroded by the wind, leaving bizarre impressions on the statues' faces.

Surrounding the city is the Salento, a flat landscape dotted with figs, stone walls, and some very interesting real estate. There are a few *trulli,* pink limestone Baroque homes, and some unusual buildings with almost African architecture and mosaics of Arabic patterns. You'll even find a posh, St. Tropez–like enclave of wealth right here in Puglia, in a little town called Tricase. Its Moorish architecture, with carved windows, and long, tree-lined approaches to princely estates make it perhaps the most attractive town in the region. Unfortunately, there is no such thing as a free lunch, even in Puglia, and the estates' prices closely reflect their ostentation. Other towns near Italy's southern tip, such as **Galatina** and **Gallipoli,** offer decent prices for concrete monsters—about €150,000 or €200,000 for a massive town house—but expect to pay closer to a half million for a beautiful villa in the Salento countryside. Then again, this isn't exactly Chianti, so who knows what you might come up with after a little bit of hunting? And renting a place is much closer to reasonable—in Lecce, you can rent a nice two-bedroom apartment downtown for about €500 per month.

Sicily

Most people from Sicily don't necessarily consider themselves Italians. They are first and foremost Sicilians, they'll tell you. They'll even describe themselves as "islanders" before they say they're Italian. The island, which at almost 26,000 square kilometers is the largest in the Mediterranean, has its own soul, its own rhythm, and its own language. Until the highly debated bridge across the Straits of Messina to the mainland is built, Sicily will remain a place unto itself in every respect.

© JOHN MORETTI

the wheel from a traditional Sicilian carriage

Sicilians have good reason to feel attached to their land. It is like no other place in the country. It holds the only two active volcanoes in Europe, Stromboli and Mount Etna (though there are several dormant ones in Italy, such as Vesuvius), and is blanketed by lemon and almond trees, olive groves, and vineyards. The local mix of Arabic and Norman cultures gives a unique flavor to the architecture and food, and reflects the diverse ethnic background of the Sicilians themselves.

The Greeks were the first to leave their mark on the island. Their traces are found everywhere, from the well-preserved temples of Agrigento to the amphitheaters of Syracuse and Taormina, to the lonely temple of Segesta. Many of these ruins now provide the backdrop for performing arts, one of the many perks to living in Sicily. The other advantages are more obvious: a fine selection of beaches, nice weather, great wines, top-quality seafood, and more ancient archaeological sites than you can shake an olive branch at.

As a foreigner, you may find Sicily a little harder to get used to than other regions. The roads can be rugged, and seemingly simple services like water can be spotty. Although everyone can speak clear Italian if prompted, the dialect is very thick, as in Naples and Puglia.

And, also as in Naples and (to a lesser extent) Puglia, there is organized crime. What separates Sicily from the rest of the South in this category is just how deeply rooted the Mafia is, and yet at the same time how much energy is now devoted to doing something about it. (Probably the best recent example is the arrest in 2006 of top Cosa Nostra boss Bernardo Provenzano, who had been "in hiding" for more than 40 years.) This is not quite the case with the Camorra in Naples or the Sacra Corona Unita in Puglia,

ANTI-MAFIA OLIVE OIL

Though the political winds of change in Palermo in the late 1990s and a crackdown by investigators in Rome have helped bring Mafia activity under control in Sicily, organized crime and corruption make a tough stain to rub out from the island's culture. The region's roots are some 1,000 years old, and much of the land still belongs to families of the Cosa Nostra. Mafia-owned lands here never bore much fruit, as they were rarely tended or cultivated, but five towns around Palermo are now reaping a long-awaited harvest.

In 1999, 500 acres of agricultural land confiscated from the Cosa Nostra in the towns of Corleone, Monreale, Piana degli Albanesi, San Cipirello, and San Giuseppe Jato were awarded to a group of nonprofit organizations, which used the fields for organically grown produce. It was part of a larger plan to seize property that has so far taken more than €125 million in Mafia holdings and turned them into parks, farms, and public buildings such as schools and police stations.

One of the more famous products to grow out of the mob's old turf is the olive oil created by the Libera association, an anti-Mafia group founded by Turin priest Luigi Ciotti and Rita Borsellino, sister of the Palermo prosecutor Paolo Borsellino, who was assassinated by gangsters in 1992. (The city's airport, Falcone-Borsellino, is named after him and another slain judge, Giovanni Falcone.)

The olive trees sit on an estate that once belonged to Bernardo Provenzano, the Cosa Nostra's presumed *numero uno,* who had been wanted by police for more than three decades before he was arrested in 2006. That symbolic provenance has helped Father Ciotti and his youths to sell about 10,000 bottles of their "anti-Mafia" brand oil per year.

where it's still monkey business as usual. The newspapers in Palermo and Catania hit the subject hard, and many Sicilians now speak openly about the problem, whereas before there was only *omertà,* or fearful silence.

In general, travelers need not worry about being the victims of organized crime. In fact, many Americans come to Sicily precisely to see the land of the mob, to cavort in the town of Corleone on packaged tours aimed at historic Mafia sites. (There's even a Mafia museum there.) One should be cautioned, however, that starting a restaurant or some other retail business could expose you to a real kind of risk that you may never have dealt with back home.

A footnote in some history books, and one that you should be aware of as an expat living in Sicily, points out that the United States was partly responsible for putting the Mafia back in power after Fascism by installing allegedly shady figures in seats of power in exchange for their loyalty when the United States liberated the island during World War II.

This does not mean that Sicilians are anti-American. That historical detail is hugely overshadowed by a strong bond between the island and Sicilian families that emigrated to the United States. For example, one of them, a fisher named Giuseppe di Maggio, moved from the small island of Isola delle Femmine outside Palermo to a fishing village near San Francisco, and his son became one of the greatest baseball players of all time. Those immigrants are not forgotten in Sicily, and indeed many come back to visit every year. Even Joltin' Joe made an appearance in Isola delle Femmine a few years before he died, and he was welcomed back with great fanfare.

Another reason for the close transatlantic ties is the strong military presence at the

Sigonella base, near Catania. If NATO bases in other parts of Europe are sometimes the source of friction, this is rarely the case in Sicily. Overall, North Americans in Sicily will feel welcomed by the locals, and those whose ancestors left 100 years before might wonder if a permanent return ticket is in order.

WHERE TO LIVE

Sicily is no stranger to foreign homeowners. Most of them have settled in glitzy **Taormina,** where nice homes start at €400,000 and skyrocket northward from there. Others have moved to **Modica,** once Sicily's fourth-largest city, an up-and-coming expat settlement and a beautiful town to visit in the summer, though it is isolated in a valley near Ragusa and, frankly, pretty depressing in the winter.

Then there are pockets of U.S. military families living near the Sigonella base, outside Catania. Catania is more maligned for crime and urban blight than any other city in Italy, though it should be pointed out that it has come a long way since its nadir in the 1970s, having cleaned up its black-lava-paved streets and returned culture to its downtown. That may not be enough to lure homeowners, however. Mount Etna has wiped out the city no fewer than seven times, and potential buyers may feel some trepidation about living in the shadow of an active volcano, especially in residential areas to the north.

While these and other sites—such as the Aeolian Islands, the Egadi Islands, the Greek temples of Agrigento, the mosaics of Piazza Armerina, and the ruins of Siracusa—are great places to visit, the most appealing choice for homeowners is likely the northwestern corner around **Palermo.** After all, any two points in Sicily are an afternoon's drive away at the most, and day trips are easy from the northwest corner where the island's two highways meet.

Palermo is Sicily's capital, and its historical significance is hard to exaggerate. In the Middle Ages, when Arabs enriched the island and the Normans made it their southern stronghold, much of the rest of Italy was in the depths of decay. Yes, the tables have turned on the once great southern cities, but like Naples, Palermo cleaned up its city center for tourists in the 1990s, pouring light into the dark spaces that once sheltered drug dealers, and these days it is a very livable city for those willing to forgo employment for year-round sunshine.

Since those who choose to live in Sicily—or anywhere in the deep South, for that matter—probably aren't looking for a nine-to-five job, they would get more out of the countryside near Palermo than in the city itself. Some of the nicest spots in rural Sicily lie just to the east of Palermo, near Cefalu, or to the southwest, near Alcamo and Segesta.

Cefalu is a gorgeous beach resort, as well as the home to one of southern Italy's most impressive cathedrals. The mix of Norman architecture, lively shopping, good seafood dining, and spectacular scenery makes it an excellent choice for anyone looking for a home, especially as it is so well-connected to the rest and best of Sicily. The inland highway and the one that practically circumnavigates the island (the part from Cefalu to Messina remains mysteriously unfinished) meet here. There is a daily ferry from Cefalu to the Aeolian Islands in the summer. The place is so inviting that many Italians have vacation homes here and on the islands, and finding one for sale takes just a little bit of work. Expect prices of around €200,000 for a modern villa. For renters, a nice villa just outside town can go for as little as €300 per month.

Alcamo is Tuscany on a budget. Here you can find vineyards of white Catarratto grapes and a lovely whitewashed town, where modest houses sell for around €150,000. It sits near the northwestern corner of the island, close to the Zingaro natural park, with its seaside hikes. Also nearby are the elegant hilltop town of Erice, the Greek temple of Segesta, the sweet-wine producers of Marsala, and the red-tuna fisherfolk on the Egadi Islands. You could hardly ask for more within a one-hour radius.

RESOURCES

Embassies and Consulates

IN THE UNITED STATES
EMBASSY OF ITALY
3000 Whitehaven St. NW
Washington, D.C. 20008
tel. 202/612-4400
fax 202/518-2154
www.ambwashingtondc.esteri.it

ITALIAN CONSULATE GENERAL
600 Atlantic Ave.
Boston, MA 02110
tel. 617/722-9201
fax 617/722-9407
www.consboston.esteri.it

ITALIAN CONSULATE GENERAL
500 N. Michigan Ave., Suite 1850
Chicago, IL 60611
tel. 312/467-1550
fax 312/467-1335
www.conschicago.esteri.it

ITALIAN CONSULATE GENERAL
Buhl Building
535 Griswold, Suite 1840
Detroit, MI 48226
tel. 313/963-8560
fax 313/963-8180
www.consdetroit.esteri.it

ITALIAN CONSULATE GENERAL
1026 Public Ledger Building
100 South 6th St.
Philadelphia, PA 19106-3470
tel. 215/592-7329
fax 215/592-9808
www.consfiladelfia.esteri.it

ITALIAN CONSULATE GENERAL
1300 Post Oak Blvd., Suite 660
Houston, TX 77056
tel. 713/850-7520
fax 713/850-9113
www.conshouston.esteri.it

ITALIAN CONSULATE GENERAL
12400 Wilshire Blvd., Suite 300
Los Angeles, CA 90025
tel. 310/820-0622
fax 310/820-0727
www.conslosangeles.esteri.it

ITALIAN CONSULATE GENERAL
4000 Ponce de Leon, Suite 590
Coral Gables, FL 33131
tel. 305/374-6322
fax 305/374-7945
www.consmiami.esteri.it

ITALIAN CONSULATE GENERAL
690 Park Ave.
New York, NY 10021
tel. 212/737-9100
fax 212/249-4945
www.consnewyork.esteri.it

ITALIAN CONSULATE GENERAL
2590 Webster St.
San Francisco, CA 94115
tel. 415/292-9210
fax 415/931-7205
www.conssanfrancisco.esteri.it

ITALIAN VICE CONSULATE
One Gateway Center, Suite 100
Newark, NJ 07102
tel. 973/643-1448
fax 973/643-3043
www.consnewark.esteri.it

RESOURCES

IN CANADA
ITALIAN CONSULATE
3489 Drummond St.
Montréal, Canada
consolato.montreal@esteri.it

ITALIAN CONSULATE
136 Beverly St.
Toronto, Canada
tel. 416/977-1566
visit.toronto@esteri.it

ITALIAN CONSULATE
1100-510 W. Hastings St.
Vancouver, Canada
tel. 604/684-7212
consolato.vancouver@esteri.it

ITALIAN EMBASSY
275 Slater St., 21st Fl.
Ottawa, Canada
tel. 613/232-2401
ambasciata.ottawa@esteri.it

IN THE UNITED KINGDOM
ITALIAN CONSULATE
32 Melville St.
Edinbrugh
tel. 44/131-226-3631

ITALIAN CONSULATE
38 Eaton Pl.
London
tel. 44/2072-359-371

ITALIAN EMBASSY
14 Three Kings Yard
London
tel. 44/2073-122-200
emblondon@embitaly.org.uk

IN ITALY
UNITED STATES CONSULATE
Lungarno Vespucci 38
50123 Florence
tel. 055/266-951
fax 055/284-088
www.florence.usconsulate.gov

UNITED STATES CONSULATE
Via Principe Amedeo 2/10
20121 Milan
tel. 02/290-351
fax. 02/290-011-65
www.milan.usconsulate.gov

UNITED STATES CONSULATE
Piazza della Repubblica
80122 Naples
tel. 081/583-8111
fax 081/761-1869
www.naples.usconsulate.gov

UNITED STATES EMBASSY
Via Vittorio Veneto 119/A
00187 Rome
tel. 06/467-41
fax 06/488-2672
www.usembassy.it

Making the Move

ADECCO
www.adecco.it

AGRITURIST
www.agriturist.it

AMERICAN CHAMBER OF COMMERCE IN ITALY
www.amcham.it

ARCIGAY
www.arcigay.it

AUTO EUROPE
www.autoeurope.com

EXPATS IN ITALY
www.expatsinitaly.com
A nice introduction to living in Italy, especially the dozens of stories from fellow foreigners who made the move.

THE INFORMER
www.informer.it
The definitive reference for those confused by Italian red tape.

INSIDERS ABROAD, DIRECTORY
www.insidersabroad.com/italy
English-language yellow pages, with a few good listings on companies from kindergartens to accountants.

MONSTER BOARD
www.monster.it

QUANTO MI PAGANO
www.quantomipagano.it

TUSCAN DREAM
www.tuscandream.com

VEDIOR
ww.randstad.it

Housing Considerations

DIONISI PROPERTY SEARCH
www.dopropertysearch.it
An upmarket agency directed at foreigners, with a few very choice pieces of real estate.

DOMENICO MINCHILLI
www.domenicominchilli.com
Rome-based architectural firm specializing in farmhouse renovation but also working with permits and property acquisition.

GABETTI PROPERTY SOLUTIONS
www.gabetti.it
A franchise that specializes in higher-end properties.

PROPERTY ABROAD
www.property-abroad.com
A nice selection of real estate in Italy.

TECNOCASA
www.tecnocasa.it
Italy's largest real estate franchise.

TAGETE
www.tagete.agenzie.casa.it
An agency specializing in Tuscany with English-speaking staff.

RESOURCES

Language and Education

DANTE ALIGHIERI SOCIETY
www.dantealighieri.com

EDUCATION FIRST
www.ef.com

Finance

The following brokerage firms have offices in major Italian cities:

BORSA ITALIA
www.borsaitalia.it
Website of the Italian stock exchange.

MERRILL LYNCH
Largo Fontanella Borghese 19
00186 Rome
tel. 800/114-330 or 06/683-931
fax 06/683-932
www.ml.com

PROMOS SIM
Via Stazio 5
80123 Naples
tel. 081/714-2222
fax 081/645-130
www.bancapromos.it

QUANTO MI PAGANO
www.quantomipagano.it
A handy site (in Italian) that calculates how much you should be getting paid.

Communications

INTERNET SERVICE PROVIDERS
ALICE
www.alice.it

BT ITALIA
https://italia.bt.com

FASTWEB
www.fastweb.it

INFOSTRADA
www.infostrada.it

TISCALI
www.tiscali.it

CELLULAR AND INTERNET PHONE COMPANIES
I MINUTI
www.iminuti.com

TELECOM ITALIA MOBILE (TIM)
www.tim.it

THREE
www.tre.it

VODAFONE
www.vodafone.com

WIND
www.wind.it

SHIPPING COMPANIES

The following sampling of Italian shipping companies have English-speaking staff.

ALPHA INTERNATIONAL

Piazza Francese 3
80133 Naples
tel. 081/551-3905
info@alpha-international.com
www.alpha-international.com

BOLLIGER INTERNATIONAL MOVERS

Via S. Pertini 51/53
50019 Sesto Fiorentino, Florence
tel. 055/425-1086
fax 055/420-6176
firenze@bolliger.it
www.bolliger.it

DHL

www.dhl.com

FEDEX

www.fedex.com

ITALIAN MOVING NETWORK

Via Trinidad 10
00040 Pomezia, Rome
tel. 06/661-818-88
fax 06/661-821-11
italianmovingnetwork@tin.it
www.italianmovingnetwork.com

ITALIAN POSTAL SERVICE

www.poste.it

UNITED PARCEL SERVICE (UPS)

Via Fantoli 15/2
20138 Milan
tel. 800/877-877
fax 051/634-2834
www.ups.com

U.S. POSTAL SERVICE

www.usps.com

MEDIA

ADNKRONOS

www.adnkronos.it
A very good news service.

ANSA

www.ansa.it
The state news agency.

CORRIERE DELLA SERA

www.corriere.it
Italy's leading newspaper, aside from the group's sports daily *Gazzetta*.

CORRIERE LAVORO

www.corriere.it/lavoro

ENGLISH YELLOW PAGES

www.intoitaly.it

IL FOGLIO

www.ilfoglio.it
Small, conservative paper with an elite readership, controlled by Berlusconi.

LA GAZZETTA DELLO SPORT

www.gazzetta.it
The nation's number-one newspaper by circulation.

LA REPUBBLICA

www.repubblica.it
A Rome-based, left-leaning paper with one of the better news websites.

MEDIASET

www.mediaset.it
Berlusconi's private television network.

RAI

www.rai.it
The state broadcaster.

Travel and Transportation

ALITALIA AIRLINES
www.alitalia.it
The state carrier's website.

AUTOSTRADE
www.autostrade.it
The highway company's website, with an English version, very good maps, and toll calculators.

EASY JET
www.easyjet.com

EUROPCAR
www.europcar.com

EUROPE BY CAR
www.europebycar.com

TRENITALIA
www.trenitalia.it
The national railway website, including a timetable and online ticket purchase.

TOURING CLUB ITALIANO
www.touringclub.it

WHAT'S ON WHEN
www.whatsonwhen.com

Prime Living Locations

ROME
AS ROMA
www.asroma.it

ATAC ROMA
www.atac.roma.it
The Roman transportation authority's website, with maps and timetables for subways and buses.

SS LAZIO
www.sslazio.it
Websites for the city's two soccer teams, AS Roma and SS Lazio.

TURISMOROMA
www.turismoroma.it
A comprehensive portal for the traveler by the Roman tourist board.

WANTED IN ROME
www.wantedinrome.com
An expat's guide to living in Rome, with English-language classifieds for housing and jobs.

MILAN AND THE LAKES
AC MILAN
www.acmilan.com
Websites for the city's two soccer teams, Inter and AC Milan.

AZIENDA TRASPORTI MILANESI
www.atm-mi.it
The Milan transportation authority's website, with maps and timetables for subways, trams, and buses.

EASY MILANO
www.easymilano.it
An expat's guide to living in Milan, with English-language classifieds for housing and jobs.

F.C. INTERNAZIONALE
www.inter.it

MILANO PER ME
www.turismo.comune.milano.it
The website of Milan's APT tourism agency.

RESOURCES

Glossary

PRONUNCIATION TIPS

You will often find yourself spelling out words over the telephone, especially foreign names. In the United States, radio operators use Alpha, Bravo, Charlie, etc., to clarify their ABCs; in Italy, people use mostly city names:

Ancona
Bologna
Como
Domodossola
Empoli
Firenze
Genova
Hotel
Imola
Jolly
Kappa
Livorno
Milano
Napoli
Otranto
Palermo
Quartomiglio
Roma
Savona
Torino
Udine
Venezia
Wagner (or just *doppio vu*)
"Iks" (just the name of the letter)
York (or just ipsylon)
Zara

MAKING THE MOVE

ambasciata: embassy
assessore: inspectors
commune: town; also town hall or city hall
consulato: consulate
direttore: director
Ministero del Lavoro: Labor Ministry
Ministero dell'Estero: Foreign Ministry
nulla osta: a document issued by the police headquarters affirming that there is no legal reason to keep you from applying for a stay permit, or from the Labor Ministry for a work permit
permesso di soggiorno: stay permit that comes in several different forms-for work, for family, etc.
questura: police headquarters
visto: a visa, which comes in as many forms as stay permits do

HOUSING CONSIDERATIONS

affitare: to rent
agriturismo: rural bed-and-breakfast
arredato: furnished
bollette: utility bills (gas, electric, telephone, etc.)
bombola: a tank (usually methane or propane, for the home)
box: garage
camera: room
condominio: homeowner's association, which collectively pays for such things as elevators and garbage removal
gattara: woman who adores cats
geometra: surveyor/deputy architect
inquilino: tenant
mansarda: slanted ceilings
masseria: farmhouse
monolocale: one-bedroom apartment (a two-bedroom is a *bilocale*, a three-bedroom is a *trilocale*, and so on)
palazzo: a building
portinaio: doorman or building superintendent
ristrutturato: renovated
rogito: deed of sale
soffitta: ceiling, or else top-floor apartment
sottodichiarazione: underdeclaring the value of a house during a sale for tax purposes (commonplace, but illegal)
spese: normally, this means "shopping," but in reference to housing, it refers to the utility costs

HEALTH

farmacia di turno: late-night pharmacy
ferito: injured
incinta: pregnant
infarto: heart attack

libretto di salute: a bill of health issued by the regional authorities

mal di testa: headache (*mal di stomaco* is a stomachache, and so on)

policlinico: health clinic, usually private (as opposed to *ospedale*, a regular hospital)

pronto soccorso: first aid, paramedics, and also emergency room

ricetta: prescription

salute: health of an individual

sanit: health, in the public sense

FINANCE

assegno: a check

azioni: shares

borsa: stock market

busta paga: a monthly statement of what has been paid to you, and what has been taken out for taxes

codice fiscale: tax identification number

commercialista: accountant

contanti: cash

deposito: deposit

in nero: "under the table"

lordo: gross

netto: net

notaio: notary public/paralegal

sindacato: union

tasse: taxes

COMMUNICATIONS

abbonamento: subscription or membership

campo: cell phone, radio, or TV reception; literally, "field"

comporre (or digitare): to dial, as in a number

destinatario: addressee

francobollo: a stamp

giornale: newspaper

mensile: a monthly publication

mittente: sender

numero verde: toll-free number

quotidiano: a daily newspaper

raggiungibile: reachable

rete: web or net, as in the Internet or a TV network

ricaricare: to recharge, as in a battery or credit on a cell phone

scheda: a card-usually the little chip behind the cell phone battery that holds your telephone number and address book information, or else the scratch-off card that holds a secret number to boost your credit

settimanale: a weekly publication

sito: website

squillo: a ring, or a call; more formally, *chiamata, telefonata,* or *colpo di telefono*

telefonino: cellular phone (literally, "little phone"; also known as a *cellulare*)

TG (telegiornale): TV news

utente: user (as in "user name")

TRAVEL AND TRANSPORTATION

autostrada: highway, usually a toll road

binario: train track

biglietteria: ticket counter

binario: train track

bollo: annual registration fee for a car, motorcycle, or moped

carabinieri: police

centro storico: historic center, or downtown

convalidare: to stamp your ticket; something you must do before getting on a train, bus, tram, or subway high-speed train (proper name)

finestrino: window (in a car, plane, or train)

galleria: a tunnel

moto: motorcycle (short for *motocicletta*)

motorino: moped

patente: driver's license

pendolino: high-speed, tilting train (literally, "little pendulum")

rallentare: to slow down

ritardo: delay

sciopero: strike

statale: state highway (smaller than an *autostrada*, and usually just two lanes)

superstrada: almost an *autostrada,* but no tolls

supplimento: additional charge for a fast train

uscita: on a highway, an exit; at an airport, a gate

Italian Phrases

Known as the language of poetry and love, Italian is perhaps the most musical language in the world. Speaking it is both fun and theatrical (moving your hands becomes natural) and not very difficult, since in most cases, words are pronounced exactly as they are written.

THE BASICS

Good day *Buon giorno* (bwon jor-no)
Good evening *Buona sera* (bwo-na say-ra)
Welcome *Benvenuto* (ben-ven-oo-to)
Excuse me *Mi scusi* (mee skoo-zee)
Pardon *Permesso* (per-mes-so)
Sir *Signore* (seen-yor-ay)
Madam *Signora* (seen-yor-ah)
Miss *Signorina* (seen-yor-ee-na)
Do you speak English? *Parla inglese?* (par-la een-glay-zay)
I don't speak Italian *Non parlo italiano* (non par-lo ee-tal-ya-no)
How are you? (formal) *Come sta?* (ko-may sta)
Very well, thank you *Molto bene, grazie* (mole-tow be-nay grat-see-ay)
How's it going? (informal) *Come va?* (ko-may va)
It's going fine *Va bene* (va be-nay)
My name is... *Mi chiamo...* (mee kee-a-mo)
What's your name? *Come si chiama?* (ko-may see kee-a-ma)
Please *Per favore* (payr fa-vor-ray)
Thank you *Grazie* (grat-see-ay)
You're welcome *Prego* (pray-go)
I'm sorry *Mi dispiace* (mee dees-pee-ah-chay)
Goodbye *Arrivederci; ciao* (ar-ree-ve-der-chee; chow)
Yes *Sí* (see)
No *No* (no)

GETTING AROUND

How do I get to...? *Come posso andare a...* (ko-may pohs-so an-da-ray a...)
Where is...? *Dove* (do-vay)

the subway *la metro* (la met-ro)
the airport *l'aeroporto* (lay-ro-por-to)
the train station *la stazione di treno* (la stats-yo-nay dee tray-no)
the train *il treno* (eel tray-no)
the bus stop *la fermata dell'autobus* (la fair-ma-tah day-la-ow-to-boos)
the bus *l'autobus* (la ow-to-boos)
the exit *l'uscita* (le oo-shee-ta)
the street *la strada* (la stra-da)
the garden *il giardino* (eel jar-dee-no)
the tourist office *l'ufficio turistico* (loof-fee-cho too-rees-tee-ko)
a taxicab *un taxi* (oon tak-see)
a hotel *un albergo* (oon al-bair-go)
a toilet *la toilette* (la twa-let)
a pharmacy *una farmacia* (oo-na farm-a-chee-a)
a bank *una banca* (oo-na bang-ka)
a telephone *un telefono* (oon te-le-foh-no)

HEALTH AND EMERGENCY

Help! *Aiuto!* (a-yoo-to)
I am sick *Mi sento male* (mee sen-to ma-lay)
I am hurt *Mi sono fatto male* (mee son-no fat-to ma-lay)
I need... *Ho bisogno di...* (o bee-zon-yo dee)
the hospital *l'ospedale* (los-pe-da-lay)
a doctor *un medico* (oon me-dee-ko)
an ambulance *un'ambulanza* (oon am-boo-lant-sa)
the police *la polizia* (la po-leet-see-a)
medicine *medicina* (me-dee-chee-nah)

EATING

I would like... *Vorrei...* (vor-ray)
a table for two *un tavolo per due* (oon ta-vo-lo payr doo-ay)
the menu *il menù* (eel me-noo)
breakfast *la colazione* (la ko-lats-yo-nay)
lunch *pranzare* (pron-tsar-ay)
dinner *cenare* (chey-nar-ay)
the bill *il conto* (eel kon-to)
nonsmoking *non-fumatore* (non foo-ma-to-ray)

a drink *una bibite* (oon-a bee-bee-tay)
a glass of... *un bicchiere di..* (oon beek-ye-ray dee)
water *acqua* (ak-wa)
beer *birra* (beer-ra)
wine *vino* (vee-no)
I am... *Sono...* (so-no)
a vegetarian *vegetariano/a* (ve-jay-ta-ree-a-no/a)
diabetic *diabetico/a* (dee-a-be-tee-ko/a)
allergic *allergico/a* (al-ler-jee-ko/a)
kosher *kosher* (ko-shur)

SHOPPING
Do you have...? *Avete...?* (a-vet-ay)
Where can I buy...? *Dove posso comprare...?* (do-vay pos-so kom-pra-ray)
May I try this? *Potrei provarlo?* (po-tray pro-var-lo)
How much is this? *Quanto costa?* (kwan-to kos-ta)
cash *in contanti* (een kon-tan-tee)
credit card *la carta di credito* (la kar-ta dee kre-dee-to)
Too... *Troppo...* (trohp-po)
small *piccolo/a* (peek-ko-lo/a)
large *grande* (gran-day)
expensive *caro* (ka-ro)

TIME
What time is it? *Che ora sono?* (kay or-a so-no)
It is... *Sono...* (so-no)
eight o'clock *le otto* (lay oht-toh)
half past ten *le dieci e mezza* (lay dee-ay-chee ay med-za)
noon *mezzogiorno* (med-zo jor-no)
midnight *mezzanotte* (med-za-noht-tay)
during the day *durante il giorno* (doo-ran-tay eel jor-no)
in the morning *di mattina* (dee mat-tee-na)
in the afternoon *nel pomeriggio* (nel po-may-reed-jo)
in the evening *la sera* (la say-ra)
at night *a notte* (a not-tay)

DAYS OF THE WEEK
Monday *lunedì* (lee-ne-dee)
Tuesday *martedì* (mar-te-dee)
Wednesday *mercoledì* (mair-ko-le-dee)
Thursday *giovedì* (jo-ve-dee)
Friday *venerdì* (ven-air-dee)
Saturday *sabato* (sa-ba-toh)
Sunday *domenica* (do-me-nee-ka)
this week *questa settimana* (kwesta set-tee-ma-na)
this weekend *questo fine settimana* (kwest-o fi-nay set-tee-ma-na)
today *oggi* (oj-jee)
tomorrow *domani* (do-ma-nee)
yesterday *ieri* (yair-ee)

MONTHS
January *gennaio* (jen-na-yo)
February *febbraio* (feb-bra-yo)
March *marzo* (mart-zo)
April *aprile* (a-pree-lay)
May *maggio* (maj-jo)
June *giugno* (joon-yo)
July *luglio* (lool-yo)
August *agosto* (a-gos-toh)
September *settembre* (set-tem-bray)
October *ottobre* (ot-to-bray)
November *novembre* (no-vem-bray)
December *dicembre* (dee-chem-bray)
this month *questo mese* (kwest-o me-se)
this year *quest'anno* (kwest-an-no)
winter *inverno* (een-vair-no)
spring *primavera* (pree-ma-vair-a)
summer *estate* (es-ta-tay)
fall *autunno* (ow-toon-no)

NUMBERS
zero *zero* (dze-ro)
one *uno* (oo-no)
two *due* (doo-ay)
three *tre* (tray)
four *quattro* (kwat-troh)
five *cinque* (cheen-kway)
six *sei* (se-ee)
seven *sette* (set-tay)
eight *otto* (ot-toh)
nine *nove* (no-vay)
10 *dieci* (dyay-chee)
11 *undici* (oon-dee-chee)
12 *dodici* (do-dee-chee)
13 *tredici* (tray-dee-chee)
14 *quattordici* (kwat-tor-dee-chee)

RESOURCES

15 *quindici* (kween-dee-chee)
16 *sedici* (se-dee-chee)
17 *diciasette* (dee-chias-set-tay)
18 *diciotto* (dee-chiot-to)

19 *dicianove* (dee-chian-no-vay)
20 *venti* (ven-tee)
100 *cento* (chen-toh)
1,000 *mile* (meel-lay)

Suggested Reading

The best way to prepare for any first trip to Italy is to read travel journals, learn the geography, study the language, and, of course, peruse some cookbooks for recipes to try to taste the flavor of the place. Those travelers who already know something about the country, and by now there are many, should start to look behind Italy's facade to get a real understanding of the nation and its people. The following are a few of the better-regarded books in English (or in translation) by journalists, authors, and historians who do dig well beneath the surface:

Barzini, Luigi. *The Italians.* Carmichael, CA: Touchstone Books, 1964 (reprint).

Duggan, Christopher. *A Concise History of Italy.* New York, NY: Cambridge University Press, 1994.

Friedman, Alan. *Agnelli: Fiat and the Network of Italian Power.* New York, NY: Penguin, 1989.

Ginsborg, Paul. *A History of Contemporary Italy: Society and Politics 1943-1988.* New York, NY: Penguin, 1990.

Ginsborg, Paul. *Italy and Its Discontents: Family, Civil Society, State.* New York, NY: Palgrave Macmillan, 2003.

Jones, Tobias. *The Dark Heart of Italy.* London: Faber & Faber, 2003.

King, Ross. *Brunelleschi's Dome: How a Renaissance Genius Reinvented Architecture.* New York: Walker & Company, 2000.

Levi, Carlo. *Christ Stopped at Eboli: The Story of a Year.* New York, NY: Farrar, Straus & Giroux, 1947; Noonday Press, 1995 (reprint).

McCarthy, Patrick. *The Crisis of the Italian State: From the Origins of the Cold War to the Fall of Berlusconi & Beyond.* New York, NY: St. Martin's Press, 1995.

Rizzo, Sergio, and Gian Antonio Stella. *The Caste: How Italian Politicians Have Become Untouchable.* Rome: Saggi Italiani, 2007.

Saviano, Roberto. *Gomorrah.* Milan: Mondadori, 2007.

Stille, Alexander. *Excellent Cadavers.* New York, NY: Vintage Books, 1996.

Suggested Films

Amarcord. Directed by Federico Fellini. 124 min. F.C. Produzioni, 1974. A year in the life of a Northern coastal Italian town in the 1930s.

The Bicycle Thief. Directed by Vittorio De Sica, 93 min. Produzioni De Sica, 1949. A poor father in postwar Rome chases a thief who stole his bicycle.

Big Deal on Madonna Street (I Soliti Ignoti). Directed by Mario Monicelli. 106 min. Cinecittà, 1960. A gang of petty thieves bungle the robbery of a pawn shop.

Caro Diario, Directed by Nanni Moretti. 100 min. Sacher Film, 1994. The director, playing himself, cruises around Rome on his moped and Sicilian islands on a ferryboat, wryly commenting on Italian society in the 1990s.

Cinema Paradiso. Directed by Giuseppe Tornatore. Cristaldifilm, 1990. A famous director living in Rome in the 1980s reminisces about his childhood movie theater in a Sicilian village.

Death in Venice. Directed by Luchino Visconti. 130 min. Alfa Cinematografica, 1971. Based on the 1930 novel by Thomas Mann, a composer travels to Venice to relax and finds no peace when he falls in love with an adolescent boy.

Divorce, Italian Style. Directed by Pietro Germi. 105 min. Lux Film, 1962. An aristocrat falls in love with his cousin, but in order to marry her he must first end the marriage with his wife. In 1960s Italy, this can only mean ending her life.

Habemus Papam (We Have a Pope). Directed by Nanni Moretti. 102 min. Sacher Film, 2011. A newly elected Pope realizes he has no interest in leading the Catholic world and hides out in secular Rome.

I Cento Passi. Directed by Marco Tullio Giordana. 114 min. RAI Cinemafiction, 2000. Based on a true story, a young Sicilian activist dares to speak out against the Mafia and pays with his life.

Il Gattopardo (The Leopard). Directed by Luchino Visconti. 187 min. Titanus, 1963. Based on the 1958 novel by Giuseppe Di Lampedusa, with tones of Chekhov's *The Cherry Orchard,* the Sicilian aristocracy of the 19th century struggles against the tide of the increasingly wealthy peasantry.

Io Non Ho Paura (I'm Not Scared). Directed by Gabriele Salvatores. 108 min. Cattleya, 2003. Based a true story of a young man abducted in Milan, Salvatores tells the story of a boy's imprisonment in a hole with another kidnapped adolescent.

Johnny Stecchino. Directed by Roberto Benigni, 102 min. Cecchi Gori Group, 1991. The famed Tuscan director and comic plays a likeable fool who is unwittingly caught in a Mafia murder plot.

La Vita è Bella (Life Is Beautiful). Directed by Roberto Benigni. 116 min. Cecchi Gori Group, 1997. Benigni turns in an Oscar-winning performance as an Italian-Jewish father who pretends that his family's internment in a Nazi concentration camp is just a fun game in order to protect his only son.

Le Fate Ignoranti (His Secret Life). Directed by Ferzan Ozpetek. 106 min. R&C Produzioni, 2001. The lead character's husband is killed when he is run over by a car, but her grief is short-lived when she learns that he had been cheating on her with a handsome young man named Michele. The widow soon befriends the lover and is taken with the gay and transgendered subculture in Rome.

Mediterraneo. Directed by Gabriele Salvatores. 96 min. A.M.A. Film, 1991. Marooned on a quiet Greek island, a group of Italian soldiers in World War II are left with no enemy to engage. As they realize the war, for them, is over, their thoughts turn philosophical.

Mio Fratello è Figlio Unico. Directed by Daniele Lucchetti. 108 min. Cattleya, 2007. A coming-of-age story in 1960s southern Italy about two brothers. One brother is a left-leaning revolutionary and the other is a seminarian who sympathizes with the Fascists. They struggle to overcome their sometimes violent politics to rediscover the importance of family.

1900 (Novecento). Directed by Bernardo Bertolucci. 245 min. PEA, 1976. This four-hour epic film follows the lives of two boy-a landowner's son (played by Robert DeNiro) and the illegitimate child of a peasant (played by Gerard Depardieu)-growing up between 1900 and 1945. As the peasants embrace Communism, it sets the stage for conflict with the rising tide of Fascism in the South.

Pane e Cioccolata. Directed by Franco Brusati. 100 min. Verona Produzioni, 1973. A hilarious look at an easy-going southern Italian immigrant's attempt to fit into the rigid Swiss society he has adopted.

Pane e Tulipani. Directed by Silvio Soldini. 114 min. Istituto Luce, 2000. An underappreciated housewife is mistakenly abandoned by her family's tour bus at a gas station in Northern Italy. Instead of going home to her miserable life, she decides to hitch a ride to Venice and start all over.

A Room with a View. Directed by James Ivory. 117 min. Goldcrest Films International, 1985. Based on the 1908 novel by E. M. Forster, an English couple on vacation in Florence, in a room without a view, will unknowingly have their marriage challenged by the offer of an upgrade from a young man and his father.

Roma Città Aperta. Directed by Roberto Rossellini. 100 min. Excelsa Film, 1945. This fill tells the story of a leader of the Italian resistance in Rome in World War II and the woman and heroic priest who aid in his struggle against the Gestapo.

Roman Holiday. Directed by William Wyler, 118 min. Paramount, 1953. Audrey Hepburn and Gregory Peck star in this classic romance between a foreign correspondent and a princess during Rome's roaring 1950s.

Romanzo Criminale. Directed by Michele Placido. 152 min. Cattleya, 2005. During the troubled "Years of Lead" of 1970s Italy, a band of Romans decide to try their hands at organized crime.

The Talented Mr. Ripley. Directed by Anthony Minghella. 139 min. Miramax, 1999. Matt Damon plays a talented con-artist, forger, and impersonator who tries to overcome his humble roots by usurping those of a wealthy American living in Italy.

Un Americano a Roma. Directed by Steno. 94 min. Excelsa Film, 1954. This is the story of an Italian so in love with all things American in the 1950s that he pretends to be just another visitor from the Midwest. The image of Alberto Sordi wearing a baseball hat and slurping spaghetti is one of the most endearing images from Italian cinema.

Index

Acknowledgments

I'd like to thank those people who have been very generous with their time, their ideas, and their hospitality, especially Monica Larner, Christopher Emsden, Elisabetta Povoledo, Davide and Safia Danovi, Susan Briggs, and of course my parents, Lynne and Joe. Writing books over the years has been a lot of fun, but it couldn't have happened without the help of friends and family.

www.moon.com

DESTINATIONS | ACTIVITIES | BLOGS | MAPS | BOOKS

MOON.COM is ready to help plan your next trip! Filled with fresh trip ideas and strategies, author interviews, informative travel blogs, a detailed map library, and descriptions of all the Moon guidebooks, Moon.com is all you need to get out and explore the world—or even places in your own backyard. While at Moon.com, sign up for our monthly e-newsletter for updates on new releases, travel tips, and expert advice from our on-the-go Moon authors. As always, when you travel with Moon, expect an experience that is uncommon and truly unique.

KEEP UP WITH MOON ON FACEBOOK AND TWITTER

JOIN THE MOON PHOTO GROUP ON FLICKR

MAP SYMBOLS

▭▭▭▭ Expressway	○ City/Town	✈ Airfield	🔺 Archaeological Site
▭▭▭ Primary Road	◉ State Capital	✈ Airport	⚱ Church
▭▭▭ Secondary Road			⛽ Gas Station
▪ ▪ ▪ ▪ Unpaved Road	⊛ National Capital	▲ Mountain	▨ Mangrove
⋯⋯⋯ Ferry	★ Point of Interest	♣ Park	▨ Reef
▭▭▭ Railroad	▪ Other Location	🎿 Skiing Area	▨ Swamp

CONVERSION TABLES

°C = (°F − 32) / 1.8
°F = (°C x 1.8) + 32
1 inch = 2.54 centimeters (cm)
1 foot = 0.304 meters (m)
1 yard = 0.914 meters
1 mile = 1.6093 kilometers (km)
1 km = 0.6214 miles
1 fathom = 1.8288 m
1 chain = 20.1168 m
1 furlong = 201.168 m
1 acre = 0.4047 hectares
1 sq km = 100 hectares
1 sq mile = 2.59 square km
1 ounce = 28.35 grams
1 pound = 0.4536 kilograms
1 short ton = 0.90718 metric ton
1 short ton = 2,000 pounds
1 long ton = 1.016 metric tons
1 long ton = 2,240 pounds
1 metric ton = 1,000 kilograms
1 quart = 0.94635 liters
1 US gallon = 3.7854 liters
1 Imperial gallon = 4.5459 liters
1 nautical mile = 1.852 km

MOON LIVING ABROAD IN ITALY

Avalon Travel
a member of the Perseus Books Group
1700 Fourth Street
Berkeley, CA 94710, USA
www.moon.com

Editor: Erin Raber
Series Manager: Elizabeth Hansen
Copy Editor: Ashley Benning
Graphics and Production Coordinator:
  Lucie Ericksen
Cover Designer: Lucie Ericksen
Map Editor: Kat Bennett
Cartographers: Chris Henrick, Kat Bennett
Indexer: Greg Jewett

ISBN-13: 978-1-61238-508-2
ISSN: 1548-6486

Printing History
1st Edition – 2004
3rd Edition – March 2013
5 4 3 2 1

Title page photo: Tuscany vineyard © lianem/123RF
Interior color photos: page 4: © perseomedusa/123RF; page 5 and 8 bottom: © Lucie Ericksen; pages 6, 7, and 8 top: © purestock

Printed in Canada by Friesens

KEEPING CURRENT

Although we strive to produce the most up-to-date guidebook that we possibly can, change is unavoidable. Between the time this book goes to print and the time you read it, the cost of goods and services may have increased, and a handful of the businesses noted in these pages will undoubtedly move, alter their prices, or close their doors forever. Exchange rates fluctuate—sometimes dramatically—on a daily basis. Federal and local legal requirements and restrictions are also subject to change, so be sure to check with the appropriate authorities before making the move. If you see anything in this book that needs updating, clarification, or correction, please drop us a line. Send your comments via email to feedback@moon.com, or use the address above.